Approaches to Teaching the Novels of Henry Fielding

Approaches to Teaching World Literature

For a complete listing of titles,
see the last pages of this book.

Approaches to Teaching the Novels of Henry Fielding

Edited by

Jennifer Preston Wilson

and

Elizabeth Kraft

The Modern Language Association of America

New York 2015

Library of Congress Cataloging-in-Publication Data
Approaches to teaching the novels of Henry Fielding / edited by Jennifer Preston Wilson
and Elizabeth Kraft.
pages cm.—(Approaches to teaching world literature ; 139)
Includes bibliographical references and index.
ISBN 978-1-60329-223-8 (hardback)—
ISBN 978-1-60329-224-5 (paper)—
ISBN 978-1-60329-225-2 (EPUB)—
ISBN 978-1-60329-226-9 (Kindle)
1. Fielding, Henry, 1707–1754—Study and teaching.
2. Fielding, Henry, 1707–1754—Criticism and interpretation.
I. Wilson, Jennifer Preston, 1966– editor. II. Kraft, Elizabeth, editor.
PR3457.A6 2015
823'.5—dc23 2015024885

Approaches to Teaching World Literature 139
ISSN 1059-1133

Cover illustration of the paperback and electronic editions:
Mr. Oldham and His Guests (c. 1735–45), by Joseph Highmore (1692–1780). © Tate, London (2015)

Published by The Modern Language Association of America
85 Broad Street, suite 500, New York, New York 10004-2434
www.mla.org

CONTENTS

PREFACE TO THE VOLUME

In a letter of 1742, Elizabeth Carter reflects on what an "agreeable entertainment I have met" in reading *Joseph Andrews*, praising its "surprising variety of nature, wit, and morality, and good sense, as is scarcely to be met with in any one composition." She finds that this diverse "entertainment" even extends into "some particular instances of inhumanity which can only be hit in this kind of writing." Carter's contemporary reaction goes a long way toward explaining why we enjoy the works of Henry Fielding three hundred years later. We still experience comic pleasure and surprise from his volatile combination of tradition and originality. His depiction of humanity verges into darker questions concerning inhumanity, and part of that interrogation asks what kind of writing and reading can best offer insight into our own mixed nature.

While the innovation and didacticism of Fielding's novels make them a natural for the classroom, their extensive referentiality and self-reflexive irony can impede comprehension. To address this challenge, our volume brings together insights and resources from those who have experimented with teaching the works of this experimental writer. Fortunately, Fielding's novels are remarkably serviceable for the time they require on the syllabus. They engage the twenty-first-century student with numerous features of eighteenth-century life: travel, inns, masquerades, political and religious factions, the '45, prisons and the legal system, gender ideals and realities, social class. At the same time that readers enter into this heteroglossic cultural system, they interact with large-scale questions about genre that are foregrounded in discussion of "what Kind of a History this is; what it is like, and what it is not like" (Fielding, *Tom Jones* 75 [bk. 2, ch. 1]).

This volume in the MLA series Approaches to Teaching World Literature appears at a time of opportunity for Fielding studies. The tercentenary celebration of his birth brought about three excellent collections of essays that assess and further enrich the criticism extant today. Moreover, the Wesleyan edition of Fielding's works is now complete, and, for what limited information we have about Fielding's life, excellent comprehensive and thematic biographical works are available. From this vantage, Henry Fielding is ready for a new century of readers, and with greater emphasis now on global and interdisciplinary studies in higher education, his works are well situated for new investigation in a changing pedagogical environment. Just as Fielding can be taught to great effect in an eighteenth-century English context, his novels are equally at home in genre courses ranging back to the early epic, romance, or drama and forward to modern works.

Fielding was a borrower, a virtuoso of the pastiche; he was especially drawn to the conventional and clichéd, finding ways to perform or unsettle the hackneyed truism to engage his audience's judgment. Recent criticism has found new ways to unsettle our conceptions about Fielding, too, offering exciting avenues of classroom discussion. The lack of consensus on his social and political agenda offers students entrance into a dynamic interpretive realm; they cannot passively sum up what others have decided but instead must enter into the ongoing discussion. Students also will find that the authorial image of a beneficent, moral Fielding is in flux; his habitual recourse to disturbing laughter and skepticism encourage further close reading of ambiguities throughout his works.

Fielding has lately found numerous advocates who foreground his role as a writer of history or of romance, changing our expectations of what his works are or attempt to do. Another growth area is performance studies, encompassing a myriad of cultural practices—gambling and lottery playing, acting, masquerading, gender, and authorship, among others. This range of self-conscious enactments often brings together analysis of Fielding's theatrical and fictional works. In short, new critical directions abound, joining a tradition of accomplished Fielding scholarship with notable rhetorical and historicist responses to his novels. Students will benefit from the diversity of interpretive views as they formulate their own understandings of Fielding's texts.

This volume has a two-part structure. Part 1 considers the materials available to teachers and students of Fielding. It lists the currently available editions of *Joseph Andrews, Tom Jones, Shamela, Jonathan Wild*, and *Amelia* and discusses useful critical and contextual works. It also presents the findings of the MLA survey taken of teachers of Fielding's novels and suggests visual, audiovisual, and electronic supporting resources.

The introduction to part 2 identifies ideas that emerge in the ensuing pedagogical essays, connecting them with currents in Fielding criticism. The essays, divided into "Backgrounds," "*Joseph Andrews*," "*Tom Jones*," and "*Shamela, Jonathan Wild*, and *Amelia*," provide quick reference for instructors seeking focused advice on a particular subject. Readers will find, however, that many of the methods and models described for one novel can easily be adapted for other Fielding works as well.

We would like to acknowledge the expertise and enthusiasm of our contributors, outside readers, and MLA editors, Sonia Kane, James C. Hatch, and Michael Kandel. We also thank our student assistant, Maura Springstead. Their support along with continuing inspiration from colleagues and students, family and friends has made this a fulfilling project that will shape our teaching of Fielding for years in the future.

The editions of Fielding's novels used in this volume are:

Amelia. Ed. Linda Bree. Peterborough: Broadview, 2010.

The History of Tom Jones, A Foundling. Ed. Fredson Bowers. Introd. and commentary by Martin C. Battestin. 2 vols. Oxford: Clarendon, 1974. Wesleyan Edition of the Works of Henry Fielding.

Jonathan Wild. Miscellanies: Volume Three. Ed. Hugh Amory. Introd. and commentary by Bertrand A. Goldgar. Oxford: Clarendon, 1997. Wesleyan Edition of the Works of Henry Fielding.

Joseph Andrews. Ed. Martin C. Battestin. Oxford: Clarendon, 1967. Wesleyan Edition of the Works of Henry Fielding.

Shamela. The Journal of a Voyage to Lisbon, Shamela, *and Occasional Writings*. Ed. Martin C. Battestin, with the late Sheridan W. Baker, Jr. and Hugh Amory. Oxford: Clarendon, 2008. 133–95. Wesleyan Edition of the Works of Henry Fielding.

JPW

Part One

MATERIALS

Texts for Teaching

Editions

Teachers of Henry Fielding's novels are fortunate these days to have plenty of choices (in most cases) and worthy options (in all cases) for classroom texts. There are three editions that present *Joseph Andrews* and *Shamela* in a single volume: Penguin Classics (ed. Judith Hawley), Oxford World's Classics (ed. Douglas Brooks-Davies, rev. Thomas Keymer), and the Norton Critical Edition (ed. Homer Goldberg). All offer useful introductions, notes, and bibliographies. The Norton Critical edition, as is the practice of that series, also provides contextual and critical material. For those instructors who do not include *Shamela* on their syllabi, there are two carefully compiled classroom editions of *Joseph Andrews*, the Broadview text (ed. Paul A. Scanlon) and the Longman Cultural Edition (*History of the Adventures*, ed. Adam Potkay). Both include contextual and critical materials (with excerpts from *Shamela*). Catherine Ingrassia's Broadview *Shamela* is available in a single volume with Eliza Haywood's *Anti-Pamela*, providing another way to contextualize Fielding's response to Richardson while offering an opportunity to discuss his professional relationship with Haywood, as well.

Tom Jones enjoys similar wealth and quality of choice for classroom use. The Norton Critical edition (ed. Sheridan Baker) has served many generations of students. It has been joined more recently by other options: the Penguin Classics edition (*History*, ed. Keymer and Alice Wakely) and the Oxford Classics edition (ed. John Bender and Simon Stern). Both the Oxford and the Penguin texts are also available for download on Kindle and Nook (as is the Oxford, though not the Penguin, edition combining *Joseph Andrews* and *Shamela*).

Although *Jonathan Wild* and *Amelia* each offer only one classroom print option, teachers of Fielding are fortunate in those excellent editions: the Oxford World's Classics *Jonathan Wild* (ed. Hugh Amory [2008], with an introduction by Claude Rawson and notes by Linda Bree) and the Broadview *Amelia* (ed. Bree).

The standard scholarly edition of Fielding's corpus is the recently completed "15 volumes in 16" edition of his works, published by Oxford University Press (*Wesleyan Edition*, 1967–2011). In a comprehensive review essay published after the appearance of the final volume, Robert D. Hume offers a retrospective evaluation of the edition as a whole, which instructors, as well as advanced undergraduate and graduate students, will find informative ("Fielding's *Plays*"). The edition's introductions and annotations are valuable and reliable, but Hume notes the intrusion of some critical biases (Martin Battestin's moral readings in particular); he also raises significant questions regarding the choice of copy-text for *Amelia* and, to a lesser extent, for *Tom Jones*. These matters will be worth mentioning to students interested in book history and editing. Graduate students encountering Fielding's work for the first time should profit from the kind of awareness encouraged by Hume's review. Students writing on Fielding's *Amelia* will want to be aware of Hume's recommendation that scholarly research cite Bree's Broadview edition of the text, as it, unlike the Wesleyan edition, is based on the first edition of the novel, whereas the copy-text for the Wesleyan edition is the suspect 1762 edition of Fielding's novel, published nearly a decade after the author's death.

Caveats notwithstanding, the Wesleyan edition is a most valuable resource for the classroom instructor who wishes to review in detail the circumstances surrounding the publication of Fielding's fiction. Furthermore, it offers annotations that explicate each novel's literary allusions and identify references to the world in which Fielding lived and wrote. The currently popular classroom texts—which have had the benefit of the Wesleyan edition—also provide grounding and glossing of this sort, not coincidentally.

Biographical Materials

Henry Fielding was not much of a letter writer, and that would be true even if we didn't compare him with the letter writer to end all letter writers, Samuel Richardson. Fielding does not seem to have relished epistolary communication, and, with the exception of his final letters from Lisbon, he did not treat his correspondence as writing with future value, as did some of his notable contemporaries. Still, given the times and his circumstances, he had to take pen in hand every once in a while to write for the post rather than the press. *The Correspondence of Henry and Sarah Fielding*, edited by Battestin and Clive T. Probyn, contains all the letters known to have survived. Hugh Amory's "Fielding's Lisbon Letters" describes the author's final correspondence and its afterlife in accounts of Fielding's last days.

Biographies abound. Both Wilbur Cross's eminently readable three-volume *The History of Henry Fielding* (1918) and F. Homes Dudden's somewhat derivative two-volume *Henry Fielding: His Life, Works, and Times* (1952) gloss over some of the irregularities of Fielding's behavior in favor of a moral reading of his life. Both works were superseded in 1989 by *Henry Fielding: A Life*, by Battestin, with Ruthe R. Battestin. This fullest and only scholarly biography of the author was a major achievement but not an unproblematic record of the author's life. Battestin's biography made a splash with its treatment (a corroboration, in effect) of the suggestion that the young Fielding engaged in inappropriate sexual conduct with his sisters—a charge made during the court battle between his father and his maternal grandmother over the Fielding children's inheritance. Given the prominence of the theme of (potential) incest in Fielding's novels, instructors might find the scholarly skirmish over Battestin's discussion of the charge worthy of remark. But they will also wish to point out the frequency of the theme in eighteenth-century fiction in general, a topic central to Ellen Pollak's *Incest and the English Novel, 1684–1814*, to which students interested in the subject should be referred.

Without weighing in on one side or the other of the truth of Fielding's youthful incestuous behavior, we recommend Claude Rawson's review of Battestin's biography ("Fielding in the Dock"), which will help instructors show their students the basis for the skeptical reception of what is widely regarded as the standard biography of Fielding. Rawson fully rehearses the scholarly community's concerns regarding the acceptance of the charge of incest and in addition notes another problem: the cache of political publications newly (at that time) identified by Battestin as Fielding's work. This caution can become a teaching moment, alerting advanced undergraduate and graduate students to the difficulty of attribution in the world of eighteenth-century literature and the ever-changing canons of authors' works as a result. Rawson's criticism of Battestin's attributions has analogues in the scholarship devoted to other eighteenth-century writers—Daniel Defoe and Laurence Sterne, notably.

Harold E. Pagliaro's *Henry Fielding: A Literary Life*, Pat Rogers's *Henry Fielding: A Biography*, and Donald Thomas's *Henry Fielding* provide sound general reviews of Fielding's life that student readers will find accessible and engaging. Bree offers a lively and usefully concise biography in the *Cambridge Companion to the Works of Henry Fielding*, ideal for instructors not wishing to spend time on the minutiae of the life at the expense of careful readings of the works ("Henry Fielding's Life"). For teachers who would like to avoid sensationalist controversy yet go into biographical detail, intersections between Fielding's various professional commitments and his novelistic writings are elaborated in Ronald Paulson's *The Life of Henry Fielding*, Lance Bertelsen's *Henry Fielding at Work: Magistrate, Businessman, Writer*, and J. A. Downie's *A Political Biography of Henry Fielding*. Battestin's *A Henry Fielding Companion* offers materials not found elsewhere, at least in handbook format—for example, a guide to Fielding's residences, family, and household and a list of all his characters from both fiction and drama.

General Background Reading

Compact general background texts (not specifically focused on Fielding but resonant with his works in ways that some may find useful in preparing introductory lectures) are Donald Greene's *The Age of Exuberance*, W. A. Speck's *Society and Literature in England, 1700–1760* as well as his *Literature and Society in Eighteenth-Century England, 1680–1820*, Roy Porter's *English Society in the Eighteenth Century*, and James Sambrook's *The Eighteenth Century: The Intellectual and Cultural Context of English Literature, 1700–1789*. Although lengthier, John Brewer's *Pleasures of the Imagination: English Culture in the Eighteenth Century* is also an excellent background source for instructors and students who wish to understand the place of arts and letters in Georgian culture—and it has the great virtue of being quite an interesting read as well. Edgier and less obviously tied to Fielding's work but nonetheless thought-provoking in ways resonant with his world are Jonathan Israel's *Radical Enlightenment: Philosophy and the Making of Modernity* and *A Revolution of the Mind: Radical Enlightenment and the Intellectual Origins of Modern Democracy*. Of course, for instructors seeking general surveys of the historical, cultural, social, and literary aspects of eighteenth-century England, the introductions to the eighteenth century in the standard anthologies of British literature (Norton, Broadview, and Longman) are reliable and informative.

The most important background materials for teaching Fielding's fiction may well be those monographs having to do with the novel as genre, most of which focus on the eighteenth-century novel and all of which treat it and Fielding as crucial to the genre's development and definition. Though Ian Watt does not accord him the admiration that he showers on Defoe and Richardson, he devotes a chapter to Fielding in his seminal *Rise of the Novel*. His triple-rise theory (the rise of literacy, the middle class, and the novel), his dismissive attitude toward fiction written before Defoe (especially fiction by women), and his underappreciation of Fielding's self-conscious narrator, in particular, have been challenged, reframed, rejected, and recast by later scholars who nevertheless acknowledge the importance of Watt's book—because, if for nothing else, it started the conversation.

Some of the more forceful revisionings of the rise of the novel in the eighteenth century are Paulson's *Satire and the Novel in Eighteenth-Century England*, Lennard J. Davis's *Factual Fictions: The Origins of the English Novel*, Michael McKeon's *The Origins of the English Novel, 1660–1740*, Nancy Armstrong's *Desire and Domestic Fiction: A Political History of the Novel*, J. Paul Hunter's *Before Novels: The Cultural Contexts of Eighteenth-Century English Fiction*, and Margaret Anne Doody's *The True Story of the Novel*. Paulson, Davis, and Hunter are particularly valuable in complicating Watt's sense of the novel's separateness from other forms of eighteenth-century writing as well as for challenging his thesis regarding the readership addressed by the new genre. Each scholar makes significant statements about Fielding. Indeed, Paulson devotes three chapters to Fielding (as satirist, antiromanticist, and novelist). Davis's book concludes with a chapter on Fielding and politics, interesting for its situating of *Tom Jones* in the context of the Jacobite rebellion (a thesis explored later by John Allen Stevenson in *The Real History of Tom Jones* and Peter J. Carlton in "*Tom Jones* and the '45 Once Again"). Hunter's comments on Fielding's fiction are dispersed throughout his engagingly written and comprehensively conceived treatment of the emergence of the novel; instructors will find especially valuable his discussion of Fielding's digressions or "stories within" (*Before Novels* 47).

Paulson and Davis have much to say about resituating the novel vis-à-vis romance, a theme elaborated by McKeon and Doody as well. McKeon discusses the novel's specific interventions in questions of truth and virtue as distinct from those interventions offered by romance. His history of the novel tracks the dialogic engagement of narratives of romance idealism and naive empiricism first and of naive empiricism and extreme skepticism later (Fielding's novels being examples of extreme skepticism). Doody, on the other hand, regards questions of origin as the novel's primary concern. Her "true story" of the novel takes us back to ancient narratives and directs our attention to the way the novel has always expressed fundamental human desires. She references Fielding throughout. Many instructors of Fielding's work will find most useful her chapter devoted to the rise of realism, but some may find equally stimulating her final section on tropes of the novel, several of which suggest creative approaches to Fielding's novels. The section on the "tomb, cave, and labyrinth" contains brief but quite provocative comments on *Joseph Andrews*. Armstrong devotes her attention to the domestic novel; she has little to say about Fielding's works specifically, though her focus on the novel's creation of the domestic woman certainly has bearing on *Amelia*, as Jill Campbell (*Natural Masques*) and Betty Schellenberg (*Conversational Circle*) demonstrate. Instructors teaching *Shamela* in conjunction with *Pamela* will find Armstrong's extensive engagement with Richardson's text essential background in presenting Fielding's ironic treatment of the domestic ideal.

Additional scholarly grappling with Watt's thesis can be documented and demonstrated for students in the essays collected in *Reconsidering the Rise of the Novel*, a special issue of *Eighteenth-Century Fiction* edited by David Blewett. It can be accessed in full online at http://digitalcommons.mcmaster.ca/ecf/vol12/iss2/.

Other works with significant attention to Fielding in their consideration of broad thematic contexts central to the eighteenth-century novel are John Richetti's examination of the novel and social change in *The English Novel in History: 1700–1780*, Terry Castle's study of the eighteenth-century novel's disruptive and subversive forces in *Masquerade and Civilization: The Carnivalesque in Eighteenth-Century English Culture and Fiction*, Everett Zimmerman's treatment of the novel as a critique of history in *The Boundaries of Fiction: History and the Eighteenth-Century British Novel*, William Warner's presentation of the eighteenth-century novel as a phenomenon of emergent media culture in *Licensing Entertainment: The Elevation of Novel-Reading in Britain, 1684–1750*, and Bender's discussion of eighteenth-century novels as agents of cultural change and institutional formation in *Imagining the Penitentiary: Fiction and the Architecture of Mind in Eighteenth-Century England*. Teachers of *Amelia* and *Jonathan Wild* will be particularly rewarded by engagement with Castle (for *Amelia*) and Bender (for both).

The Cambridge Companion to the Eighteenth-Century Novel, edited by Richetti, has several features useful to the teacher of Fielding. The volume begins with a chronology spanning 1660–1793 and situating the publication of the most important eighteenth-century novels in relation to the major historical and literary events of the times. Richetti's introduction (Introd.) and Hunter's opening essay ("Novel") provide excellent grounding for students and instructors alike. Rawson's essay on Fielding surveys all the novels and is valuable for its deep engagement with the Scriblerian influence on Fielding as well as its treatment of the relationship between the author of *Joseph Andrews*, *Tom Jones*, and *Amelia* and his rival, Richardson ("Henry Fielding"). Richetti's edited *Columbia History of the British Novel* also contains several good essays on the period, and Fielding receives a chapter of his own in Campbell's "Fielding and the Novel at Mid-Century," an exploration of the novelist's fictions as negotiations of individual identity under the pressure of political and historical change. *The Cambridge History of the English Novel*, edited by Robert L. Caserio and Clement Hawes, provides excellent contextual material on matters such as biography and the novel (Downie, "Biographical Form"), domesticity and the novel (Wall, "Domesticities"), legal discourse and the novel (Shevlin, "Legal Discourse"), novelistic history (Hawes), cognitive theory and the representation of interiority (Zunshine, "Cognitive Alternatives"), and obscenity and erotics in the novel (Keymer, "Obscenity"). There is no single essay devoted to Fielding in this volume (as there is to Richardson), but the thought-provoking nature of many of the discussions of eighteenth-century fictional contexts will enrich the study of Fielding's novels.

Finally, in Cheryl Nixon's *Novel Definitions* instructors will find an anthology of eighteenth-century commentary on the novel. Designed for classroom use, this volume presents the period's own responses to the emerging form and allows students to witness the evolution of critical reception and response to the novel as genre as well as to individual authors and works.

Bibliographies

Two annotated bibliographies, one by H. George Hahn and the other by John A. Stoler and Richard D. Fulton, supplemented by Stoler, and a reference guide by L. J. Morissey are available to guide students to useful secondary materials written before 1992. For more current bibliographic help, students and instructors should consult the *MLA Bibliography*, which provides the most complete listing of works published on a given author in a given year—with cross-listings to Festschrifts and monographs not solely devoted to the author concerned. For those seeking evaluative remarks on the Fielding commentary that appears in print, *Studies in English Literature* offers yearly reviews of scholarship and criticism in Restoration and eighteenth-century literature (published in the summer issue), and the review publication *The Scriblerian*, helpfully indexed by author's name, has incisive evaluations of significant scholarship appearing in either monograph or essay form.

Though not a bibliography per se, Hume's 2010 retrospective essay "Fielding at Three Hundred: Elusive, Confusing, Misappropriated, or (Perhaps) Obvious?" provides a comprehensive overview and evaluation of Fielding scholarship from the author's time to ours; it also outlines potential areas of growth for Fielding scholarship.

Fielding's Library: An Annotated Catalogue, edited by Frederick G. Ribble and Anne G. Ribble, provides insight into Fielding's reading. This highly admired reference will be of particular interest to graduate students. Keymer has described this book as "an essential resource for anyone doing serious work on Fielding in the future" ("Fielding's Library" 365).

Critical Collections

Instructors wishing to give the fullest view of the range and scope of Fielding criticism without compiling bibliographies on their own are in luck because of the resources available. We suggest beginning with the following collections, which gather critical commentary on Fielding from his own time to the 1990s: Paulson and Thomas Lockwood's *Henry Fielding: The Critical Heritage*, Paulson's *Fielding: A Collection of Critical Essays*, Rawson's *Henry Fielding: A Critical Anthology*, and Albert Rivero's *Critical Essays on Henry Fielding*. Neal Compton's *Henry Fielding:* Tom Jones, *a Casebook* offers a collection of critical materials helpful to the undergraduate reader.

Three more recent collections of essays will bring the instructor up-to-date: *The Cambridge Companion to Henry Fielding*, edited by Rawson; *Henry Fielding in Our Time: Papers Presented at the Tercentenary Conference*, edited by Downie; and *Henry Fielding, 1707–1754: Novelist, Playwright, Journalist, Magistrate: A Double Anniversary Tribute*, edited by Rawson. The *Cambridge Companion* includes essays on all the novels: Lockwood's "*Shamela*," Paul Baines's "*Joseph Andrews*," Jenny Davidson's "*Jonathan Wild*," Nicholas Hudson's "*Tom Jones*," and Peter Sabor's "*Amelia*." It treats the rest of Fielding's career as well, with essays on his theatrical, periodical, and legal writings. Rawson himself offers a discussion of Fielding's style ("Fielding's Style"), and Jane Spencer writes on Fielding's treatment of women's authority, an issue at issue, as it were, in many of the novels. *Henry Fielding in Our Time* is a publication of papers delivered at the tercentenary conference on Fielding held at the University of London in April 2007. It features essays by both established and emerging scholars, including an opening essay on Fielding's laughter by Battestin ("Fielding's Anatomy"). Commentary on the novels is amply represented in this volume: *Joseph Andrews* (Drake; Lund, "Augustan Burlesque"); *Tom Jones* (Black, "Adventures"; Burke; Chibka; Evans; Langille); *Amelia* (Lupton). In addition, this volume offers provocative essays, pertinent to the teacher of Fielding's novels, on the relationship between Fielding and Eliza Haywood (King), Fielding's work as magistrate (Downie, "Henry Fielding"), the omniscient narrator (McCrea, "Fielding's Omniscient Narrator"), teaching Fielding in the American South (C. Johnson), Fielding and his "misguided reader" (Janes), and Fielding's sexuality (Butler, "Fielding's Disruptive Heterosexuality"). *Henry Fielding, 1707–1754*, includes essays by Lockwood, who discusses *Shamela*, *Joseph Andrews*, and *Jonathan Wild* in relation to Fielding's work in the theater ("Fielding"); Rawson, on *Jonathan Wild* and other literary works about "the Tyrant thug" ("Avatars"); Simon Dickie, on *Amelia* and sex (and the woman question) ("*Amelia*"); Bree, on the Fielding novelist siblings ("Henry and Sarah Fielding"); Frédéric Ogée, on Fielding and William Hogarth ("'O, Hogarth'"); and Rogers, on Fielding and the law ("Poacher").

Criticism

From the beginning, certain aspects of Fielding's fiction seemed to need explanation: his self-conscious narrator, his treatment of character, his emphasis on form, and the moral worth of his artistic vision. Consequently there is a wealth of critical commentary on all these topics. But we also hope that instructors will encourage students to keep looking for new takes on these old matters.

The self-conscious narrator is Fielding's signal contribution to the emerging genre we now call the novel. Wayne C. Booth's chapter "Fielding in *Tom Jones*" in his *Rhetoric of Fiction* is a grounding text for treatment of this narrator. Robert Alter's *Fielding and the Nature of the Novel* and his later *Partial Magic: The Novel as a Self-Conscious Genre* are also centered on the self-conscious narrator, and though neither is in extended conversation with Booth, each offers valuable insights into Fielding's method of narration and its influence on the development of the novel. Essay-length studies of Fielding's narrators and their self-reflexivity regularly appear in scholarly journals—for example, Howard Anderson's "Answers to the Author of *Clarissa*: Theme and Narrative Technique in *Tom Jones* and *Tristram Shandy*," Leland Warren's "Fielding's Problem and Ours" and "History as Literature and the Narrative Stance of Henry Fielding," Timothy D. O'Brien's "The Hungry Author and Narrative Performance in *Tom Jones*," Sandra Sherman's "Reading at Arm's Length: Fielding's Contract with the Reader in *Tom Jones*," and Henry Power's "Henry Fielding, Richard Bentley, and the 'Sagacious Reader' of *Tom Jones*."

Fielding's treatment of character was given an early negative review by Samuel Johnson, who famously quipped that there was "as great a difference between" Richardson and Fielding "as between a man who knew how a watch was made, and a man who could tell the hour by looking on the dial-plate" (389). James Boswell, who reports this view, understands the distinction as one of drawing characters of nature as opposed to characters of manners. He objects to the notion that one is better than the other, but we are left with the judgment of the authoritative Johnson—and with the undeniable preference the genre eventually revealed for the psychological narrative as prefigured by Richardson. Were Fielding's characters exclusively exterior creatures? Elizabeth Kraft argues that they were not, in her *Character and Consciousness in Eighteenth-Century Comic Fiction*, with particular emphasis on *Tom Jones*, which in her view elaborates parallels among the thought processes of narrator, reader, and characters. Deirdre Shauna Lynch's *Economy of Character: Novels, Market Culture, and the Business of Inner Meaning* also takes issue with Johnson's distinction. Concerned with the legibility of character, Lynch finds that Fielding and Richardson share a language of exteriority derived from the urban culture that sustained the book trade in which they both participated. Baker focuses on the relation between plot and character in "Bridget Allworthy: The Creative Pressures of Fielding's Plot." John S. Coolidge's "Fielding and 'Conservation of Character'" and Cheryl Wanko's "Characterization and the Reader's Quandary in Fielding's *Amelia*" offer helpful treatments of character in Fielding's final novel, especially the ways in which Fielding's approach in it differs from that employed in his earlier fiction.

Some scholarship regarding Fielding's characters is devoted to identification of real-life models. The Wesleyan edition is replete with annotations that give this identification, as is Battestin's *A Henry Fielding Companion*. While such an approach may seem to have limited classroom applicability, an instructor might find, in such allusions, an opportunity to encourage student research. Miriam Allott's brief discussion of *Tom Jones*'s Square as a portrait of the theologian Samuel Clarke is elaborated by K. K. Ruthven in "Fielding, Square, and the Fitness of Things," providing a strong example for instructors who wish to demonstrate that exploration of topical allusion can yield critical insight.

Instructors interested in the depiction of characters in terms of Fielding's approach to class should consult Hudson's essay in Rawson's *Cambridge Companion*, Kay Weeks's "Fielding Looks Down: *Tom Jones* and the Lower Orders," Stevenson's *Real History of Tom Jones*, Richetti's "Representing the Underclass: Servants and Proletarians in Fielding and Smollett," and Christopher Parkes's "*Joseph Andrews* and the Control of the Poor." Hal Gladfelder's *Criminality and Narrative in Eighteenth-Century England: Beyond the Law* offers insight into Fielding's treatment of the criminal class in the full range of his fiction as well as in his legal writings. Scott MacKenzie's "Stock the Parish with Beauties: Henry Fielding's Parochial Vision" provides a different view of class, with a focus on the parish system of surveillance as reflected and depicted in *Joseph Andrews*. Kristina Straub's exploration of the servant class in her *Domestic Affairs: Intimacy, Eroticism, and Violence between Servants and Masters in Eighteenth-Century Fiction* is useful both for its examination of *Joseph Andrews* and for its reading of Fielding's "A Clear State of the Case of Elizabeth Canning" in relation to Richardson's *Pamela* and the "servant problem."

Some of Fielding's nonfictional prose may help instructors deal with his approach to character. His *Essay on the Knowledge of the Characters of Men* is a fascinating meditation on how to assess another person. Its observations hold relevance even today. His recounting of the legal cases of Bosavern Penlez and Elizabeth Canning have novelistic overtones. An incisive essay relating these works to Fielding's fiction is Arlene Wilner's "The Mythology of History, the Truth of Fiction: Henry Fielding and the Cases of Bosavern Penlez and Elizabeth Canning." That Josephine Tey's mystery novel *The Francise Affair* is based on the Canning case underscores the novelistic worthiness of this tale—it also opens up avenues for investigation into the novelizing of trauma.

Those who wish to emphasize the formal properties of Fielding's fiction can begin with Eleanor Hutchens's *Irony in* Tom Jones and Glenn W. Hatfield's *Henry Fielding and the Language of Irony*. Hume notes in "Fielding at Three Hundred" that for decades these two studies were the only monographs available for readers interested in the analysis of Fielding's style. More recent work by Campbell ("Fielding's Style") and Rawson ("Fielding's Style") has reopened the topic and provides contexts for further classroom investigation. Nancy A. Mace's *Henry Fielding's Novels and the Classical Tradition* alerts us to the fact that many of Fielding's formal choices are rooted in classical literature, particularly with regard to the narrative personae Fielding employs.

In terms of larger formal questions, plots and plotting received seminal consideration in R. S. Crane's "The Concept of Plot and the Plot of *Tom Jones*" (1950) and Frederick Hilles's "Art and Artifice in *Tom Jones*" (1968). Andrew Wright's *Henry Fielding: Mask and Feast* (1965) was concerned, as many later studies have been, with Fielding's generic choices. Wright's book discussed *Joseph Andrews* (as comic epic), *Tom Jones* (as epic comedy), and *Amelia* (as domestic epic) and contained a section on character in each novel and a chapter on language. Paulson's *Satire and Novel in Eighteenth-Century England* (discussed above) and Thomas E. Maresca's *Epic to Novel* include significant analysis of Fielding's work. Rawson's *Fielding and the Augustan Ideal under Stress* and Hunter's *Occasional Form: Fielding and the Chains of Circumstance* critique Fielding's formal choices in relation to various kinds of cultural change, while Sheldon Sacks's *Fiction and the Shape of Belief: A Study of Henry Fielding* explores the connection between literary form and moral purpose in Fielding's novels.

Many works have been devoted in whole or in part to study of Fielding's narrative form. James J. Lynch's *Henry Fielding and the Heliodoran Novel: Romance, Epic, and Fielding's New Province of Writing* discusses *Joseph Andrews*, *Tom Jones*, and *Amelia* as versions of heroic romance. Simon Varey's *Space and the Eighteenth-Century English Novel* brings architectural theory to bear on *Joseph Andrews*, *Jonathan Wild*, *Tom Jones*, and *Amelia* (more fruitfully on the latter two). Patricia Meyer Spacks's *Desire and Truth: Functions of Plot in Eighteenth-Century English Novels* discusses Fielding's plots of power in comparison with Richardson's. Her chapter on the two novelists begins, interestingly enough, with an analysis of the power dynamic in John Cleland's *Fanny Hill*. Sandra Macpherson's *Harm's Way: Tragic Responsibility and the Novel Form* reads the eighteenth-century novel (including Fielding's comic novels) as tragically structured demonstrations of the power of inexorable fate over individual character. Ashley Marshall's *The Practice of Satire in England, 1658–1770*, on the other hand, presents readings of *Joseph Andrews* and *Tom Jones* as sympathetic satires. Scott Black discusses significant elements of *Tom Jones* as essays in his *Of Essays and Reading in Early Modern Britain*. Not strictly a study of form, Bender's *Imagining the Penitentiary* is essential reading for teachers of *Jonathan Wild* and also valuable for its insights as to the juridical themes and narrative strategies that inform Fielding's other novels.

Finally, Black's "Anachronism and the Uses of Form in *Joseph Andrews*," Roger D. Lund's "Augustan Burlesque and the Genesis of *Joseph Andrews*," and Paula McDowell's "Narrative Authority, Critical Complicity: The Case of *Jonathan Wild*" offer insights into the formal choices Fielding makes in *Joseph Andrews* and *Jonathan Wild*. McDowell's essay takes issue with some of Bender's central claims and, paired with his chapter on Wild in *Imagining the Penitentiary*, will be valuable for encouraging classroom discussion and debate for instructors including *Jonathan Wild* in their courses.

Occasionally (though perhaps less often than in the past) instructors who would prefer to concentrate on form and its implications find themselves dealing with student concern about morality. Much of this concern comes from traditional Fielding scholarship: students researching Fielding will inevitably encounter secondary sources that frame engagement with the author in moral terms. Also, the twentieth-century emphasis on moral vision was a corrective to the view, dating back to Richardson and Johnson, that Fielding's novels forwarded immoral models of behavior. Today's teachers who wish to take a nuanced approach to the question of morality in Fielding's novels will also want to acknowledge the reason for the twentieth-century emphasis. The most important statements in the debate are Battestin's *The Moral Basis for Fielding's Art: A Study of* Joseph Andrews, which makes the case for Fielding as a moral writer, and Bernard Harrison's *Henry Fielding's* Tom Jones*: The Novelist as Moral Philosopher*, which makes an even stronger case, elaborated on and extended by Potkay in "Liberty and Necessity in Fielding's *Amelia*."

Instructors who wish to treat the moral vision of both Fielding and Richardson should consult Allen Michie's *Richardson and Fielding: The Dynamics of a Critical Rivalry* and Warner's "The Elevation of the Novel in England: Hegemony and Literary History." Michie brings reception theory to bear on the perception of Fielding's inferior moral reputation with regard to his literary enemy and thereby usefully disturbs some of the truisms about the enmity as well as tracing many of its effects. Warner, on the other hand, examines the way Fielding and Richardson change the very notion of what narrative fiction is by asserting moral purpose in order to differentiate their works from the fictional narratives that preceded them (particularly the amatory novels). Allison Conway's reading of *Tom Jones* in her *The Protestant Whore: Courtesan Narrative and Religious Controversy in England 1680–1750* places Fielding's major novel in conversation with Defoe's *Roxana* and Aphra Behn's *Love Letters between a*

Nobleman and His Sister and rejects the moral reading privileged by Battestin. Jesse Molesworth's *Chance and the Eighteenth-Century Novel: Realism, Probability, Magic* flatly renounces interest in defending the eighteenth-century novel's moral stature, preferring instead to examine its investment in transgressive behavior. Molesworth devotes two chapters to Fielding and discusses *Jonathan Wild*, *Tom Jones*, and *Amelia* in connection with Hogarth and with Sterne. Simon Dickie's *Cruelty and Laughter: Forgotten Comic Literature and the Unsentimental Eighteenth Century* might be a bit challenging for undergraduates, but its decided turn away from moral readings of the period should be factored into classroom discussion of Fielding's moral vision. (Dickie has much to say about Fielding's jokes about parsons and rape). Moving in a different direction, Brian Schroeder reads *Joseph Andrews* as an ethical as opposed to a moral text—a distinction rooted in Levinasian philosophy, to which he is indebted.

Paul Kelleher's "'The Glorious Lust of Doing Good': *Tom Jones* and the Virtues of Sexuality" takes a provocative approach to the question of male sexual morality, arguing that Fielding's project in *Tom Jones* is to demonstrate that lust is actually the source of moral behavior and ethical practice. Kelleher's essay provides a good transition into new critical approaches to Fielding—new concerns, new cruxes—because it speaks to the emphasis on gender that emerged in Fielding studies in the late 1970s and the 1980s with essays such as Katherine M. Rogers's "Sensitive Feminism vs. Conventional Sympathy: Richardson and Fielding on Women," April London's "Controlling the Text: Women in *Tom Jones*," Anthony J. Hassall's "Women in Richardson and Fielding," and Gene S. Koppel's "Sexual Education and Sexual Values in *Tom Jones*: Confusion at the Core?" This focus culminated in two monograph-length treatments of the subject: Angela Smallwood's *Fielding and the Woman Question: The Novels of Henry Fielding and Feminist Debate, 1700–1750* and Campbell's *Natural Masques: Gender and Identity in Fielding's Plays and Novels*, both essential reading for students interested in Fielding's treatment of women. Earla Wilputte's "Ambiguous Language and Ambiguous Gender: The 'Bisexual' Text of *Shamela*," her "'Women Buried': Henry Fielding and Feminine Absence," and Nina Prytula's "'Great Breasted and Fierce': Fielding's Amazonian Heroines" are also recommended.

There has been a good deal of work on Fielding's treatment of eighteenth-century constructions of masculinity as well. Two essential books on this topic are Tiffany Potter's *Honest Sins: Georgian Libertinism and the Plays and Novels of Henry Fielding* and Brian McCrea's *Impotent Fathers: Patriarchy and Demographic Crisis in the Eighteenth-Century Novel*.

Instructors wishing to point students toward the future of Fielding studies might well begin with David H. Richter's edited *Ideology and Form in Eighteenth-Century Literature*, which includes essays employing materialist, queer theorist, and feminist-forward approaches as well as those that reflect more traditional methods but are reinvigorated by new theoretical challenges. This volume does more than collect a series of discrete arguments; instead, the contributors engage, sometimes heatedly, with one another's ideas and positions. Fielding is featured in essays by Richter ("Closing"), Richetti ("Ideology"), Spacks ("Ideology"), Ralph W. Rader, Gerald J. Butler ("Making"), and Carol Houlihan Flynn, in which *Tom Jones* and *Jonathan Wild* receive significant attention. Many of the areas of concern revealed in Richter's volume will be attractive to today's instructors and students.

Another publication that explores new theoretical approaches to Fielding is Castle's treatment of Fielding's "The Female Husband" in her *Female Thermometer: Eighteenth-Century Culture and the Invention of the Uncanny* (67–81). The use of Fielding's essay and Castle's reading of it can provoke interesting classroom discussions about Fielding's treatment of gender in his novels. Additional work that opens up discussion about gender issues in Fielding's novels is Carl R. Kropf's "A Certain Absence: *Joseph Andrews* as Affirmation of Heterosexuality," Richter's comments on this essay ("Closing"), and George E. Haggerty's "Amelia's Nose; or, Sensibility and Its Symptoms." Consideration of Fielding and disability studies could begin with Lennard Davis's "Dr. Johnson, Amelia, and the Discourse of Disability," in his *Bending Over Backwards: Disability, Dismodernism, and Other Difficult Positions* (47–78). For those interested in treating Fielding through the lens of cultural materialism, Sophie Gee's *Making Waste: Leftovers and the Eighteenth-Century Imagination* ends with an afterword focused, in part, on Sophia's muff. Lisa Zunshine's "Lying Bodies of the Enlightenment: Theory of Mind and Cultural Historicism" is a good introduction to cognitive theory and eighteenth-century literature, including *Tom Jones*, as is her "Cognitive Alternatives to Interiority."

Visual, Audiovisual, and Electronic Resources

The prints of Hogarth enhance the teaching of Fielding's novels to such a degree that we recommend considering their inclusion on syllabi. Sean Shesgreen's affordable Dover edition of Hogarth's engravings is the best print option if they are to be fully integrated into a course as physical text. Online options are also available but offer less selection. The Tate Britain Web site (www.tate.org.uk/visit/tate-britain) has images for many Hogarth paintings and prints and excellent notes as well. At the time of this writing, the *Wikipedia* links to Hogarth's various series are accompanied with high-resolution images that work well when projected for classroom analysis; the explanations given are also worthy. For authoritative commentary, instructors should consult Paulson's masterful two-volume *Hogarth's Graphic Works*. Peter de Voogd's *Henry Fielding and William Hogarth: The Correspondences of the Arts* and David Bindman, Ogée, and Peter Wagner's *Hogarth: Representing Nature's Machines*, which includes a number of comparisons of Hogarth and Fielding, are also recommended resources.

The 1963 Oscar-winning film *Tom Jones* (screenplay by John Osborne, directed by Tony Richardson) is a handy means to convey the spirit of Fielding's narrative. (We are much less enthusiastic about Richardson's film adaptation of *Joseph Andrews*, though we note its existence for instructors who wish to consider it for classroom use.) The 1997 BBC miniseries version of *Tom Jones* (*History*) is a faithful treatment of that text, though not as much fun as the 1963 film. For helpful commentary on these two *Tom Jones* films, visit the blog of Ellen Moody at www.ellenandjim.wordpress.com (search "Tom Jones"). There are also several good essays on the adaptations: Laurence Behrens's "The Argument of *Tom Jones*," Lawrence F. Laban's "Visualizing Fielding's Point of View," and Battestin's "Adapting Fielding for Film and Television." The films are available for purchase (as DVDs or through online streaming) from Amazon.com.

One interesting online resource for those teaching *Jonathan Wild* and *Amelia* is the fully searchable *Old Bailey Proceedings Online*, which can be accessed at www.oldbailyonline.org. Another popular resource is *Eighteenth-Century Collections Online* (*ECCO*), if one's university is able to subscribe. With *ECCO* the instructor has access to images of Fielding's works (useful for teaching book history) as well as to a searchable database for topics and concerns shared, in print, by Fielding and his contemporaries.There are several worthy free-access Web sites, and more are added daily, it seems. Recommended are

Bridewell Prison and Hospital, which has information about Newgate, policing, and the justice system as well
www.londonlives.org/static/Bridewell.jsp

"Divine Providence," an entry in the *Stanford Encyclopedia of Philosophy*—the encyclopedia covers other philosophical topics one might deem relevant to Fielding
http://plato.stanford.edu/entries/providence-divine

The World Upside Down: Eighteenth Century Masquerades (Hees, Mangla, Porentas, and Reece)
www.umich.edu/~ece/student_projects/masquerade/index.html

Five: The Later History of "Coram" (Banarjee), an entry in *The Victorian Web* about the Foundling Hospital
www.victorianweb.org/history/orphanages/coram5.html

Methodism (Cody), an entry in *The Victorian Web*
www.victorianweb.org/religion/methodist.html

Locating London's Past: digital resources relating to early modern and eighteenth-century London, connected with John Rocque's 1746 map
www.locatinglondon.org/

Like all Web sites, these must be reviewed and assessed by instructors before they are employed in class. It is always wise to search terms used in lecture for their Internet presence, because new sites emerge frequently, and some can be very useful.

Classroom Contexts

Fielding's novels are taught in a wide variety of courses, as was demonstrated by a survey we conducted before the compilation of this volume. We present the results of that survey here. The answers to our questions about classroom practice may inspire new instructors to think of ways to include Fielding's extraordinary novels in courses that do not, on the surface, seem to demand their presence. These answers may also validate the practice of those who already include Fielding in the classroom.

Joseph Andrews finds a place in courses devoted to a survey of British literature (Milton to the Romantics), in undergraduate eighteenth-century novel courses, in graduate-level courses in the eighteenth- and nineteenth-century British novel, in special-topics courses (e.g., on novel rivalries; Fielding's novels; satire; Richardson, Fielding, and Sterne; the legacy of *Don Quixote* in Western literature; religion and the novel), in history-of-the-novel courses, in courses devoted to seventeenth- and eighteenth-century comic fiction, and in a special three-hundredth-anniversary course on Fielding and his circle of rivals and imitators. *Tom Jones* enjoys a place in similar courses (often instructors mentioned they chose *Joseph Andrews* sometimes and *Tom Jones* other times) and is also featured in senior seminars, world literature surveys, classes on the European novel, and courses with such titles as Faith and Reason and Readers and Rogues. Instructors occasionally teach excerpts of *Tom Jones* when they do a full reading and discussion of *Joseph Andrews*, but most prefer teaching one or the other novel in its entirety.

Shamela was mentioned less often than *Joseph Andrews* or *Tom Jones* as a novel regularly taught in the classroom. Predictably it is discussed in conjunction with *Joseph Andrews* and appears in novel courses (both graduate and undergraduate) that begin with readings of Richardson's *Pamela*. There was an interesting exception to this rule: one professor designed a unit in which *Shamela* was paired with *Jonathan Wild*.

Jonathan Wild has a surprisingly active classroom life these days. It is a popular choice for British literature survey courses (one respondent mentioned including *Jonathan Wild* in a unit with Defoe's *Journal of the Plague Year* and Behn's *Oroonoko* in order to focus on the storytelling strategies and truth claims of early fiction). It is also a good example of the protonovel in courses on eighteenth-century literature or the origins of the novel. One instructor pairs the text with John Gay's *Beggar's Opera* in London: High and Low Life; another pairs it with Defoe's *Roxana* in a course on the rise of the novel. Some instructors included the work in courses devoted to satirical crime fiction, the picaresque, and criminal narrative.

Amelia has been taught less frequently than any of Fielding's novels, but a few respondents used the work in graduate and undergraduates courses on the eighteenth-century novel, on Fielding's works, and on sensibility. With the recent publication of the Broadview *Amelia*, we expect this novel will find its way into syllabi of various sorts.

How do instructors apportion time and designate reading assignments in a course not devoted solely to the reading of a Fielding novel? Our survey revealed a fairly consistent pattern of allotting two weeks to *Joseph Andrews*, three weeks to *Tom Jones*, and two weeks to *Amelia*. Some instructors found a week and a half sufficient for *Joseph Andrews*, especially as it generally followed extensive discussion of Richardson's *Pamela*; others needed two and a half weeks, especially if they included *Shamela* in the unit. For graduate courses, one week on *Joseph Andrews* and two on *Tom Jones* were the norms, though summer courses made for a more intense experience—one week of four two-and-a-half-hour sessions were spent on *Tom Jones* by one respondent who taught a graduate-level novel course during the compressed term. All survey respondents felt that time was an issue for students and the reading load demanding, but both instructors and students felt that the effort was worth it. Some instructors employ strategies to help students with the reading, especially for *Tom Jones*. Some assign *Tom Jones* at the beginning of the semester, to build reading muscle at the outset when the reading load in other classes tends to be less demanding; some make sure they assign the text over a period that includes a holiday—spring or fall break, perhaps—so that students can use the extra time if they wish to catch up. Some even devote a class period to a screening of the 1963 *Tom Jones* in order to give the students a bit of a breather. Focused questions can also help. As one instructor observed, "During the road section in the middle of *Tom Jones*, I urge them to think about the relation between the inn episodes and the digressions with respect to the plot so far and the expectations of the plot to come." Another employs brief quizzes to reward basic knowledge of plot and character and thereby encourage reading.

Instructors revealed a few common goals, and some individual objectives, in teaching Fielding's novels. Most wish to convey a sense of Fielding's narrative strategies, his voices, his playful style, his humor, his imaginative sympathy, and his use of irony. Many desire to address Fielding's moral vision, his construction of gender and class, and his innovations with regard to the novel form. There are more-specific goals. One instructor emphasizes Fielding's interactions with his contemporaries—not only Richardson but also Sarah Fielding, Eliza Haywood, and Colley Cibber. Another places the novels in conversation with the romance tradition (Heliodorus, Cervantes, et al.) and with various theories of comedy (Hobbes to Bergson). Another uses Fielding to "address the shift in cultural consciousness from brittle Augustan satire to the softer contours of sensibility." Another finds it important to present Fielding's "feminist approaches to questions of gender, sexuality, family, marriage, and heroism."

Survey respondents were asked to name the most important features of *Joseph Andrews*, *Tom Jones*, or *Amelia* for their students to understand. Some say it is the balance of universal and topical satire. Others stress Fielding's narrative voice as it differs from Richardson's and that of the epistolary novel. Several commented that it was important to them to convey Fielding's moral vision. One respondent mentioned the particular concern that students grasp Fielding's moral reasoning for avoiding psychological depth. The literary and social implications of his work are also high on the list of priorities, as are questions of genre (epic, romance, the picaresque) and gender (the construction of masculinity, femininity, sexuality, and marriage). In general, the survey showed that Fielding's development of the omniscient authorial voice in *Tom Jones*, his representation of a panoramic view of English society, and his articulation of the novel's potential as a literary form are at the center of classroom practice today.

Instructors find Fielding's novels amenable to a variety of theoretical approaches, ranging from historicist to feminist to new historicist to queer theorist. Many take a comparatist approach in arguing the transnational significance of the novel as genre and Fielding's contribution to that significance, and just as many situate their discussions in a British-English context of national literature and identity. One respondent (of the comparatist persuasion) found this disagreement important enough to highlight it in class: "My students will typically encounter these novels having looked at Cervantes's *Don Quixote* for two to three weeks, and having read excerpts from Watt, Davis, and Hunter that argue the Englishness of the novel and that dismiss European antecedents. They are left to make up their own minds about the adequacy of nationalist approaches to a transnational genre."

Our survey suggests that many new pedagogical strategies are being employed to engage the imagination of students as they read and discuss Fielding's novels. One instructor mentioned the efficacy of reading aloud "to tease the reluctant into participation." Another described a class devoted to playing "the dating game" with the characters of *Tom Jones*: "Students are required to craft answers and questions as bachelors and bachelorettes on the basis of close readings and character analysis." Graded assignments range from the tried-and-true to the innovative. Most survey respondents mentioned critical papers, close readings of brief passages, journals that follow prompts, comparison-contrast essays (on the satiric strategies of Fielding and Swift, for example, or on the relationship between Fielding and his reader as compared with that of another eighteenth-century novelist). Some instructors require presentations on secondary sources, weekly short papers, and examinations. A few responses described more unusual assignments. One instructor emphasized illustration, asking students to choose one of three options: design a frontispiece or book cover for the novel, create a six-panel storyboard for a scene in the novel, or draw a set of five illustrations for the novel and consider their placement in the text. The same instructor assigns a "shifting voice" essay, asking students to rewrite one of the key moments of the novel from another character's perspective. Another instructor asks students to compare a self-selected scene from *Joseph Andrews* with one engraved plate from Hogarth's *Harlot's Progress* or *Rake's Progress*. The same instructor sometimes asks students to write a letter in the voice of one of the characters describing the incidents of the plot.

In classrooms today, Fielding's novels are keeping company with a host of interesting authors and works. One survey respondent describes a course featuring Fielding with Boswell (*London Journal*), Addison and Steele (*Tatler* and *Spectator*), Defoe (*Journal of the Plague Year*) and Pope (*Rape of the Lock* and *The Dunciad*). Examples of novelistic company are Richardson's *Pamela*, of course, but also Frances Burney's *Evelina*, Eliza Haywood's *Love in Excess*, Horace Walpole's *Castle of Otranto*, Sarah Scott's *Millenium Hall*, Jane Austen's *Northanger Abbey* and *Mansfield Park*, Jonathan Swift's *Tale of a Tub*, Charlotte Lennox's *Female Quixote*, Laurence Sterne's *Tristram Shandy*, and novels by Behn and Jane Barker were mentioned as well. Courses that go beyond the eighteenth century place Fielding in conversation with William Godwin, Amelia Opie, Eliza Fenwick, Mary Shelley (*Frankenstein*), Charles Dickens (*Hard Times*, *Tale of Two Cities*, or parts of *David Copperfield*), Elizabeth Gaskell (*Cranford*), Emily Brontë (*Wuthering Heights*), and Oscar Wilde (*Dorian Gray*). Courses that go beyond England situate Fielding in company that includes Cervantes (*Don Quixote*), Calderón (*La vida es sueño*), Gustave Flaubert (*Madame Bovary*), Fyodor Dostoevsky (*The Idiot*), Luigi Pirandello (*Six Characters in Search of an Author*), Jorge Luis Borges ("Pierre Menard, autor del Quijote"), Benito Pérez Galdós (*La desheredada*), Alexandre Dumas (*Three Musketeeers*), Mark Twain (*Huckleberry Finn*), Clarín (*La regenta*), and Miguel de Unamuno (*Niebla*). One instructor mentioned requiring Clara Reeve's essay "On the Progress of Romance" and excerpts from *Arabian Nights' Entertainments* "to underscore the importance of Fielding's work with moralizing and modernizing what Reeve calls 'an epic on prose.'"

Fielding's novels are also taught in conjunction with other of his works. Specific pairings mentioned are: *Joseph Andrews* and *The Author's Farce*, *Amelia* and *The Covent-Garden Journal*, *Shamela* and *The Journal of a Voyage to Lisbon*, *Tom Jones* and *Tom Thumb*. One instructor advises students to read Bruce Alexander's modern detective novels featuring Sir John Fielding. Those who do, this respondent reports, "tell me they really like them for the ways in which they shed light on Henry Fielding's London milieu."

In short, while teaching Fielding's novels presents its share of challenges, today's college professors are rising to the occasion—and taking advantage of the ever-growing wealth of resources on which to draw.

Part Two

APPROACHES

Introduction

Jennifer Preston Wilson

The "Approaches" part of this book is divided into four headings. The first offers contextual background for understanding Henry Fielding's career as a novelist, his recurrent themes, and the intertextualities in his work; the next two deal with teaching each of his longer comic novels, *Joseph Andrews* and *Tom Jones*; the fourth contains essays on engaging students with his early and late works—*Shamela*, *Jonathan Wild*, and *Amelia*.

As our contributors present ways to study Fielding in the twenty-first-century classroom, commonalities emerge that surmount the differences among the novels. These shared pedagogical strategies include finding means to invest students with influence and purchase over the text; foregrounding depictions of authority and leadership in Fielding's works; theorizing his fictional thinking and connecting his novels to larger transnational traditions; using techniques of contrast and debate to enter into his highly ironic, often self-conflicted texts; situating his works amid questions of gender and genre by complicating the narrative of the rise of the novel; and teaching Fielding as part of modern material culture in classes designed for visually oriented, multimedia-literate audiences.

Confidence Games

Respondents to the survey for this volume often asked how students might best be helped with the sheer length and complexity of Fielding's works. A number of our essays suggest that a concentrated, close-reading approach keeps students engaged as they work through the portions of the plot they must navigate on their own. This method of modeling in-depth inquiry can give students a sense of self-confidence and motivate further reading. One of our contributors, Pamela S. Bromberg, calls this process "building students' reading muscles," and she begins her class with *Tom Jones* just for this effect. Of course, as J. Paul Hunter has pointed out, the more carefully readers read Fielding, the greater becomes their awareness of the instability of his texts (*Before Novels* 50), and discussion of interpretive mistakes comes into play in the classroom as well.

Through discussion of specific passages, Jill Campbell shows how in *Tom Jones* Fielding's themes are grounded in his characteristic stylistic techniques. She begins with what students first notice about the novel—its wide and unfamiliar vocabulary—and asks how Fielding's lexicon might "be acknowledged, celebrated, wondered at, and puzzled over." When students take this inductive approach, they are ready to discuss Mikhail Bakhtin's concept of heteroglossia and to question how the novel as genre incorporates polyphony. Campbell also looks at examples of Fielding's extended rhetorical effects, discussing periphrasis, the mock epic, syntactic gymnastics, and double irony and urging students to take note of further examples of these inset performances as they progress in their reading.

Christopher D. Johnson also finds close reading rewarding in the classroom. For example, he helps his students interpret the symbolism of Parson Adams's torn cassock to understand the religious background of *Joseph Andrews*. Beginning with digital images of ecclesiastical vestments from the eighteenth century, Swift's clothing allegory from *The Tale of a Tub*, and passages depicting Adams's ragged appearance, Johnson draws students into analysis of Fielding's mixed satire on the clergy. His method allows them to ponder a complex message: the ridiculous appearance of Adams costs him traditional clerical authority, but at the same time he gains "a more authentic ethical authority" in contrast to his religious brethren in the novel.

In an essay that demonstrates how seemingly small moments can lead to large discussion of characterization and theme, Eric Leuschner explores the allusion to Jenny Cameron in *Tom Jones*. Drawing on different articulations of the myth of Cameron—popular ballads, fictionalized biographies, paintings—he lets his students debate the interpretation of this cultural icon and the effect the reference creates in our understanding of Sophia and of the national political-religious conflict of the '45.

Nicholas Hudson's essay on Fielding's social contexts extends close reading to the realm of critical biography. Fielding has often been too easily labeled as a conservative or opposition writer although his class identifications and political affiliations wavered throughout his lifetime. When students perceive this complexity in his personal history, they are much more likely to question his didactic goals and suspend judgment on his writings until all the evidence is in. Some reliability can be found, however, in the consistency of Fielding's turn to comedy "as an antidote to a decline of English society into avarice, self-interest, and hypocrisy."

"Fielding" on Authority

Another group of essays considers how the classroom might uncover deep-rooted themes of authority in Fielding's fiction. A large body of criticism informs this topic: John Bender (*Imagining*) and John Richetti ("Ideology") are notable for their analyses of ideological structures in Fielding's works, while critics such as Hudson and Paula McDowell argue for his recurrent "distrust of the vehicles of control" (McDowell, "Narrative Authority" 222). All agree that Fielding is self-conscious in his treatment of authority and that a reading of this motif is central to the interpretation of his novels.

In her essay, Rivka Swenson looks at the "patriliterary" anxiety that manifests itself in "Fielding," the narrative presence in *Tom Jones*. Uniting formalist study of narrative instability and historicist contextualization of the early-eighteenth-century crisis in authorship (Statute of Anne of 1710, Actor Rebellion of 1733, and Stage Licensing Act of 1737), she cultivates a paradoxical reading of the novel's depiction of authority. Through her comparisons of *Tom Jones* and *The Author's Farce*, the struggle between *auctor* and audience comes to the fore in the novel.

Elizabeth Kraft describes how her classroom builds on Eric Rothstein's "Virtues of Authority in *Tom Jones*," which refers to Richard Sennett's *Authority* (and its modes of paternalism and autonomy) and Max Weber's categories of leadership (traditional, legal-rational, and charismatic). Encouraging students to read Tom as a potential leader who "will or will not develop the skills necessary to properly govern," Kraft charts her class between Bolingbroke and Hegel to give a politically vital reading of *Tom Jones* as a didactic conduct book for leaders that still has resonance today.

Carl Fisher establishes the hero myth in *Jonathan Wild* through the theories of Machiavelli, Hobbes, and Carlyle. He then asks his class to explore Fielding's ironic undercutting of the heroic, from Fielding's characterization of "Pollitricks" (*Jonathan Wild* 67) to the mob at the gallows awaiting Wild's execution. Fisher finds that his students' enjoyment of satire in modern media makes them receptive to *Wild*'s themes, including that of the "antithetical relation between greatness and goodness."

The depictions of control and power in Fielding's novels corollate significantly with those in his legal and journalistic writings. J. A. Downie notes the consistency of the author's outrage at the ignorance and corruption of the legal system. Citing Squire Allworthy as the rare exception of a skilled magistrate amid a slew of bad ones, Downie shows that throughout his career Fielding railed against abuses of the law at all levels of practice but especially against the assignment of capital punishment to petty offenses. The language of law permeates Fielding's writing, and Fielding often utilizes Roland Barthes's *scriptible* mode of discourse, which requires the reader to adjudicate meaning.

Fielding's Fictional Thinking

Nancy A. Mace, Stephen C. Behrendt, and Anthony J. Hassall foreground literary authority, asking their students to contemplate Fielding's modes of fictional thinking. Their approaches invite students to reflect on aesthetic theory across centuries and disciplines. As a result, Fielding is portrayed as an artist in lively conversation with his predecessors, contemporaries, and successors.

Appraising Fielding's numerous influences and borrowings, Mace helps instructors guide their students through what can be a very ambiguous subject. As she notes, Fielding often "simultaneously imitates and undercuts the genres from which he derives his novels." She demonstrates the epic, romance, and theatrical conventions that frequently appear in his fiction and tracks his narrators' comments about genre (whether or not those remarks about literary kinds run counter to Fielding's own use of them).

In an undergraduate course on British fiction populated by both majors and nonmajors, Behrendt uses analogies to music, visual arts, religion, and philosophy to make students aware of their participatory role in the construction of *Joseph Andrews*. He engages his class in discussion of the narrator, finding that it helps students "respond to the familiarity of [the narrator's] rhetoric and the appearance of candor." The narrator's conversational style and the instability of the information he provides ultimately leads back to a consideration of the preface and its trompe l'oeil description of what *Joseph Andrews* is—trompe l'oeil in that the preface defines the novel by defining the space of what it is not.

Hassall teaches *Tom Jones* as a sui generis work and encourages students to think of the first chapter of each book as an "art of fiction" or instruction manual for users of the text. Reading thus becomes an active process that balances different cognitive functions, such as judgment, entertainment, and sympathy. He has students respond in class discussion and written analysis to the narrator's divergent rules, contradictions, and ironies, helping them see that "[s]tripped of its commentary . . . the story of Tom and Sophia is unremarkable." Like Mace and Behrendt, Hassall presents Fielding as a strategic innovator.

Fielding and Wider Traditions

Several essays in this volume connect Fielding's work to maps of fiction wider than the specifically English tradition. They suggest that Fielding should appear on many more syllabi than solely that of a course on the eighteenth-century English novel. This approach coincides with recent critical studies by Margaret Anne Doody, Michael McKeon, Steven Moore, and Franco Moretti (*Novel*) that reframe the development of the novel.

Attuned to the way that "Fielding's novels challenge the epistemological, moral, and aesthetic premises of realism," Scott Black offers an alternative concept of literary history that avoids narrow definitions and instead maximizes the novel's dialogic and polychronic form. His essay situates Fielding's work in a wide expanse from Cervantes to Milan Kundera and makes a case for the enduring "open-ended ironic dialogism" of Fielding's fiction.

Adam Potkay places *Joseph Andrews* in line with theories of modern romance. This genre, adhering to verisimilitude and the portrayal of virtuous and vicious character types, constitutes a tradition that extends from Homer to Heliodorus, Cervantes, Paul Scarron, Alain-René Lesage, Pierre de Marivaux, and Fielding. Potkay's discussion of Fielding's role in the European tradition examines these roots and expands to Kundera, Salman Rushdie, and other writers students will know from their course work in world literature. Given the increasing prominence of global studies in higher education and the number of double majors, Potkay's approach is well suited for comparative English and Romance-language study.

Joseph Andrews also features in Chloe Wigston Smith's course Travel Literature, which "[contemplates] the expansion of the press alongside the period's growing tourist industry." The course considers the interplay among travel, narrative structure, and the book trade in *Joseph Andrews*, and the readings move from depictions of imaginary destinations to real-world settings, ranging from early America to eastern locales such as Turkey and India.

James Evans teaches Fielding in a course that explores comic theory from Aristophanes to Martin Amis, arguing that *Tom Jones* is "a practical encyclopedia of comic forms, among which are festive comedy, social comedy, manners comedy, intrigue comedy, humors comedy, romantic comedy, sex comedy, farce, parody, and burlesque." Evans explains the methodology behind his choice of texts, showing how cohesion can be built into a set of readings that spans several hundred years.

Jennifer Preston Wilson likewise connects *Amelia* forward in time to nineteenth-century "choice of life" novels featuring a domestic heroine who must devise a course of action under duress. The experimental realism of Fielding's last novel resonates with Romantic and Victorian narratives that portray the psychological toll of social inequity. Wilson shows how the works that most productively interact with *Amelia* often follow its lead in sidestepping the courtship plot, providing an alternative line of development in the novel.

Sham, Opposition, and Debate

Fielding's investigations of deceit, including his depictions of affectation, masquerade, and misinformation, have inspired a number of double-edged classroom techniques. These techniques enter into the spirit of Fielding's comic vision by avoiding commonplace or straightforward modes of communication.

Earla Wilputte offers suggestions for ways that *Shamela*, with its short satiric structure and portraits of audacity and gullibility, might be taught on its own, without the contexts of *Pamela* or *Joseph Andrews*. She looks at how the text exposes sham in the realms of literature, politics, and religion—themes that pervade many other literary and visual works of the eighteenth century—but does not lose sight of Fielding's participation in the exploitative culture he is satirizing. Wilputte asks her students to complete two short written assignments, one a vocabulary list of the tainted "words of wisdom" that permeate the text's discussion of "Vartue," the other a set of character sketches of Shamela, Williams, and Booby. Students often must confront their own preference for the sham spirit over more foolhardy honesty.

Presenting Fielding's *Jonathan Wild* as a puzzle piece that fits into a great many class syllabi, Manushag N. Powell shows the text's versatility by describing how it might work in two very different classes: a performance theory class with *The Beggar's Opera* and a protonovel class in which Mrs. Heartfree's narrative is linked to other travel tales by Jane Barker, Penelope Aubin, and Eliza Haywood. While "Wild is an evil actor run amuck in fiction," Mrs. Heartfree is the heroine of "a feminocentric travel tale," and these contrary identities reside together in *Jonathan Wild*'s "jagged mix" of genres.

Regina Janes builds argument and dissent into her teaching of *Amelia*. Recreating Fielding's own trial of his "favorite child" in the *Covent-Garden Journal*, she invites student participation in an unresolved critical debate. Through this process she finds that students learn to engage not only with the text but also with "Fielding's contemporaries, modern critics, and their own assumptions about the craft of fiction."

Gender Matters

Our contributors find Fielding an excellent resource for considering the performance of eighteenth-century gender, themes of friendship and marriage, and conditions of male and female authorship. As Robert D. Hume notes in his assessment "Fielding at Three Hundred," gender issues in Fielding's fiction veer from transvestite husbands to attempted rape to female warriors (249). Although this is a thriving area of Fielding studies, much remains to be clarified, offering graduate students a possible avenue of research.

In revising his eighteenth-century-novel course, Brian McCrea changed his lineup to include *Joseph Andrews* rather than *Tom Jones*. He discovered that when placed next to works by Eliza Haywood, Frances Burney, Charlotte Lennox, and Elizabeth Inchbald as well as Samuel Richardson's *Clarissa*, *Joseph Andrews* emerges as a significant innovation of the traditional trope of the feminizing birthmark. This theme runs through McCrea's semester and culminates in Burney's *Evelina*, another story of a nobody who is eventually recognized through possession of her mother's appearance and writing.

Pamela S. Bromberg uses juxtapositions to construct a conversation on eighteenth-century gender conventions. She disrupts chronology in her course The English Novel through Austen and begins with *Tom Jones* because of the questions it raises and readerly habits it instills. This novel provides a cornerstone in many ways—offering theories on the emergent genre but also representing women, marriage, and gendered authors and readers, depictions that will come into dialogue with "the different kinds of knowledge and experience, of women's lives and stories, that inform the works of writers such as Behn and Haywood."

In teaching *Amelia*, George E. Haggerty emphasizes its innovation as a "deeply felt account of the complexities of contemporary life and the burdens to be borne by a young married couple of limited means." Fielding tests the strength of social bonds throughout his novel; in particular, male friendship is complicated by conflicting codes of honor and rivalry. Same-gender friendships are marred by competition and deceit in *Amelia*, but at the same time the novel advances a new model of marriage as friendship.

Material Culture Connections

A final group of essays in this volume describes how to teach Fielding through the material culture of the book. By foregrounding the media market of his time, this approach bridges the eighteenth and twenty-first centuries, meeting media-savvy students on familiar ground and interesting them in another era of textual abundance.

Joshua Grasso uses the debate about reading plays versus acting them in *The Author's Farce* to segue into *Joseph Andrews* and its intense concern about what art should do. Establishing the idea that this novel is "a performance about performance itself," he teaches his students about Fielding's theatrical career and the market reality of reading plays intended for print as opposed to acting plays intended for ephemeral enjoyment. This interplay between meaning and entertainment appears in conversations throughout the novel, and Grasso shows students how the manner of performance skews our ideas about what is meaningful and what delightful.

Lisa Maruca teaches a unit entitled "The *Pamela* Media Event," which incorporates *Shamela* and *Joseph Andrews* in a look at eighteenth-century print culture. Her approach includes historical accounts of developments in the book trade, copyright, and modes of print dissemination, and in the class her students develop multimedia forms of writing. Through blog postings, group Web site creation, digital humanities projects, interaction with images from the *ECCO* database, and like activities, the students learn about their own media market while studying the interactions of one predating it by three hundred years.

One further material culture essay is offered by Leigh G. Dillard, who uses illustrated editions of *Joseph Andrews* and *Tom Jones* in her classroom with carefully chosen written prompts that ask students to play the role of illustrator: "What scenes are worthy of visual depiction and why?" "How would you rewrite one of Fielding's novels as a children's book, and what illustrations would you include?" "How would you create a storyboard for a scene to be adapted to film?" By engaging students with creative and evaluative questions, she deepens their knowledge of the novel. When she displays the illustrated texts, she first establishes the history of the publications, then has students compare them. In evaluating visual depictions of Fielding's work, her students must establish ideas of character, scene, and plot against which to articulate their analysis of the artistic rendition.

The essays in this volume demonstrate the adaptability of Henry Fielding's writing to a wide range of contexts, contexts that are highly informed by historical period and national boundaries and contexts that operate beyond those categories. Fielding's vivid portrayal of eighteenth-century society and complexities of language make classroom study of his novels a site of shared interpretive endeavor. Fielding's political and dramatic works may be beyond the scope of this volume, but they inform his performative model of gender identity, self-conscious discussion of authorship, and persistent questions about authority.

Social Contexts: Politics, Law, Religion, Class, and Gender

Nicholas Hudson

Few authors have been as successful as Henry Fielding in creating a broad and various panorama of his age. He seems to capture the very temperament of English life in the mid–eighteenth century. As this temperament is usually vigorous and buoyant, full of life and comedy, teaching his novels and plays is a pleasure that may lead us to forget that he was also a serious social critic, a man who had suffered a great deal personally during a time that he regarded as corrupt and wished to influence and change for the better. Particularly as a novelist, he was driven by a sense that he had something important to say. A contextual reading of his work is useful because it teaches us why he was so concerned, and why he formulated a style that responded with comedy and irony to a social reality that struck him as bleak and dangerous. Although he would not have wanted us to forget his brightness and comedy, he would have liked us to see that they were meant as an antidote to a decline of English society into avarice, self-interest, and hypocrisy. If these themes still resonate with us, it is because he was reacting to the emergence of a political and commercial society that remains part of our modern experience.

Modern scholarship has often linked Fielding to a conservative, aristocratic, and patriarchal tradition (Zirker 136; Battestin and Battestin, *Henry Fielding: A Life* 514). In this way he seems to contrast unfavorably with, especially, his novelistic rival Samuel Richardson, who seems comparably modern, middle-class, and feminist. This comparison is in many respects misleading. The background of Fielding was indeed privileged and elitist insofar as he had aristocratic connections on his father's side and belonged to a large and wealthy clan of landowners, merchants, and clergymen. Always conscious that he was a gentleman, he often reminds us, as in *Tom Jones*, that he was endowed with a splendid classical education at Eton, a college reserved for England's social and political elite. Nonetheless, this background did him little good financially. Well down in the family's scale of inheritance and largely estranged from his father, an erratic and decadent army officer, Fielding had to fend for himself. It is important to keep in mind that the young man was essentially prohibited from merely getting a job. Going into regular trade would have been a disgrace to his family. Though genteel, he appears to have been unattracted by the usual choice of the professions—the military, the law, the cloth, or medicine—yet eventually embraced the law. Instead the twenty-year-old Fielding chose to write for the stage, joining a large group of young men, and some women, with some pretense of social respectability who tried to make a living in London's theatrical and publishing world. Beginning with a fairly routine stage comedy, *Love in Several Masques* (1728), he sought to be a professional writer.

It was an exciting time, and Fielding belonged to what, at some risk of anachronism, we might call a bohemian society. What was termed freethinking was in the air, which meant that the truth of Christianity itself was being challenged in the burgeoning scene of London's taverns and coffeehouses. During the early 1730s, Fielding became acquainted with freethinking writers like James Ralph and Thomas Cooke, and also with aspiring political leaders, like George Lyttelton, who combined freethinking attitudes with wealth and influence. Although Fielding would later reflect deeply over the improvidence of his youth, this period in his life had an abiding influence on his writing. He was recognized by a widening group of people in this set; he was not just any writer drinking in the local tavern. Rebuffed by the theatrical establishment at Drury Lane Theatre, he scored a major success at the Little Haymarket Theatre by satirizing that establishment in *The Author's Farce* (1730). Another great success, *Tom Thumb* (1730), soon after expanded into *The Tragedy of Tragedies* (1731), took aim at some of the most esteemed writers of English tragedy, including John Dryden, as well as the bombastic conventions of tragic acting.

Fielding's talent for farce and his willingness to ridicule the establishment made him an attractive figure for the leaders of the political opposition during a time of rising dissent against the prime minister, Sir Robert Walpole. *Prime minister* was a new coinage, for no minister of the crown had previously assumed so much power. According to the opposition, this power was wielded through bribes and lucrative appointments to friends, along with frequent attempts to intimidate the press. With *Pasquin* (1736), Fielding turned his satire against Walpole's government, scoring a huge success with his audience but also prompting the prime minister to impose the Theatrical Licensing Act of 1737. Driven by this measure from the stage, Fielding would continue to satirize Walpole in the journal he coedited, *The Champion*, while also studying for a career in the law.

The possible insincerity of Fielding's attacks on Walpole has raised much controversy in modern scholarship (see Downie, *Political Biography* 111). Fielding may have accepted a bribe to suppress an earlier stage satire, *The Grub-Street Opera* (1731), and to stop writing for *The Champion* in 1741. He even wrote a satire against his erstwhile political allies, *The Opposition: A Vision* (1741), which portrays Walpole as a benign and maligned figure working for the good of the nation. In certain respects, the political outlook of Fielding was consistent: he was a strong Whig with a patriotic commitment to English "Liberty" (Fielding, *Miscellanies: Volume One* 36–41 and *Jonathan Wild* [*Miscellanies: Volume Three*] 140). He also ardently opposed the exiled Stuart claimants to the throne and, despite some gentle satire of the royal family in early plays, upheld the right of the reigning monarch, George II. But it is dismaying to suspect that, having impugned Walpole principally for his use of bribes, Fielding accepted bribes himself. The evidence of this susceptibility should be kept in mind in teaching *Jonathan Wild* (1743), which certainly contains renewed satire of the "Great Man" (as Walpole was derisively named) at a time when the prime minister had been ousted from power and had evidently disappointed Fielding's hopes of income and promotion.

One defense of Fielding's inconsistency was that Fielding actually cared little about "Pollitricks," as he cynically dubbed the machinations of Parliament (*Shamela* 190; *Jonathan Wild* [*Miscellanies: Volume Three*] 67). Dependent on his pen for his livelihood, he accepted the need to take advantage of financial support offered by either the opposition or the government. His real commitment, however, was to morality, social order, and finally the law. Although his talent for crowd-pleasing farce was profitable, he had always wanted to make his name as a serious social commentator. This aspiration is evident in his dark play *The Modern Husband* (written in 1730, performed in 1732), in which a husband pimps his wife to a fashionable lord and other wealthy men. The play is worth consulting, for its moral concerns remained central to Fielding's writing to the end of his life. Sexual love between married couples was sacred for Fielding, and the corruption of marriage by the love of money reflected the general degradation of a society dominated by avarice and self-interest. Though proud of his connection with the upper classes, he had no illusions about the infections of vice and self-interest in the aristocracy, whose representatives are not generally positive in either his drama or fiction. Long before entering the law, moreover, he was deeply concerned about the corruption of the legal system, as particularly evident in his comedy *Rape upon Rape* (1730), later renamed *The Coffee-House Politician*.

The moral alternative of Fielding to this corruption was generosity, benevolence, and love for others, what he later called "Good-Nature" (*Miscellanies: Volume One* 158; Harrison 89–112). For a number of reasons, this alternative was controversial among his enemies and critics, such as Richardson. First, Fielding tended to rate good nature above all other virtues—for example, above sobriety or a pious respect for the church and clergymen. Though he became inclined to Anglican orthodoxy late in his life, he had much in common with the freethinking circles of his youth in his willingness to berate the clergy for using the church as a vehicle for personal advancement, living the high life while hypocritically preaching the virtues of temperance and chastity. It seemed to many that he had elevated his own notoriously libertine lifestyle as a young man into a kind of moral code, flouting every precept of virtue and religion with the excuse that he was essentially a good-hearted fellow who spent and gave away his money freely. Ironically, Fielding struck others who had comparatively impoverished and obscure backgrounds, such as Richardson and Samuel Johnson, as low or coarse. He indulged in vulgar humor and, according to many reports, was nowhere as happy as in the bibulous company of a low-life tavern. Theoretically, good nature could exist in the breast of a footman or chambermaid, as his novels seem to attest. In practice, however, Fielding set a high premium on his own superiority as a gentleman and increasingly regarded the lower classes as a mob that needed to be controlled. The same inconsistency characterized his attitudes toward women: he demanded chastity from respectable and marriageable women but was a sexual libertine among lower-rank women and in brothels, at least as a young man.

These inconsistencies would be the subject of much repentance in his later life, as dramatized in the apparent self-portrait of Mr. Wilson in *Joseph Andrews* (1742). Nonetheless, Fielding remained convinced that the only cure for the avarice, self-interest, and hypocrisy of modern society was the generosity and love of a good-hearted man or woman. His problem was finding a literary vehicle for these values. His attempt to stage serious social critique, as in *The Modern Husband*, met with limited success, as his audience wanted to laugh. He achieved much greater success in blending social critique with comedy in two adaptations of Molière, *The Mock Doctor* (1732) and *The Miser* (1733). This use of comedy as a medium for social commentary would characterize him when he turned to prose fiction in the early 1740s, beginning with *Shamela* (1741), his parody of Richardson's *Pamela* (1740).

The spectacular success of Richardson's first novel struck Fielding as revealing the corruption of English society. Richardson not only elevates chastity above good nature and all other values but also implies that this virtue is consistent with self-interest and social advancement. Fielding's portrayal of Shamela as a shameless lower-rank hussy suggests snobbery in the author, but this impression is somewhat corrected by *Joseph Andrews*, his novelistic alternative to *Pamela*. Although it is true that his heroically principled footman, Joseph, turns out to be the son of a gentleman, aligning his benevolence with a genteel heritage, Fielding also indicates that the difference between "high People and low People" is really only dress, and he endows his illiterate heroine, Fanny, with "natural Gentility" (153 [bk. 2, ch. 12], 156–58 [ch. 13]). In the eccentric and good-hearted Parson Adams, Fielding presents a truly worthy clergyman left in virtual penury by the establishment. Adams is theologically broad-minded, or latitudinarian, believing that a virtuous Muslim will go to heaven before a vicious Christian. But his commitment to the physical and spiritual welfare of his parishioners fulfills his vocation properly and suggests that Fielding had already distanced himself from the heterodox freethinking of his early acquaintances. Adams also despises Methodism, particularly as championed by George Whitefield, because this emerging populist movement elevated mere faith over the good works that Fielding regarded as the primary commandment of Christianity (82 [bk. 1, ch. 17]; see Battestin, *Moral Basis*).

Adams's lack of advancement in the church is due to his refusal to cooperate with cynical political machinations, the "Pollitricks," also satirized soon after in *Jonathan Wild*. In this second novel, however, Fielding was satirizing not just the recently deposed Walpole but more generally a prevailing value system that rated self-interest, cunning, power, and wealth over the vulnerable good nature of Mr. Heartfree and his wife. In both *Jonathan Wild* and *Joseph Andrews*, he was experimenting with an ironic narrative voice and episodes of broad comedy that, given his talents, were more effective than grave declamation in conveying his moral and social concerns. It was his masterpiece, *Tom Jones*, that completely integrated his comic technique with his moral and social vision. Fielding set this novel during 1745 in the midst of a major political event, the invasion of Prince Charles Edward Stuart with the aim of restoring his Catholic father James to the throne. Although Fielding generally took a cynical view of politics, the '45 galvanized him into action, for he shared the antipathy of most English Protestants to the Church of Rome. He rallied the nation against the Jacobites (supporters of the exiled Stuarts) in his journal *The True Patriot* and later *The Jacobite's Journal*. In *Tom Jones*, the hero joins the troops heading northward to encounter Charles Stuart's army. Fielding was by now loyally reconciled to the government, which included former members of the opposition, such as George Lyttelton, the dedicatee of *Tom Jones*.

Interestingly, Tom's experience mirrors that of the exiled Stuart monarch. Just as the Jacobites claimed that George II was a usurper whose family had deposed the rightful monarch, so Blifil ousts Tom from his legitimate claim to Mr. Allworthy's estate. In Fielding's version, however, the self-interested and hypocritical villain robs the inheritance of a hero who, for all his deviations from chastity and sobriety, exemplifies the instinctive generosity of good nature. If Allworthy's estate, Paradise Hall, can be understood in part as a microcosm of the nation, then Tom's final ascendance to authority, forgiven for his errors by Allworthy and the virtuous Sophia, represents the ideal of an England ruled by benevolence rather than greed and ambition. In this better world, political divisions can be tolerated—even the Jacobitism of Squire Western, who is finally harmlessly comic rather than threatening. Yet Fielding strongly implies throughout the novel that this is a utopian vision, possible in a comic novel but not in reality: in reality, Blifil would have succeeded and Tom would have been hanged. Fielding's deep concern about the state of modern society is evident in the Old Man of the Hill's pessimistic story of corruption and betrayal. Fielding greatly admired Richardson's tragic novel *Clarissa* (1747–48). Although the comedy of *Tom Jones* conveys Fielding's values of generosity and tolerance, Fielding still wished to write something as serious and monitory as *Clarissa*, which he attempted in his decidedly unfunny last novel, *Amelia* (1752).

Some scholars have argued that Fielding finally lost faith in his benign vision of human goodness because of his experience as a London magistrate (Rawson, *Henry Fielding and the Augustan Ideal* 67–98). For many years a hard-working lawyer, he was raised to the bench as chief magistrate for the borough of Westminster in 1748 and later became the chief justice for London. It is important, however, not to exaggerate this loss of faith. The darkness of *Amelia* is not so distant from the vision of corruption in *The Modern Husband* some twenty years before. What we can say is that Fielding became far more conservative socially and politically in his last years. His daily encounters with the violence and depravity of inner-city London, captured in the early prison scenes of *Amelia*, convinced him that only a strict and steady application of the law could control crime and immorality. In practice, he tempered justice where he thought possible, yet his legal pamphlet *An Enquiry into the Causes of the Late Increase of Robbers* (1752) counseled against charity to able-bodied beggars and maintained that magistrates must enforce capital punishment even against the dictates of compassion. He also became more orthodox with regard to the church, arguing in his *Covent-Garden Journal* that the clergy should not tolerate impiety and freethinking. The clergyman in *Amelia*, Dr. Harrison, in his fierce moralism is a far cry from Parson Adams. Meanwhile, the free living of Fielding's early years had taken a terrible physical toll. Fielding traveled to Lisbon in search of the restorative powers of a warm climate but soon died there, in 1754, at the age of only forty-seven. His journal of this voyage presents a depressing picture of a dying man who despaired of the possibility of human goodness.

Viewed in the context of his time, Fielding emerges as a highly independent commentator on English society. Politically, he was a solid Whig who believed in liberty, though he generally had little faith in the virtues of politicians. His greatest concerns were moral and social. His belief that morality was grounded in benevolence toward other human beings, even to the neglect of other virtues, was highly controversial. Only love and compassion, he insisted, could correct the greed and self-interest fostered by a commercial society. He believed in open-mindedness and latitude until near the end of his life, though he became increasingly suspicious of non-Christian morality, such as espoused by the philosopher Square in *Tom Jones*. Fielding has been frequently criticized, both then and now, for his superficial view of women and idealized notion of male erotic passion (see Smallwood 15–32). But he believed strongly that healthy love between men and women was a redemptive force in a world where human relations were too often dictated by avarice and self-obsession. Above all, he embraced the full range of English society and, despite his self-conscious gentility, was distinctive for his capacity to value goodness in the humblest settings.

Literary Contexts: Epic, Romance, Drama, and the Novel

Nancy A. Mace

One of the most important features of the novels of Fielding is the way he engages with other literary genres, including the epic, the romance, and the drama. He could assume that his original readers were familiar with the ancient epic and with the romance, whose development stretches from the medieval chivalric narratives to the French romances of his own time, but his references to epic, romance, and eighteenth-century drama present difficulties to many of his modern readers, who are unacquainted with these literary traditions. Although Fielding drew liberally from a wide range of literary types, his use of his sources reflects both his admiration for and his discomfort with them. In particular, his statements about genres like epic and romance often run counter to his use of these literary forms. A review of these sources reveals that he adopts features from them in his "new species of writing" (*Essay on the New Species*), while at the same time it demonstrates how his work differs from the literature that has preceded him.

The relationship of his novels to various literary genres has been the subject of much debate. For years scholars have struggled to interpret his often quoted statement that "a comic Romance is a comic Epic-Poem in Prose" (*Joseph Andrews* 4), reaching no consensus about the extent to which the epic and the romance influenced his novels. Such critics as Sheridan Baker ("Fielding's Comic Epic-in-Prose Romances" and "Idea"), James Lynch, and Henry Knight Miller have argued that Fielding's novels reflect a close connection to the romance tradition; others, like Thomas E. Maresca, J. Paul Hunter (*Occasional Form*), Nancy A. Mace (*Henry Fielding's Novels*), and Lyall Powers, have noted the pervasive presence of Latin quotations and references to epic, which seem to align his narratives with the works of Homer and Vergil. A chief difficulty with this debate is the question of definition. How did eighteenth-century writers and readers distinguish between epic and romance? This question is particularly tricky because, as many scholars have observed, the early writers of romances drew plot elements, settings, and characters from the epics of Homer and Vergil. Another difficulty is whether eighteenth-century readers simply equated the terms *epic* and *narrative*, as some scholars have argued, or associated the epic with particular features.

Fielding's use of the epic is typical of the manner in which he simultaneously imitates and subverts the genres on which he bases his novels. On the one hand, he uses the term *epic* in his prefaces and alludes to Homer and Vergil so as to demonstrate that he considers his novels serious literary works of the same caliber as epic poems. Throughout his introductory chapters, he draws from René Le Bossu's description of the epic, well known to eighteenth-century readers: "The EPOPEA is a Discourse invented by Art, to form the Manners by such Instructions as are disguis'd under the Allegories of some one important Action, which is related in Verse, after a probable, diverting, and surprizing Manner" (6).

Fielding echoes this definition in the preface to *Joseph Andrews* when he mentions "Fable, Action, Characters, Sentiments, and Diction" as features related to the epic (3). He also links his concept of the novel in *Tom Jones* to Le Bossu's definition, especially in the introductory chapter where Fielding discusses probability, referring to the ancient epics and to critics like André Dacier, who wrote extensively on epic theory (*History of Tom Jones* 395–407 [bk. 8, ch. 1]). While we cannot take all his comments in this chapter seriously—for example, his remarks about introducing ghosts into novels are certainly facetious—his references to epic suggest that he considers his works comparable to this ancient genre, still considered by eighteenth-century critics to be a highly prestigious literary form.

That his novels are full of allusions to Homer, Vergil, and their commentators also suggests that he regarded his novels as a modern descendant of the epic. For example, the epigraph to *Tom Jones* is a quotation about Homer from Horace's *Ars Poetica*, "*Mores hominum multorum vidit*" 'he saw the customs of many men' (*De arte poetica liber*, line 142), a phrase that can equally describe the epic poet and Fielding's narrator (1). Scholars have also noted affinities between the structures and characters in his novels and those of ancient epics. For example, Maurice Johnson (139–56) and Powers both find similarities between the plot and characters of Vergil's *Aeneid* and Fielding's *Amelia*, and Leon Gottfried discusses patterns in *Joseph Andrews* that mirror elements of the *Odyssey*. Thus, Fielding's commentary on the novel form and imitation of epic plots and characters reveal his admiration for these ancient writers, whose work is in part the model for his own.

On the other hand, Fielding undermines his laudatory references to epic through parodies of epic scenes and his ambivalent presentation of the epic hero. Both *Joseph Andrews* and *Tom Jones* have episodes that are comic imitations of those in Homer and Vergil. For example, Fielding's description of Joseph's cudgel recalls those of Achilles's shield in *Iliad* 18.490–508 and Aeneas's armor in *Aeneid* 8.608–731 (*Joseph Andrews* 238–42 [bk. 3, ch. 6]). Other scenes echo traditional set pieces in the ancient epics. The famous battle between Molly Seagrim and the townspeople in the churchyard is a comic recreation of the battle scenes and catalogs of Homer and Vergil (*History of Tom Jones* 177–84 [bk. 4, ch. 8]). Later, the narrator uses the terms of the standard libation scene in epic poetry when Tom shares a drink with the innkeeper, his wife, and their servant (508 [bk. 9, ch. 4]). Such juxtapositions of the ancient and the modern emphasize the distance separating the heroic from the modern world, suggesting the inferiority of the latter. At the same time, these parodies mock the epic genre itself, indicating its limitations when applied to a Christian nation. Nowhere is this effect clearer than in Fielding's presentation of the epic hero. Although the epic imitations reflect the attitude of characters like Tom, who, when fighting for Molly in the churchyard, imagines himself as Achilles or Aeneas, they also underscore Fielding's discomfort with a heroic ideal that does not conform to Christian morality. As Tom discovers on his travels, real soldiers are nothing like the Greeks and Trojans of epic, and he finds the heroic concept of honor incompatible with his duty as a Christian to refrain from killing another person (367–84 [bk. 7, chs. 11–13]).

Fielding's use of the romance tradition functions in the opposite way from his use of the epic: although he repeatedly distances his work from the romance in his introductory chapters, he freely draws on this literary tradition. In *Joseph Andrews*, he identifies his work with Fénelon's *Télémaque* and Homer's *Odyssey*, contrasting these epics with the romances, which have "very little Instruction or Entertainment" (3–4). He observes in *Tom Jones* that, unlike his novels, romances do not have a unified structure and violate the rules of probability (264 [bk. 5, ch. 12]; 402 [bk. 8, ch. 1]). He reinforces his negative comments about the romance with references to satires like Scarron's *Roman comique* and Cervantes's *Don Quixote*. His most explicit statement appears in *Joseph Andrews*, where he contrasts these narratives with such works in the romance tradition as Mary Delarivier Manley's *New Atalantis* (185–91 [bk. 3, ch. 1]). By making such direct statements and associating his own work with famous parodies of romance, then, he distances his novels from a literary form largely denigrated in his time.

Yet, as many scholars have observed, Fielding adopts romance conventions in creating the characters and plots of his novels. Scholars arguing that the romance is Fielding's primary source do not agree about his usage of the term: some maintain that he turns to the chivalric romances, while others focus on postclassical Greek romances typified by Heliodorus's *Aethiopica*, a work rediscovered in the sixteenth century, or on the French romances widely available in English translation during the eighteenth century (H. Miller; J. Lynch; Baker, "Fielding's Comic Epic-in-Prose Romances" and "Idea"). Regardless of the type of romance identified as the main influence on Fielding, these scholars dismiss his references to the epic, suggesting that his usage of the term is synonymous with *narrative* and asserting that he invokes the epic analogy only to signal the serious intent of his novels. In fact, these critics virtually ignore Fielding's references to epic by arguing that the original romances grew from the ancient poems; thus, they assert, many of the epic elements in Fielding's novels come from the romance tradition.

Despite their differences, these scholars detect the same romance elements in the plots of *Jonathan Wild*, *Joseph Andrews*, and *Tom Jones*. Each of these narratives contains adventures reminiscent of the journeys undertaken by the heroes of romance. One of the most humorous is Mrs. Heartfree's account of her experiences at sea, in which she fights off the advances of ship captains and a hermit, survives a storm and shipwreck, encounters strange beasts, and eventually arrives safely home (*Jonathan Wild* 154–75 [bk. 4, chs. 7–12]). Another plot device common to the romance involves a mystery surrounding the true identities of the main characters and the revelation of their birth at the end of the narrative, for many characters in both *Joseph Andrews* and *Tom Jones* do not know who their real parents are until the last chapters of the novel. After fearing that they are brother and sister, for example, Joseph and Fanny discover their real parentage: she is actually the Andrews' daughter, kidnapped as an infant by Gypsies; he is actually Mr. Wilson's lost son, stolen from him by the same group. In typical romance fashion, Mr. Wilson confirms his son's identity from Joseph's strawberry birthmark (335–39 [bk. 4, ch. 15]). In *Tom Jones*, Mrs. Waters reveals that Tom's real mother is Bridget Allworthy; Tom, whose origin has long been a mystery, is therefore Mr. Allworthy's nephew and a suitable husband for Sophia (944–51 [bk. 18, ch. 8]). While these endings satirize the resolutions typical of romance, they also demonstrate Fielding's practice of drawing freely from other genres to forward his plot.

In addition, Fielding has his characters use the inflated diction of romance. For example, among the roles that Tom assumes is that of the romantic lover, especially in his encounters with Sophia. Typical is a lovers' meeting near the brook, when their dialogue imitates the elevated language of chivalric love (237–39 [bk. 5, ch. 6]). In his soliloquy in a later chapter, he avows that he prefers Sophia over Circassian beauties adorned with "all the Jewels of the *Indies*" (256 [ch. 10]). Thus, he imagines himself the romance hero swearing eternal fidelity to his mistress. Consequently, Fielding's use of romance conventions contradicts his statements in the prefaces distancing his work from this genre.

The use of epic and romance by Fielding has received the greatest critical attention, but his novels also reflect his earlier work in the theater, since he incorporates features taken from drama into his novels. Many of his characters deliver soliloquies without the narrator's commentary, as when Wild ponders the vanity of human greatness and Heartfree bemoans his misfortune after being arrested for debt (*Jonathan Wild* 62–63 [bk. 2, ch. 4], 94–98 [bk. 3, ch. 2]). In addition, characters engage in dialogues presented as if they were scenes in a play; such is the heated exchange between Wild and Laetitia after their marriage (112–18 [ch. 8]). Fielding includes actual stage performances, in part to explore audience response, as he does in describing Partridge's reaction to Garrick's performance in *Hamlet* (*History of Tom Jones* 636–40 [bk. 12, ch. 5]). Many scenes in the novels are theatrical in their staging, having entrances, exits, and fast pacing—the most famous example of such staging is the central episode at Upton in *Tom Jones*, full of fights, seductions, and mistaken identities (499–522 [bk. 9, chs. 3–7], 527–54 [bk. 10, chs. 2–7]). Finally, Fielding draws from his plays for many character types that populate his novels. Sir Positive Trap of his early play *Love in Several Masques* (1728) is a prototype for Squire Western in *Tom Jones*, and Lady Trap, the amorous matron, has reincarnations as Mrs. Waters and Lady Bellaston (Lockwood, "Fielding" 26; Baker, "Fielding" 110).

Fielding refers to the theater and its critics in his commentaries and prefaces, often acknowledging the connections between his novels and plays. In *Joseph Andrews*, readers hear about the vagaries of a playwright's existence in

Mr. Wilson's account of his efforts to become a writer for the stage (215–18 [bk. 3, ch. 3]), and in a later chapter, "A Discourse between the Poet and Player," a poet and player disparage both actors and playwrights of the period (259–64 [ch. 10]). Fielding's commentary in *Tom Jones* also periodically relates to the stage. In the chapter "In Which the Author Himself Makes His Appearance on the Stage," Fielding assumes the role of the chorus to interpret the actions of Blifil, Allworthy, and, most important, Tom (140–42 [ch. 7]). He introduces book 7 with a chapter entitled "A Comparison between the World and the Stage," which explores both his characters' behavior and his readers' response to it (323–29).

As theatrical as the novels appear, however, they are not plays. As Fielding does with other genres, he incorporates conventions from his work in the theater into his new form. In some cases, the theatrical presentation of a character underscores the artifice of the character. Scholars have noted that Fielding portrays Jonathan Wild as a bad comic actor whose speeches become less effective as the narrative progresses. Wild's performances reveal his hypocrisy and the distance between the roles he plays for his various audiences and his real personality (Rawson, *Henry Fielding and the Augustan Ideal* 101–259; Pettit 159–68). One of Fielding's main challenges in adapting dramatic technique for the novel was the matter of interpretation. Because Fielding does not have the assistance of actors to convey character through their speeches and gestures, he substitutes a lively style and uses the intrusive narrator as a commentator who serves the function of actors interpreting their roles for the audience. Thus, as Thomas Lockwood has argued, his narrative persona is in effect another actor on the stage, guiding the response of the audience to the scenes as they unfold ("Fielding" 21–39).

A final possible source for Fielding is the work of his contemporaries in the genre of the novel, particularly Samuel Richardson. Scholars have attempted to link Fielding's work to an earlier novel tradition, stretching back to the ancient classics. One flaw of this approach is that it relies on a very broad definition of a novel, including episodic narratives like Petronius's *Satyricon* and Lucian's *True History*. Because Fielding does not mention any of these earlier works, we have no way of determining his level of familiarity with them. Lucian has often been linked to Fielding, but the influence of the Greek satirist is overstated. In fact, Fielding rarely refers to Lucian in his work, preferring classical authors like Homer, Vergil, and Horace (Mace, *Henry Fielding's Novels* 54–57). In addition, the ancient prose narratives do not fit the definition of the genre as laid out in his prefaces and introductory chapters, which emphasize the novel's didactic purpose, narrative unity, believable characters, and realistic situations. Instead, Fielding conceives of his new species in relation to epic and the French romances of his time. Throughout his commentary on the novel genre, he demonstrates his belief that he is establishing rules for a completely new literary form. Consequently, even if one considers these earlier narratives novels, their influence on Fielding is minimal at best.

Although Fielding clearly had Richardson's *Pamela* in mind when he wrote *Shamela* and *Joseph Andrews*, neither is merely a parody. Richardson is not Fielding's only satiric object in *Shamela*; as has often been noted, in addition to *Pamela*, Fielding's targets include Conyers Middleton, Colley Cibber, and Methodists like George Whitefield (*Shamela* 137–40). Fielding draws some characters and the original premise for *Joseph Andrews* from Richardson's novel but does not imitate the epistolary form of *Pamela*, nor does his work parody Richardson after the opening chapters. *Joseph Andrews* has more plot similarities to Cervantes's *Don Quixote* than to Richardson's work (Ardila; Baker, "Fielding" 116–20). Consequently, we cannot regard many earlier novels as significant sources of Fielding's fictional practices.

Fielding drew from a wide variety of literary types in constructing his narratives—epic, romance, drama—and he was aware of the experiments in fiction made by contemporaries like Richardson. But he made those sources his own, incorporating elements that served his purposes at the same time as he asserted his independence from the literature that came before him. His true genius, then, appears in the way he transforms the literary tradition in order to create something new.

Generic Contexts: Nonrealist Traditions of the Novel

Scott Black

One of the ironies of this volume is that Fielding didn't write novels. That's an irony the author himself, one of the great ironists of the English literary tradition, would have relished, both as a joke on critics and as a nice problem in its own right. In *Joseph Andrews* and *Tom Jones*, in particular, he addresses the tricky issue of genre. He insists his works aren't romances, at least in the common sense of the term, but he's ambivalent about the category and remarks that if the genre of romance didn't have such a bad reputation, he'd be willing to adopt the name (*History of Tom Jones* 489 [bk. 9, ch. 1]). He also calls his works biographies and histories but mocks the typical biases of biographies and histories (*Joseph Andrews* 18–19, *History* 150 [bk. 4, ch. 1]). And he comes up with unwieldy and funny but quite accurate and helpful composite categories to characterize "this kind of Writing, which I do not remember to have seen hitherto attempted in our Language," which he calls in the preface to *Joseph Andrews* "comic Romance" or "comic Epic-Poem in Prose" (4) and in *Tom Jones* "Prosai-comi-epic Writing" (209 [bk. 5, ch. 1]). But Fielding never, ever calls his works novels, and the only time he refers to novels is as part of a compound genre that he dismisses, for instance, in castigating the "Swarm of foolish Novels, and monstrous Romances" he fears will clog up booksellers' shelves and readers' minds (*History* 487 [bk. 9, ch. 1]).

This is not just terminology. Fielding's novel is not our realistic novel, but Fielding's prose fictions (which I'll continue to call novels in imitation of his characteristically ironic adoption of familiar terms) fit no more comfortably into recent Anglo-American histories of the novel than into the eighteenth-century category. If not "monstrous," Fielding's novels have been the ugly ducklings of novel history, something to explain away rather than describe in their own terms. They are comic, ironic, and adaptive, and they fit awkwardly into accounts of a genre defined by formal realism and the invention of a modern form for the modern world: posttraditional, empiricist, individualist. Fielding's works were famously exceptions to Ian Watt's magisterial account of the rise of the novel and continue to be read as skeptical, conservative reactions to the genre's development (McKeon, ch. 12; Richetti, *English Novel*, ch. 5). This outsider status is certainly right, but it should be remembered that such histories adopt a perspective that Fielding criticized. His novels challenge the epistemological, moral, and aesthetic premises of realism. Assertions of truth and goodness, he loves to demonstrate, are most questionable when they come from one's own mouth, and an art formed by such testimony, pretending unmediated access to the real, depends on a fundamental mistake of reading that Fielding's work is designed to ridicule and correct. His self-consciously and playfully mediated fictions disable the illusion of such access and mock the aspiration to it. Instead of defining his work in the restricted, locally contextualized terms of realism, Fielding makes full use of the formal resources of his traditions—indigenous and imported, new and old, high and low—in works organized by the interaction, and the clash, of the many voices and many forms that make up complex, cosmopolitan cultures. If ugly ducklings in histories of the realist novel, Fielding's works fly gracefully with the swans of a longer, wider, and stranger history of prose fiction.

This essay offers some suggestions for thinking about the novel's form and history from Fielding's perspective, suggestions I've developed over the past several years in courses on long genealogies of prose fiction organized by questions of experiment and adaptation. Steven Moore bluntly states that the familiar account of the novel, "realistic narratives driven by a strong plot and peopled by well-rounded characters struggling with serious ethical issues, conveyed in language anybody can understand," is "wrong": "The tradition is wider and weirder than that" (3, 31). Less combatively, recent academic histories of the novel have sought to remap its rise (Mander) in terms that are "historically longer, geographically larger, and morphologically deeper than nineteenth-century realism" (Moretti, "Novel" 111). Such alternative histories of the genre (or histories of an alternative genre) offer a promising opportunity for presenting Fielding in terms that are closer to his own theory and practice of the novel than to an English tradition oriented by formal and historical realism. (Histories of the realist novel are organized by the realism they track; literary texts are read in relation to local contexts). Robert D. Hume wonders whether Fielding belongs in such a history at all: "We in English departments treat Fielding as a novelist in an English tradition (often, indeed, as a founding father), but he evidently saw himself as part of larger classical and Continental traditions. Scholars have rarely made much attempt to view Fielding in a supranational context" ("Fielding" 242). There are notable exceptions to this neglect (Mace, *Henry Fielding's Novels* 132; Scholes, Phelan, and Kellogg 267; Battestin, *Henry Fielding: A Life* 327–28), but Hume's larger point is morphological rather than historical: "Conscious though he is of the classics, Fielding is not trying to associate himself closely with predecessors and traditions. Conscious though he is of Continental practice, neither does he seem to become derivative of it. . . . He innovates, experiments, and takes chances." Fielding certainly was an experimental writer, and if not quite as "radically *sui generis*" as Hume suggests (259), his novels self-consciously participate in a tradition of fictions that explore and play with formal conventions. Putting Fielding's novels in such contexts allows us to read them with the grain, as self-consciously adaptive, expansively polyvocal, and elaborately multigeneric works in a genealogy of reflexive fictions.

Joseph Andrews is "written in imitation of the manner of Cervantes" (from the title page), and when Fielding introduces it as a "comic Epic-Poem in Prose," he refers to a long-standing critical trope that he may have picked up from the canon of Toledo's conversation with Quixote at the end of the first part of

Don Quixote ([trans. Smollett] 494 [pt. 1, ch. 47]). After five hundred pages of mocking the absurdities of romance, Cervantes introduces the canon of Toledo to defend it. This is one of the ways the *Quixote* answers Quixote, suggesting a better way to read romances and one that depends on the reflexive perspective Cervantes builds into his book with devices like the canon. The canon provides a different kind of answer to Quixote than either the realists who burn the dangerous books or the realism of a disenchanted world that destroys Quixote's literary illusions. The canon rehearses the arguments of the literary debate sparked by the rediscovery of Heliodorus's *Ethiopian Story*, which was taken as a classical model for a modern prose fiction that would formally regularize and morally correct the fantastic, unwieldy, and adulterous medieval romances of chivalry (Forcione 91). Such modern romances coordinated a variety of stories, genres, and levels of discourse in shapely epic designs, and this coordination stands behind the canon's praise for romance as "a web of such various and beautiful texture," which "gives the author opportunities of shewing his talents in epics, lyrics, tragedy and comedy, and all the different branches of the delicious and agreeable arts of poetry: for, epics may be written in prose as well as verse" (*Don Quixote* [trans. Smollett] 500). The canon is a metafictional mouthpiece of critique and correction in the novel, one of a long series of readers in (and readers of) *Don Quixote* who populate the work alongside its foundational reader, Quixote. (The canon pops in as one voice in this loose and baggy book; in his final work, *Persiles*, Cervantes will write a more shapely modern prose epic on the model of Heliodorus.) *Don Quixote* is a book obsessed with reading, its dangers, its difficulties, and its pleasures. Fielding's novels adopt Cervantes's narrative variety and adapt his metafictional gestures to imitate the *Quixote*'s multiperspectival critique of Quixotic reading. Like Cervantes, Fielding plays with both the limits of romance and the limits of realism: he deconstructs Tom's inflated romance rhetoric when Tom crawls into the bushes with Molly (*History* 256–57 [bk. 5, ch. 10]) but also elaborately inflates his own rhetoric when he introduces Sophia by way of literary fireworks—and includes a discussion of literary fireworks (154–56 [bk. 4, ch. 2]). The answer to the mistake of reading that Cervantes satirizes with Quixote's imitation of *Amadis* and that Fielding satirizes with Joseph's imitation of *Pamela* isn't just to sanitize and simplify fiction (so readers won't be fooled again) but to open it up to the interplay of critical judgment and readerly desire.

Fielding announces his participation in the tradition of comic epic poems in prose in a critical voice that (to either the horror or delight of students) remains with us for the rest of the book. He relaxes Cervantes's baroque play with authorship into a single, though variable, voice that is extended throughout the text. This relaxation gives both an essayistic intimacy and an epic range to the metafictional perspective (Knight, "Fielding's Afterlife" 177; Alter, "Fielding's Legacy" 319), and it allows Fielding to focalize the various problems of judgment his novels are built around. I find Mikhail Bakhtin's "Discourse in the Novel" useful for presenting to my students these aspects of Fielding's works.

Part of the "second stylistic line" of the genre that's defined by "a trial and self-critique of novelistic discourse," English comic novels like Fielding's are thoroughly dialogic representations of their cultures:

> The novel begins to make use of these languages, manners, genres; it forces all exhausted and used-up, all socially and ideologically alien and distant worlds to speak about themselves and in their own style—but the author builds a superstructure over these languages made up of his own intentions and accents, which then becomes dialogically linked with them. . . . [A]n unresolved conversation begins to sound in the image itself; the image becomes an open, living, mutual interaction between worlds, points of view, accents. (412, 409)

Fielding offers an especially performative version of this kind of authorial superstructure. He participates in the loud and busy space of the comic novel as one voice, albeit a privileged one, among many—Bakhtin notes that truth doesn't have its own word in such dialogic forms (309)—and engages readers in the experience modeled by the narrative experiment (Alter, *Fielding and the Nature* 190; Bell 238). The narrative comedy—interrupted conversations, incompatible perspectives, ironically juxtaposed social idioms and discursive levels—is continued at the level of narrative address, as Fielding responds to his own text and teases, mocks, and provokes the reader to respond, in turn, to it and to him. This dialogic comic form, where everyone gets a say but no one gets the final word, is the work space of Fielding's signature moral irony, which "shifts the function of the novel away from exemplary moral instruction and towards the comic perception of human complexity and contradiction" (Knight, "Fielding's Afterlife" 187). It's an open question whether this open form is supposed finally to be resolved or not.

This open-ended ironic dialogism also organizes Fielding's self-conscious participation in literary history, as a comic interplay of genres, idioms, and cultural forms is managed by a stagey impresario. Charles Knight discusses Milan Kundera among other novelists (like Thackeray, Gogol, and Gombrowicz) who adopt Fielding's essayistic voice and its various ironies, and Kundera himself discusses Fielding's experiments with narration: "[H]e wanted to dazzle his audience not by the illusion of reality but by the enchantment of his storymaking" (*Curtain* 13). Fielding's performative narration includes both a running commentary about the mechanics of his story and a flamboyant and usually ironic adaptation of patterns from a wide range of sources. Robert Alter writes that "his most essential procedure as a novelist is constantly to enrich his fictional world by reminding us in different ways of the literary artifice through which that world comes into being" (*Fielding and the Nature* 31). If this procedure reflexively registers the constructed nature of the artwork, it also makes clear the several contexts in which the work participates, both its own local time and what Bakhtin calls "great time" ("Response" 3–4), that space in which books respond to other books "as if on a distinct time-scale, and even time-sequence"

(Fowler 122–23). In this context of "the supranational history of its art (the *large context*)," Kundera notes, the novel looks like this: "[I]t was to Rabelais that Laurence Sterne was reacting, it was Sterne who set off Diderot, it was from Cervantes that Fielding drew constant inspiration, it was against Fielding that Stendahl measured himself" (*Curtain* 35). Fielding's play with literary artifice registers a scale of history in which texts are formed as much by future readings and adaptations as by their moments of production. "*Don Quixote* becomes more than it initially was after its transmutation into the 'Cervantick' *Tom Jones* and *Tristram Shandy*, after *The Red and the Black*, *Madame Bovary*, *Moby Dick*, *Ulysses*, and *The Castle*" (Alter, *Partial Magic* 229). We tend to think (in terms of realism) that putting texts in history means locating them in their original time. But putting texts in history also means recognizing how texts live in time, and in other times, as anachronistic hinges that join disparate epochs and as relays in a string of adaptations that more fully realize the potential of earlier experiments.

Modern literary histories work by identifying the invention of new forms that break with tradition and convention. A less modern literary history might recognize in this kind of invention an ironic trace of an older meaning (*inventio* as "finding," "adapting") as a way into a contrapuntal method of writing and reading history. Fielding answers Samuel Richardson's project in *Pamela*, which depends on a naively Quixotic practice of reading, with *Joseph Andrews*, an adaptation of the *Quixote*. In answering a local problem with a borrowed tool, he imitates Cervantes's "invention of the novel," which Anthony Cascardi describes as a refashioning of preexisting forms, not an invention of new ones, and indeed a remix that ironically undercuts such claims for novelty (59, 64). In these terms the novel is a critical genre that suggests a different way to construe its historical contexts and its history. Rather than a brand-new form for a brand-new world, it offers a way to explore the variety of forms, discourses, and genres that make up a complex, polychronic world. Self-consciously fashioned as hinges that join rather than wedges that separate, Fielding's novels model and enable the skills of literacy necessary to cosmopolitan cultures of many forms from many times and many places.

This is the literacy of the total *Quixote*, not its eponymous hero. But of course that totality includes the pleasures as well as the parody of Quixote's readerly mistakes. The totality indicates a distinction between Fielding's kind of reflexive novel and some postmodern ones. Fielding uses metafictional tools but remains firmly in a traditional project of *poiesis*, making art rather than using aesthetic forms for critical projects. The novel according to Fielding is an epic poem in prose, both adaptive and shapely, and as concerned with reusing the narrative power of its borrowed forms as with critiquing their abuses. Fielding's novels clearly aim to provide readerly pleasure. They recycle forms, that is, for both new and old purposes, adapting traditional narratives for new reasons as well as adopting them for familiar reasons. Like Cervantes—and like the writers adapted by Cervantes such as Heliodorus and Ariosto, as well as more recent novelists working on projects that critically adapt and creatively tap their own traditions, Italo Calvino, Carlos Fuentes, Salman Rushdie, Ben Okri—Fielding shows a reflexivity that is part of an "unresolved conversation" across history between still active, still potent forms and new adaptations. This is not a single conversation or a shared tradition. Rather, it's a shared gesture coded in the potential of the novel's intimately dialogic form that brings together literary history, text, and reader in an emergent experience. Rushdie writes:

> What is formed, in the secret act of reading, is a different kind of identity, as the reader and writer merge, through the medium of the text, to become a collective being that both writes as it reads and reads as it writes, and creates, jointly, that unique work, "their" novel. This "secret identity" of writer and reader is the novel form's greatest and most subversive gift. (426)

Fielding certainly belongs in genealogies of self-conscious, metafictional novels, as Alter (*Fielding and the Nature* 187), Linda Hutcheon (27), and Scott Robertson (224–25) agree, though Patricia Waugh doesn't (32). But Fielding's novels also suggest a different kind of history of the novel, one organized by the readerly contexts of anachronism and an attendant recognition of the polychronicity of history. His novels, that is, suggest a conception of literature (and of culture and consciousness) that mixes and juxtaposes, and perhaps almost integrates, a variety of forms with a self-awareness about the work that can be done on them and the pleasure that can be had with them. His genre is defined by the interaction of readerly experiences with other realities. And it is organized by the strange loops between them: not only the ways realities are uploaded into representations (the questions of realism) but also the ways texts are realized by both Quixotes and *Quixotes* (questions of reading). Fielding's kind of novel (or comic romance, or comic epic poem in prose, or maximalist megametanarrative) offers a tool of witty critique in a space of witting play—a work space and a game space in which to explore and experiment with the continual, unresolved feedback between the products of the imagination and the real world, through a readerly experience that may not fully obey the laws of either literature or history.

Authorial Contexts: Connections between Fielding's Novels and His Legal and Journalistic Writing

J. A. Downie

On 1 November 1737, a few months after his career as a playwright came to an abrupt end with the passing of the theatrical Licensing Act, Henry Fielding was admitted into the Society of the Middle Temple as a "special" student. Less than three years later, on 20 June 1740, he was called to the bar as a consequence, apparently, of his "great application and progress in the Study of the Law" (Downie, "Henry Fielding" 113). Between November 1748, when advance copies of the first two volumes of *Tom Jones* were made available to eager subscribers, and the middle of 1754, when he left for Lisbon in a vain attempt to recover his health, he implemented the series of initiatives as justice of the peace for Westminster and Middlesex that established his reputation as a reforming magistrate. During these years, he also published a series of writings addressing social issues, including *An Enquiry into the Causes of the Late Increase of Robbers, &c.* (1751; Enquiry 61–218) and *A Proposal for Making Effectual Provision for the Poor* (1753; 219–80), which offer interesting perspectives on his approach to crime and poverty. His novels not only are shot through with references to the law but also attend to the sort of issues addressed by the social pamphlets. Interrogating the ideology underpinning Fielding's other writings opens up a further dimension for students' understanding and appreciation of his novels.

Magistrates figure prominently in Fielding's novels and throughout his writings, from the corrupt Justice Squeezum of his early play *Rape upon Rape; or, The Justice Caught in His Own Trap* (1730) to Squeezum's fictional counterpart as magistrate for Westminster in *Amelia* (1752), "*Jonathan Thrasher*, Esq; one of the Justices of the Peace for that Liberty" (58 [bk. 1, ch. 2]), who outrageously sends the unfortunate Captain Booth to prison. In *Tom Jones*, both Allworthy and Squire Western are justices of the peace, even though the latter (like Thrasher) is heavily reliant for advice on his clerk, who "luckily" has "a Qualification, which no Clerk to a Justice of [the] Peace ought ever to be without, namely, some Understanding in the Law of this Realm" (*History of Tom Jones* 357 [bk. 7, ch. 9]).

Widespread ignorance of the law, especially on the part of those whose responsibility it was to dispense justice, was one of Fielding's favorite themes, not only in his fiction but also in the pamphlets he published while he was a magistrate. In contradistinction to such unworthy examples, the magistrate who commits Heartfree to prison in *Jonathan Wild* "did indeed no small Honour to the Commission he bore" and "duly considered the weighty Charge committed to him, by which he was intrusted with Decisions affecting the Lives, Liberties and Properties of his Countrymen." In fact, when we are told that he "examined always with the utmost Diligence and Caution, into every minute Circumstance" (152 [bk. 4, ch. 6]), he appears to anticipate what Fielding was to put into practice ten years later as a reforming magistrate at Bow Street, when he began to transform the role, along the lines of the Scottish procurator-fiscal, from a passive to an active one (Langbein 60–76).

However, the magistrate held up by Fielding in his fiction as a model for others to follow was Mr. Thomas Allworthy, who, according to the narrator of *Tom Jones*, was "in Reality as great a Pattern [of true Wisdom] as he was of Goodness" (282 [bk. 6, ch. 3]). Unlike Justice Thrasher, who "was never indifferent in a Cause, but when he could get nothing on either Side" (*Amelia* 21 [bk. 1, ch. 5]), Allworthy is shown to be utterly impartial. His sentiments are made apparent early on in the narrative, in his dealings with the supposed mother of the foundling he discovers in his bed. When he offers Jenny Jones "wholesome Admonition and Reproof" concerning the serious consequences of "the Violation of [her] Chastity," he observes that "no private resentment should ever influence a Magistrate" (50–51 [bk. 1, chs. 6–7]), yet his treatment of her also bears out the narrator's subsequent observation: "For such was the Compassion which inhabited Mr. *Allworthy's* Mind, that nothing but the Steel of Justice could ever subdue it" (140 [bk. 2, ch. 7]).

Allworthy is by no means the only character in *Tom Jones* to be connected with the legal profession. Fielding runs the gamut, from the "Attorney of *Salisbury*," Lawyer Dowling, who "brought the News of Mrs. *Blifil's* Death to Mr. *Allworthy*" (431 [bk. 8, ch. 8])—the circumstance on which the plot of the novel largely turns—through the person who "stiled himself a Lawyer, but was indeed a most vile Petty-fogger, without Sense or Knowledge of any Kind; one of those who may be termed Train-bearers to the Law; a Sort of Supernumeraries in the Profession, who are the Hackneys of Attornies, and will ride more Miles for half a Crown, than a Post-Boy" (431–32 [bk. 8, ch. 8]), to "those Sages of the Law, called *Newgate* Solicitors" (794 [bk. 15, ch. 4]). It is interesting that Fielding's unease at the increasing numbers of those involved at the lower end of the legal profession mirrored official concern. Early in the reign of George II, a Commons' Select Committee had inquired into the proliferation and practices of attorneys, solicitors, and entering clerks in an attempt to draw "a clear-cut line between the legitimate element in the profession and the semi-legitimate or illegitimate practitioners, something that plagued the law increasingly between the 1680s and the 1720s" (Holmes 153).

Over and above the widespread incidence in Fielding's fiction of characters who in one way or another are involved in the workings of the English legal system, his use of legal language is so pervasive, particularly in *Tom Jones*, that it does not seem unreasonable to describe it as a distinctive feature of his prose style. When Fielding offers to excuse his use of medical metaphor in a particular passage, he refers to "the violent Hands we have been necessitated to lay on several Words and Phrases, which of Right belong to them, and without which our Descriptions must have been often unintelligible" (198 [bk. 4, ch. 12]). This statement certainly applies, mutatis mutandis, to his use of legal language. At the end of the second chapter, he informs the reader that, as he is "a better Judge than any pitiful Critic whatever," he "intend[s] to digress, through this whole History, as often as [he sees] Occasion." The reason he gives is telling: until " [the Critics] produce the Authority by which they are constituted Judges, I shall [not] plead to their Jurisdiction" (37).[1] This use of legal terminology in *Tom Jones* is the first of many, such as the opening paragraph of book 4, chapter 6, "An Apology for the Insensibility of Mr. *Jones*, to All Charms of the Lovely *Sophia*," in which the narrator assumes the existence of "two Sorts of People, who I am afraid, have already conceived some Contempt for my Heroe, on Account of his Behaviour to *Sophia*"—namely, those who "blame his Prudence in neglecting an Opportunity to possess himself of Mr. *Western's* Fortune" and those who "will no less despise him for his Backwardness to so fine a Girl, who seemed ready to fly into his Arms, if he would open them to receive her." An extended legal metaphor follows:

> Now, though I shall not perhaps be able absolutely to acquit him of either these Charges; (for Want of Prudence admits of no Excuse; and what I shall produce against the latter Charge, will, I apprehend, be scarce satisfactory;) yet as Evidence may sometimes be offered in Mitigation, I shall set forth the plain Matter of Fact, and leave the whole to the Reader's Determination. (171)

Indeed, the critical tasks Fielding sets "the judicious Reader" in *Tom Jones* (117 [bk. 3, ch. 1]) bear a close resemblance to the way in which evidence is presented to the jury by both the prosecution and the defense. In this instance, the reader is invited to consider the evidence presented against Tom and to decide whether he is guilty not merely of a lack of prudence but also of a lack of awareness of the beauty of Sophia.

In addition to employing an extended legal metaphor, this passage offers a clear indication of the writerly (*scriptible*) character of Fielding's fiction. To adopt the terminology of Roland Barthes (*S/Z* 4), instead of offering his readers the easy option of telling them what to think about his characters' actions (*texte lisible*), Fielding invites them, time and time again, to choose between a number of alternatives. "The Charms of *Sophia* had not made the least Impression on *Blifil*; not that his Heart was pre-engaged; neither was he totally insensible of Beauty, or had any Aversion to Women; but his Appetites were, by Nature, so moderate, that he was able by Philosophy or by Study, or by some other Method, easily to subdue them" (283–84 [bk. 6, ch. 4]). By offering the reader information in this way, Fielding's narrator prompts the reader to speculate not about the sexuality of Blifil—he is quite clearly heterosexual—but about whatever "other Method" he might have employed to subdue his moderate appetites.

Blifil is of course a deeply unattractive character. According to the narrator, he "fell very short of" of Tom "in the amiable Quality of Mercy; but he as greatly exceeded him in one of a much higher Kind, namely, in Justice: In which he followed both the Precepts and Example of *Thwackum* and *Square*." Unfortunately, in their pursuit of "this sublime Virtue," as the narrator wryly observes, "*Thwackum* would probably have destroyed one half of Mankind, and *Square* the other half" (147 [bk. 3, ch. 10]). One of Fielding's main preoccupations in his novels is justice, and this theme inevitably involves commentary on the workings of the English legal system, especially what the narrator of *Tom Jones* calls the "many arbitrary Acts [that] are daily committed by Magistrates" (192 [bk. 4, ch. 11]). In this context, critics often cite the postilion's act of charity to the naked Joseph Andrews in offering him "a great Coat, his only Garment," followed by the narrator's parenthetical aside—"a Lad who hath since been transported for robbing a Hen-roost" (53 [bk. 1, ch. 12])—as an example of the harshness with which petty theft was punished by the English legal system. This instance is only one of several offered in *Joseph Andrews*. Lawyer Scout, described by the narrator as "one of those Fellows, who without any Knowledge of the Law, or being bred to it, take upon them, in defiance of an Act of Parliament, to act as Lawyers in the Country, and are called so" (286 [bk. 4, ch. 3]), seeks to curry favor with Lady Booby by having Joseph and Fanny committed to Bridewell. Fortunately, Mr. Booby intervenes. He then reflects on Scout's actions: "'Jesu!' said the Squire, 'would you commit two Persons to *Bridewell* for a Twig?' 'Yes,' said the Lawyer, 'and with great Lenity too; for if we had called it a young Tree they would have been both hanged'" (290 [ch. 5]).

In drawing the reader's attention to the sort of draconian punishments routinely meted out to perpetrators of crimes against property, Fielding offers a striking illustration of the extent to which, in mid-eighteenth-century England, "the rule of law" was "an instrument of the *de facto* ruling class" (E. Thompson 259). Over one hundred crimes carrying the death penalty were added to the statute books between 1688 and 1800, and the vast majority of them, like the one to which Lawyer Scout refers, were for crimes against property. Although Fielding was a magistrate, he was no advocate of the system, much less its apologist. On the contrary, he spoke out through the columns of the *Covent-Garden Journal*: "By the Law of England, as it now stands, if a Larceny be absolutely committed, however slight the Suspicion be against the accused, the Justice of the Peace is obliged in strictness to commit the Party." He went on to spell out the consequences of such a punitive regime. "Thus for a Theft of two-pence or three-pence value, a poor Wretch may lie confined and starving in a Gaol near two Months in this Town, and in the Country above half a Year, before he is brought to his Trial" ("*Covent-Garden Journal*" 409–10).

Although the practical suggestions to reform the legal system that are offered in the *Covent-Garden Journal*, involving corporal punishment and hard labor for petty crimes, might strike the twenty-first-century reader as unacceptably brutal, they clearly indicate Fielding's dissatisfaction with aspects of the system. As Fielding had previously satirized lawyers in the *Champion* in the manner of Jonathan Swift in part 4 of *Gulliver's Travels*, his criticism is scarcely surprising. Whereas Gulliver explains to his Houyhnhnm master that "there was a Society of Men among us, bred up from their Youth in the Art of proving by Words multiplyed for the Purpose that White is Black, and Black is White, according as they are paid" (210), Fielding, in an extract from the *Voyages of Mr. Job Vinegar*, "*Of the* Government, Manners, Habits, *&c. of the* PTFGHSIUMGSKI, *or the* INCONSTANTS" (*Contributions* 239–42), offered an account of "that Part of their publick Diversions, which our Men mistook for Law":

> [I]t is a Game unlike any Thing practiced in *Europe*, and may be played by one or two, or sometimes ten of a Side. There are two Balls, one of which they call PL[AIN]T[IFF], and the other D[E]F[ENDAN]T. The Gamesters are furnish'd with Rackets call'd BR[IE]FS, with which they beat the two Balls from one to the other; young robust Gamesters sometimes strike them away immediately, but those who are more experienced will keep them up till they are beaten to Pieces. As this is the most consummate Perfection in the Game, so they are reckoned the most dextrous Gamesters, who strike the Ball in such a Manner to the Adversary as he may be capable of returning it. There is sometimes one, and sometimes four Umpires of this Game; and if well played, it affords excellent Sport to the Spectators. (240–41)

Fielding's satire of the practice of lawyers who exploit their clients in order to line their own pockets is thoroughly conventional but also of a piece with his indictment, especially through the columns of the *Champion*, of corruption in the English legal system *tout court*. In the same way that Gulliver's naive comparison of English laws and customs and those of the Lilliputians serves to satirize the shortcomings of the former (Swift 47–50), so Vinegar's ironic denunciation of the laws of the Inconstants reveals Fielding's dissatisfaction not with the Ptfghsiumgski but with English criminal law: "Whether it be that these People imagine Mankind are govern'd more by Fear than Hope, or whether their original Law-givers were more cruel than generous, I can't determine; but I never could find any such Things as Rewards for the greatest and most relative Virtues, while the severest Punishments are inflicted on the smallest Crimes" (409).

While Fielding consistently argued for a scheme of rewards for good behavior to balance punishments for crimes, what I find of most interest is his insistence that petty criminals were being penalized too harshly. In his novels, the narrator often comments on the disproportionate punishment of those found guilty of petty larceny. This theme brings into question the arguments of those social historians who put Fielding in the ranks of those involved in a "ruling-class conspiracy" to exploit the criminal law as a means of keeping the lower orders in their place (Hay 27). Fielding unquestionably subscribed to a benevolent paternalism according to which the lower orders accepted their place in society, showing due deference to their superiors—the nobility and gentry who together made up the English ruling class—but he was critical of the failure of "booby squires" to care for the material and spiritual welfare of their dependents (Downie, *Political Biography* 125–27).

It was not only disproportionate punishment for petty larceny of which Fielding was critical. In the essay from the *Champion* quoted above he goes on to mount a serious attack, albeit through irony, on a legal system in which the theft of goods valued at more than a shilling (twelve pence) was classified as grand larceny and therefore carried the death penalty: "These People value the Life of a Man at the Rate of the lowest Piece of Coin in their Country, the taking of which, in a violent Manner, from another, is punish'd with Death; when I objected this to one of their Sages, he answer'd me, He believ'd it was in Respect of their Deity M[O]NEY, whose Name was common to that of their Coin" (410).

Although Fielding then proceeds to satirize the game laws—as he was to do in *Tom Jones*—the more interesting parallel between the essay and the novel is with Tom's treatment of the would-be highwayman, Enderson, who attempts to steal Sophia's £100 banknote on the road from St. Albans to London. Yet again, Fielding's method is to invite his readers to ruminate on the incident:

> Our Readers will probably be divided in their Opinions concerning this Action; some may applaud it perhaps as an Act of extraordinary Humanity, while those of a more saturnine Temper will consider it as a Want of Regard to that Justice which every Man owes his Country. *Partridge* certainly saw it in that Light; for he testified much Dissatisfaction on the Occasion, quoted an old Proverb, and said, "He should not wonder if the Rogue attacked them again before they reached *London*."
>
> (680–81 [bk. 12, ch. 14])

On this occasion, "by tempering Justice with Mercy, and by refusing to gratify the good-natured Disposition of the Mob" (59 [bk. 1, ch. 9])—represented here by Partridge—Tom is merely imitating the example set earlier on in the novel by Allworthy. "You know, Child," Allworthy explains to Jenny Jones, "it is in my Power, as a Magistrate, to punish you very rigorously for what you have done" (51 [ch. 7]). Fielding undoubtedly was preoccupied with justice as an abstract principle in his novels, but he was by no means uncritical of the way in which the criminal law tended to operate to the disadvantage of the lower orders of society.

NOTE

1 The Wesleyan Edition does not include the word *not*, but the sense seems to require it.

Book History Contexts: The Visual Fielding

Leigh G. Dillard

Many studies of Henry Fielding acknowledge his achievement in the historical trajectory of the English novel; comparatively few, however, view him from a visual perspective, even though his novels occupy an important place in the illustrated fiction of the period. The novels consistently appear in illustrated reprint editions at the end of the eighteenth century, but our modern encounters with Fielding's works often overlook them despite their broad circulation and value to contemporary readership. Growing interest in book history urges literary scholars—particularly those focused on eighteenth-century studies—to revisit works considered solely as words on a page, to read and teach them with renewed attention to the material characteristics of their early editions.

Illustration is a primarily material characteristic, and in this essay I discuss the books as artifacts to offer a basis for teaching eighteenth-century visual responses. I also provide models for assignments that encourage visual attention to and interpretation of Fielding's novels. This essay draws connections to contemporary illustrations and visual works, moving beyond the often discussed connections between Fielding and William Hogarth to the broader context of Fielding's illustrated novels. Using *Joseph Andrews* and *Tom Jones*, I select from illustrated collections of the period, including *The Works of Henry Fielding* (1783), James Harrison's *Novelist's Magazine* (1780s), and Charles Cooke's *Pocket Edition of Select Novels* (1790s). That the reprint editions published by Harrison and Cooke prominently feature Fielding novels in their opening volumes reflects the influence of both the author and his "new Province of Writing" (*History of Tom Jones* 77 [bk. 2, ch. 1]) in this richly illustrated and widely distributed form. Through the lens of these editions, I explore the importance of visual interpretations as they function in tandem and competition with the narratives on the facing pages.

To show what illustration adds to our study of Fielding's novels, I propose here a two-part approach to teaching them from a visual perspective: students are asked to create illustrations in response to their own encounters with the text, then they are encouraged to interpret the visual responses found in published editions. My hope is that through this approach my readers will find something to engage their students, regardless of the primary source material.

Background

The link between Fielding and Hogarth is well-traveled critical territory, as literary and art historians alike have pointed to the conversations between the author and artist in their most notable works.[1] The first published interaction between the two appears in 1751, when Hogarth provided the frontispiece to Fielding's *Tragedy of Tragedies*. Critics point to Fielding's reference in the preface of *Joseph Andrews* to "the Ingenious Hogarth" (6) and to the inherent similarity in the nature of Fielding's characters to those featured in Hogarth's narrative visual series. Notable, too, is the textual reference by Hogarth in the caption to his *Characters and Caricaturas* (1743), wherein he directs the viewer to the recently published novel of his literary counterpart: "For a further explanation of the difference betwixt character and caricature see ye preface to Jo^{h} Andrews." I would take this conversation a step further by suggesting that the relationship between Fielding and Hogarth should signal for us an adjusted frame of reference in reading and teaching Fielding's novels.

This connection led to the author's portrait by Hogarth in the collected works of Fielding in 1762, the first collection of its kind in England for a writer of fiction. Published by Andrew Millar, this subscription-based edition of four quarto volumes offered its readers a handsome view of the author and his writings. It gathered not only Fielding's novels but his miscellanies and judicial writings as well. Subsequent editions—stand-alone editions and collections—would do more to present the visual elements of Fielding's novels, but this early set provides a foundation for the link between image and text in his works.

The illustration history of Fielding's novels reflects the trajectory of popular novels from the middle of the eighteenth century, when the cohabitation of illustration and text was fairly uncommon, particularly in first or early editions. Despite the popularity of Hogarth's narrative series during this time—*A Harlot's Progress* (1732), *A Rake's Progress* (1733–35), *Marriage à la Mode* (1745)—illustrations were more often reserved for works of poetry or drama. Publishers of novels seeking to unite image and text would test the literary market first and commission illustrations after the novel had proved successful. Illustration for adult fiction in the 1740s and 1750s was therefore still an oddity.

Considering the uncertain market for illustrated fiction—and for the novel itself—there are few contemporary illustrated editions of Fielding's novels. Yet the novels encourage in their readers an awareness of the visual, both in terms of the physical presence of the characters and in the recognition of the nonverbal cues to assist in unraveling the narrative.[2] A generation after the initial publication of Fielding's novels, however, the 1774 *Donaldson v. Beckett* decision heralded a new publishing market. It fostered the proliferation of reprinted classics, ranging from legitimate to pirated and all points in between, and many of these publications both enhanced and challenged the authors' words by the addition of engraved plates.

Consistency in these collected reprints extended from pagination and typesetting to margins and illustrations. Although designed and engraved by many hands, the illustrations display common characteristics in the form of frames, captions, or other textual references to tie image to passage. Many also bear a statement of copyright or printerly attribution along with the publication date to ensure proper placement in the desired edition. Among these collected editions are highly descriptive and often richly decorated title pages that deliver matching volumes to the reader. These elements not only unify but also advertise, announcing to the readership the publisher's intention to build collected, personal editions of the nation's best authors.

In this reprint market, Harrison and Cooke offered to the public improvements on earlier attempts by publishers such as John Bell, best known for *The Poets of Great Britain Complete from Chaucer to Churchill* (1776–82). In Harrison's collection, *Novelist's Magazine*, twenty-three volumes were published in octavo numbers from 1780 to 1788, and Fielding's novels occupied space in two of the first three.[3] Instead of crafting volumes dedicated to one author alone, Harrison cobbled together works by many authors in a single volume, combining long and short works to contribute to the uniform appearance of the collection. The first volume, for instance, pairs John Hawkesworth's *Almoran and Hamet* with Fielding's *Joseph Andrews* and *Amelia*; *Tom Jones* is bound with Charles Morrel's *Tales of the Genii.* The text appears in double columns with minimal decoration, leaving the engraved title page and the plates to enhance visually the contents of each volume. Compared with Harrison's neatly numbered volumes appearing with regularity from 1780 to 1788, the publication history of *Cooke's Select British Novels; or, Novelist's Pocket Library* is more difficult to trace, because of the inconsistent numbering of the volumes: historians of the set rely largely on the statements of the publisher about what he planned for the series. These octodecimo volumes, with their "elegant Engraving in every number," delivered novels to their readers in paper wrappers advertising the past and future volumes in the set while also hawking Cooke's edition of poems, which began appearing in 1794.[4] Cooke formally articulates his vision for this reprint series in the *Plan and Catalogue of Cooke's Uniform, Cheap, and Elegant Pocket Library*, promoting the size, paper, print, and embellishments of his new venture, offered to the public in both superior and cheap editions:

> The Embellishments which accompany this Pocket Library possess an uncommon Degree of high Finishing and beautiful Effect, and are, without Exception, more *chaste and elegant* Productions than ever accompanied any Editions of similar Works. They are taken from the Paintings and Drawings of *Kirk, Graham, Corbould, Burney* and *Singleton*; and engraved by *Heath, Neagle, Anker Smith, Warren, &c.* whose Abilities are too well known to need any Eulogium. (1–2)

Fielding's novels headline this series too: *Tom Jones* was published as the opening volume in 1792, and *Joseph Andrews* appeared in 1793. Cooke employed a number of designers and engravers to complete the new designs for the collection. For Fielding's novels, Richard Corbould contributed eight of the thirteen plates; additional designs were done by Henry Singleton, Hugh Hamilton, and Charles Riley, all less known. The Cooke editions feature ornate frames to contain and reinforce the narrative scenes, particularly in the editions reissued at the turn of the century. Cooke and Harrison both used these elements to distinguish their products in the highly competitive literary market.

Authorial collections too sought to capitalize on the newly loosened copyright laws by delivering the complete works of popular authors to an increasingly voracious reading public. Illustrations became part of this process. The 1783 collection titled *The Works of Henry Fielding*, published by a collective led by Strahan, Rivington and Sons, and Longman appeared in twelve duodecimo volumes. Expanding on the contents of the 1762 collection, the chronological organization of this set places the novels *Jonathan Wild*, *Joseph Andrews*, *Tom Jones*, and *Amelia* in the middle: volumes 5–11. The first volume contains the familiar Hogarth portrait reengraved by Isaac Taylor, but each subsequent number features a frontispiece designed by Michael Angelo Rooker and engraved by Joseph Collyer. The move to illustrate works beyond the novels is also noteworthy, because authorial editions often neglected illustrations, even frontispieces, for nonfiction and shorter works.[5]

The insertion of illustrations in the reprint editions published by Harrison, Cooke, and their contemporaries added to the marketability of the novels and of the growing number of collections containing them. Although reviews for these illustrated editions are difficult to find—a consequence of the negative perception of the reprint trade by some in the literary market—the appearance of multiple reprints and reengraved plates through the 1790s and into the early 1800s attests to their staying power. The variety of illustrative responses evident in *The Works of Henry Fielding*, Harrison's *Novelist's Magazine*, and Cooke's *Pocket Edition of Select Novels* not only helps us see Fielding's novels differently by providing visual support to his narrative but also points to a trend in literary collections and library building. It became increasingly fashionable to own a personal copy of the nation's literary classics and at the same time to invest in a set of books that was enriched by engravings.

Digitization of texts from the past has opened access to modern readers that otherwise would have been reserved primarily for scholars and collectors. Equally exciting are continual improvements in the field of digital humanities that present new opportunities for students and scholars interested in the intersection of technology and the written word.[6] Key players in this regard are large projects like *18thConnect* and its sister Web site *NINES* as well as focused author-specific projects such as the *William Blake Archive*. *Eighteenth Century Collections Online* (*ECCO*) provides one of the primary digital resources to these works, even if it remains prohibitively expensive and contains fairly low-quality images—dark black blobs in place of finely engraved lines. Reproduction is predictably poor when illustrations have undergone duplication and scanning from a microfilm copy. Scholars of the period frequently lament plate condition among other problems, such as OCR translation, with what is otherwise an enlightening electronic resource. Fortunately improvements are being made as *ECCO* expands its scope.[7]

Those without access to *ECCO* can find fine examples of period illustrations through a variety of other online sources. Although more selective than the titles on *ECCO* and the *English Short Title Catalogue* (*ESTC*), helpful and high-quality visual records exist in the online database of the British Museum www.britishmuseum.org/research. For instance, a search there for the phrase "Tom Jones" returns results from Harrison's *Novelist's Magazine* and Cooke's *Pocket Edition*. Also accessible are Thomas Rowlandson's 1791 stipple designs for the Edinburgh edition and Luke Clennell's plates for the 1811 edition, published by Sherwood, Neely, and Jones as part of the popular British Novelists series. Such fine digital examples give students of Fielding a sense of the longevity of the author's visual influence. With a little patience, copies of the *Novelist's Magazine* can even be found on *Google Books*, with free access to illustrated editions of both volumes 1 and 3, containing *Joseph Andrews* and *Tom Jones*, respectively.[8]

Assignments

It is a challenge for teachers to facilitate learning for an ever-changing student population. Transforming the traditional lecture-and-discussion formats into a participatory, visual environment will enhance classroom dynamics by offering the unexpected, and providing a visual means of interpretation will encourage student engagement with the text.

I confine my discussion to the undergraduate classroom, but my two-part approach to teaching Fielding from a visual perspective could easily be adapted for graduate students interested in the intersection of word and image, particularly as it appears in the novels of the eighteenth century. Students in literature classes are often hesitant to treat illustrations as anything more than decoration, elements they can skim in their otherwise attentive reading. But my assignments are designed to integrate visual responses into the discussion, fostering a skill set for reading and interpreting graphic elements along with the text. Likewise, I recall my own curiosity about the image-and-text relation prompted by a course on the eighteenth-century novel in graduate school. I recall my first attempt to read illustrations and how, as a student of literature, I felt intimidated. This experience helps me help students who feel that intimidation. In his early study on illustrations in English literature, Edward Hodnett urges students to create illustrations themselves and suggests guidelines for teachers to implement an illustration activity as part of a graduate seminar (22):

> For the student of book illustration, the ability to put himself in the place of an artist and reconstruct his actions with something like tactile understanding is an extremely valuable extension of mental understanding. The more proficient in drawing the student of book illustration becomes, the more likely he is to understand the technical aspects of a project and to judge correctly the decisions made by an artist. (23)

Hodnett encouraged me, both as a teacher and a scholar, to think differently about illustration and to consider its placement in a text as part of the discussion of a novel, even when an illustration appeared after the novel's early editions. While the definition of illustration employed here is conservative—Hodnett judges the quality of artistic interpretation in his illustrative studies, which is not my intention—there is something appealing in having students design their own illustrations for texts.

The assignments I have employed in the undergraduate classroom range from short, in-class activities to longer, essay-length considerations and are written in two parts: the italicized portion addresses the student, and the text that follows provides a brief pedagogical discussion. The activities are described broadly, without application to specific scenes in Fielding's novels, in the hope that they will provide greater resonance across literary works taught in the undergraduate (and perhaps graduate) classroom. The assignments can be enhanced by having students write to justify their visual decisions.

> *A publisher has contacted you about creating a new critical edition of* Tom Jones *or* Joseph Andrews. *The publication agreement allows you to include eight to ten original illustrations. You must justify or describe each illustration in terms of placement, composition, and significance to the text.*

The above assignment works well in small groups as a follow-up to discussions of the main scenes of the novel. I often begin by asking students to brainstorm about the scenes or a particular selection. Individual illustrations come next, then students work together in small groups to defend the choices they made to illustrate scenes and to collaborate with others to create a complete set of illustrations for the edition we are reading.

> *Make a poster to advertise the novel.*

I employ this assignment in tandem with Robin Williams's *Non-designer's Design and Type Books*, which defines the design concepts of contrast, repetition, alignment, and proximity using the acronym CRAP.[9] Making a poster allows students to move from a visual mode of expression to one that combines visual and written elements to deliver a message.

> *Make a poster to advertise a film adaptation of the novel.*

This assignment allows students to convey what they know about the generic standards of both movies and movie posters. Options here might include a screening of Tony Richardson's raucous film starring Albert Finney or a more general consideration of how best to adapt the novel for a modern audience.

> *Create a new book jacket for your edition, including both images and text to entice a modern audience to buy the novel. Work in groups for this assignment, using the design principles discussed in Williams's book.*

This assignment helps students articulate the rationale behind their design decisions. I ask students to formulate their ideas before joining a group, so that they are more likely to contribute something to the collaborative editorial experience.

> *Consider the key points of the narrative action in the novel and rewrite the story in the form of a children's book. Keep in mind the conventions of this genre. The book should contain at least seven original illustrations.*

This assignment allows students to merge what they know of illustration with recognition of a particular audience.

> *You have been given the task of filming a scene from the novel and must first create a storyboard for it. Draw eight to ten boxes on your page, then start filling them in with details of each shot. Be sure to label the primary action with a short phrase.*

Storyboarding can be productive in gauging student understanding of the key moments of a text. I have used and participated in many iterations of this assignment. Typically, it follows an in-class discussion of a set of scenes in the narrative. Requesting students to reflect on one scene allows them to showcase their attention to detail and narrative structure and to demonstrate their understanding of the crucial elements of scene composition—setting, lighting, transitions, and so on.

It is important to avoid showing students printed illustrations before they complete their own visual interpretations. Because published responses possess a level of authority by virtue of their attachment to a particular edition, they may inhibit originality in students preparing their own scene selections. It also helps to remove the expectation of talent: I am interested more in the scope and composition of the illustration than in its artistic merit. I introduce visual analysis with an exercise in seeing and articulating the meaning of a visual form, such as an advertisement from a popular magazine. This exercise is most productive in small groups and often serves as an icebreaker, to get students talking about what they see and what they know about visual interpretation. Some discussion points and activities for published illustrations follow:

> *Prepare a close reading of a particular illustration, evaluating the characters in the frame along with the setting and overall composition of the image.*

This type of compositional analysis demands close attention to the lines on the page. Students' first response to illustrations, particularly eighteenth-century engravings, is confusion. I ask students to simply describe what they see, so that we as a class can arrive at possible interpretations. Hogarth's engravings provide fertile ground for this type of preliminary activity. Students are eased into interpreting elements they are more comfortable with, such as facial expressions, setting, and action, before moving to more nuanced symbolism.

Compare an illustration with its corresponding scene in the novel.

Students might be asked to compare the differences—omissions, additions—between the text and the image and to consider whether the image contains elements from many scenes instead of depicting a specific event.

Compare one scene with illustrations in different editions.

Focusing on one scene from the novel—Allworthy's discovery of the infant Tom or Tom's finding Square in Molly's room—allows students to consider stylistic variation between editions.

Discuss the characteristics of a complete set of illustrations.

Attention to a complete set of illustrations makes students consider tone, theme, setting, and so on. For instance, how might Harrison's *Novelist's Magazine* present the character of Tom Jones?

Compare your set of illustrations with those appearing in a published edition. Defend your choices.

Interesting discussions arise when students compare their designs with those published elsewhere, particularly when they consider not only their selection of scenes but also the composition of their selections and the rationale behind them.

Admittedly some of these assignments stretch the boundaries of what we might typically do in a composition or literature classroom, but they can provide significant entry points into the texts that we explore. I find helpful a combination of individual and collaborative work in these assignments.

Implications

As scholars and teachers of eighteenth-century works, we are undoubtedly concerned with the balance between the discussion of a lengthy novel and an activity, like my suggested assignments, that goes beyond the words on the page. The pedagogical implications of this mode of reading are far-reaching. We are allowed to vary the structure of our courses to maintain student engagement with the novel. Our interactions with the texts we read become more nuanced and expressive when the visual perspective is added. These assignments ask students to understand, interpret, and articulate responses to things they read and see—illustrations among them—and they stimulate a range of skills that can be transferred to the writing process. Close reading is crucial in both forms of these activities: readers must consider textual details and convey their thoughts, whether visually or verbally, to a specific audience. Because alternative kinds of organization spring from these exercises, students will see—in the tradition of *Tristram Shandy*—that narrative action need not always be linear.

Visual analysis encourages us along with our students to explore more thoroughly the publication history of literary works. It reminds us that the novels we encounter most frequently in newly printed anthologies and critical editions, with regularized spellings and pages typically devoid of decoration, looked quite different to earlier generations of readers. It encourages us to make this fluctuating visual identity part of the conversation, critical or otherwise, about the novel as it reflects the culture from which it emerged. Such questions echo the widening field of literary history, allowing us to discuss the history of the book and the collaborative nature of the publishing process along with more traditional modes of literary interpretation.

To celebrate the two-hundredth anniversary of Charles Dickens's birth on 7 February 2012, the Museum of London launched an iPhone and iPad app titled *Dickens: Dark London*, an interactive graphic novel based on *Sketches by Boz* and illustrated by David Foldvari. Although no such project heralded the tercentenary of Fielding's birth celebrated in 2007, perhaps the next milestone birthday of Fielding will be greeted by a multimedia project that is equally engaging and challenges the new literary historian whose interests span the visual as well as the verbal traces of his novels. Along these lines, Christina Ionescu expresses the sentiment, in her edited collection *Book Illustration in the Long Eighteenth Century*, that we should explore the "visual history of the text" with the same vigor that past literary historians have used to unearth the foundations of the novel.[10] Students of Fielding's works must encounter and interrogate illustrations as part of the complex and collaborative history of the novel.

NOTES

[1] Consider the work of Ronald Paulson (*Hogarth*, vol. 2, and *Popular and Polite Art*), Robert Moore, and Peter Jan de Voogd as a starting point. Scholars of Hogarth and Fielding will find that most current discussions of either man reference the other, at least in passing.

[2] These points are discussed more thoroughly in Dillard.

[3] For more detail about this series, see Benedict; Ezell; Shevlin, "Exploring"; and Taylor.

[4] Thomas Bonnell's monograph on the poetry reprints of this period describes Cooke's project as "a vast reprint operation that turned Cooke into a full-service purveyor of English classics, the first to offer parallel series of poems, novels, essays, histories, and devotional works in matching formats" (227–28). Bonnell's study focuses on the poetic reprints, but his analysis of the publishers engaged in this market provides a relevant corollary, in that many of the same parties were involved across genres.

[5] The five-volume *Works of Laurence Sterne*, for instance, includes only a frontispiece portrait of the author at the head of the first volume, which contains *Tristram Shandy*, while subsequent volumes, containing part 2 of *Tristram, Sermons of Yorick*, and *Sentimental Journey*, remain unillustrated. A 1774 Dublin edition extends illustration to the complete volumes of *Tristram Shandy* (with three plates by Hogarth) but still resists decoration for *Sermons of Yorick, Posthumous Works,* and *Sentimental Journey.*

[6] Although his essay is now dated by its mention of programs like *HyperCard* and *ToolBook*, Joel Haefner discusses the teaching and learning potential of getting students in a Romantic poetry course to create hypertexts of the works they read as they "import texts, link texts to their essays, and attach comments" (48).

[7] This issue, one of the ongoing topics of discussion for eighteenth-century scholars, was recently addressed by Patrick Spedding.

[8] Other sources that have merit are the *HathiTrust Digital Library* (www.hathitrust.org) and *Gallica* (gallica.bnf.fr).

[9] Williams simplifies Gestalt principles through this acronym but still manages to convey the nuances of visual design to her readers.

[10] Ionescu defines the "visual history of the text" as "the visual complement of or supplement to textual matter, designed as part of the material presentation and packaging of various editions throughout the publication history of a text" (8).

JOSEPH ANDREWS

Staging the Reading Play in *Joseph Andrews*

Joshua Grasso

> As a good play is certainly the most rational, and the highest Entertainment, that human Invention can produce, let that be my Apology (if I need any) for having thus freely delivered my Mind, in behalf of those Gentlemen, who, under such calamitous Hazards, may hereafter be reduc'd to write for the Stage.
>
> —Cibber, *Apology for the Life of Colley Cibber*

Any survey of literature of the eighteenth century—or any course that covers Fielding's novels—should include the following mock-serious aside about the period: that most of its writing occurred onstage. The mania for plays, operas, farces, and orchestral works far outpaced the ability of critics to decide what was what. Composers and playwrights were improvising on a grand scale, mixing *buffa* and *seria*, replacing gods with highwaymen, and inserting minuets in all the wrong places. This abundance allowed theatergoers to experience these works as critics themselves, ushering in an unprecedented aesthetic of novelty. Not that the artists didn't try to steer them in the right direction. In 1786, Antonio Salieri wrote an opera entitled *Prima la musica e poi le parole* ("First the Music, Then the Words"), which dramatizes the primacy of music over verse. Despite its lighthearted tone, Salieri addressed a question that lingered in the mind of every artist: When genres combine, what one quality or aspect reigns supreme? Words or music, actors or composers—who has the final say? This question was all the more intriguing when the debate toppled offstage, as it did most significantly in the time of Daniel Defoe, Samuel Richardson, and Fielding.

Fielding's contribution to the debate appeared in 1742 with the publication of *Joseph Andrews*, a work that fits uneasily beside its contemporaries in the age of the novel. No work betrays his debt to the stage more profoundly, and with good reason: that year represented an important leave-taking for Fielding, as Walpole's Licensing Act of 1737 had brought down crushing censorship on Fielding's ballad operas and farces. His greatest rival, the playwright-director Colley Cibber, reflected the mood against Fielding in his 1740 memoir, decrying his "Farces, that seem'd to knock all Distinctions of Mankind on the Head: Religion, Laws, Government, Priests, Judges, and Ministers, were all laid flat, at the Feet of this *Herculean* Satyrist!" ([1968] 156). Fielding returned the compliment, claiming that Cibber "lived [his] life only in order to write it" (*Joseph Andrews* 18 [bk. 1, ch. 1]). Yet Fielding never lost the belief—expressed by Cibber himself—that plays were indeed "the most rational, and the highest Entertainment, that human Invention [could] produce" (100). Though effectively ending his playwriting career in 1742–43, Fielding merely left one stage for another, finding an even more fitting medium to "knock all Distinctions of Mankind on the Head." Reading *Joseph Andrews* as a natural extension of his work in the theater, particularly in the context of the classroom, offers a unique response to the eighteenth-century question "Words or music?"—or, in this case, "Reading or acting?"

Fielding launches into the debate from the first sentence of the novel's preface, the narrator offering a pedantic defense of his "comic Romance," which might well befuddle "the mere *English* Reader." Like many who attended the premieres of Fielding's ballad operas, these readers "may have a different Idea of Romance with the Author of these little Volumes; and may consequently expect a kind of Entertainment, not to be found, nor which was even intended" (3). What, then, did Fielding intend in his comic-epic-romance-burlesque-satire? Responding to claims that burlesque has no place in classical art, the narrator writes:

> I have less Abhorrence than [Lord Shaftesbury] professes for it: and that not because I have had some little Success on the Stage this way; but rather, as it contributes more to exquisite Mirth and Laughter than any other; and these are probably more wholesome Physic for the Mind. . . . Nay, I will appeal to common Observation, whether the same Companies are not found more full of Good-Humour and Benevolence, after they have been sweeten'd for two or three Hours with Entertainments of this kind, than when soured by a Tragedy or a grave Lecture. (5)

Here, in short, is Fielding's theatrical aesthetic. By inserting it in the narrator's defense, Fielding slyly suggests that we read his novel as a comedy, a form he clearly felt to be of more public value than a "Tragedy or a grave Lecture." In the context of the novel, Richardson was certainly guilty of such grave performances, which treated readers as so many maidservants to be instructed through a five-hundred-page letter. Did the novel—like its contemporary cousin, the symphony—have room for burlesque and satire, or must gravity obtain in every line and bar? Fielding's answer is much like that of Joseph Haydn, who decades later transformed the symphony from a staid opera overture into a work of dynamic, emotional, and farcical contrasts.

Fielding knew his readers would be puzzled by a work that presented so many performances on one stage. What should they be watching or listening for? In *The Grub-Street Opera* (1731), the Poet famously remarks that since audiences rarely care for the plot (so long as they have good tunes and horseplay), he took the liberty of removing it altogether (4). While Fielding makes no such claims for *Joseph Andrews*, the same technique emerges in the preface, which tells readers what they will not find in the novel but little of what they will. Only when we wander through the novel do we find the true preface, hidden like a careful aside in book 3, chapter 1:

> I describe not Men, but Manners; not an Individual, but a Species. Perhaps it will be answered, Are not the Characters taken from Life? To which I answer in the Affirmative; nay, I believe I might aver, that I have writ little more than I have seen. The Lawyer is not only alive, but hath been so these 4000 Years . . . when the first mean selfish Creature appeared on the human Stage, who made Self the Centre of the whole Creation, would give himself no Pain, incur no Danger, advance no Money, to assist or preserve his Fellow-Creatures; then was our Lawyer born; and whilst such a Person as I have described exists on Earth, so long shall he remain upon it. (189)

Here Fielding's aesthetic has become a manifesto: to mistake a character for a person would be to mistake the reflection of the moon for reality. The role of art—and particularly of Fielding's burlesque—is to upset the surface of the water so that the moon disappears and viewers see their own astonished faces. In short, the masks of the actors are the masks we all wear, costumes that belong not to the province of the stage but in every drawing room and coffeehouse in London.

Joseph Andrews parades an entire troop of recognizable English men and women before the reader, from Lady Booby to Madam Slipslop; yet despite their unmistakable accents, they are not as English as roast beef. They are the same lawyers who ambled across the human stage in Plato's time and should continue to be read by an enlightened audience. Yet few audiences of any generation are skilled at reading art—much less themselves—with the eye of an accomplished playwright. How should a playwright make those interested in an evening's entertainment appreciate their likenesses onstage? More important, how should a playwright defend that ambition in the name of art? A passage from Fielding's first theatrical success, *The Author's Farce*, offers a second preface to *Joseph Andrews* and its concern with art and audience. The poet, Luckless, is unable to sell his play to the bookseller, Bookweight, since "a Play which will do for [actors] will not always do for us. There are your Acting Plays and your Reading Plays." When Luckless's companion, Witmore, fails to see the distinction, Bookweight elaborates:

> Why, Sir, your Acting Play is entirely supported by the Merit of the Actor, without any Regard to the Author at all. In this Case, it signifies very little whether there be any Sense in it or no. Now your Reading Play is of a different Stamp and must have Wit and Meaning in it. These latter I call your Substantive, as being able to support themselves. The former are your Adjective, as what require the Buffoonry and Gestures of an Actor to be joined to them to shew their Signification. (237)

Here again is the distinction between words and music: words have the sense, music the effect. The condescending bookseller (who commands a galley of hack writers in Grub Street) confirms the narrator's fear in *Joseph Andrews*: that a work of burlesque, having no classical precedent, cannot be true art. Only a true reading play, substituting wit for farce and substance for gestures, can enter the marketplace. How then does Fielding classify *Joseph Andrews*: as a reading or acting play?

Fielding resurrects the argument in book 3, chapter 10, of *Joseph Andrews*, in the delightful dialogue between the Poet and the Player. Each character blames the other for the failure of the Poet's play; however, they momentarily come to a truce and fall to excusing the other's efforts. In a comic mea culpa, the Poet exclaims that "the Works of most modern Authors, like dead-born Children, cannot be murdered. It is such wretched, half-begotten, half-writ, lifeless, spiritless, low, groveling Stuff that I almost pity the Actor who is oblig'd to get it by heart, which must be almost as difficult to remember as Words in a Language you do not understand."

The Poet allies himself with the Bookseller and Lord Shaftesbury, suggesting that anything written for laughs is mere nonsense, a corruption of wit and substance. The Player demurs, "I am sure . . . if the Sentences have little Meaning when they are writ, when they are spoken they have even less. I know scarce one who ever lays an Emphasis right, and much less adapts his Action to his Character" (261). Although the two eventually return to abusing each other, Fielding has cleverly dramatized the tension between reading and acting, the yin and yang of the eighteenth-century playwright. The question is even more pointed than Salieri's opposition between words and music: How can wit carry the day in a garbled performance of "half-writ" lines?

In *The Author's Farce,* Luckless's response to the public's reading/acting distinction is to abandon his conventional play and fashion a grotesque extravaganza entitled "The Pleasures of the Town," a full-blown ballad opera (with puppets, no less) crammed full of every theatrical convention and cliché known to London. As so often with Fielding's plays, it proved a resounding success, playing for forty-two performances and appearing in print (as a reading play) the very day after its premiere—something of a novelty for the time (Hume, *London Theatre World* 314). This work set a precedent for Fielding's theatrical career: Fielding was not just a playwright but also a theater manager who rivaled Cibber himself. Arthur H. Scouten describes him as "a bold and shrewd contriver intent on being a trouble maker, a promoter who did not scruple at persuading Charlotte Charke to play a role which ridiculed her father, Colley Cibber . . . and who was both sensitive toward criticism and ready to take extraordinary measures to secure publicity" (lxxxvi).

One of the most controversial innovations of Fielding was to offer plays during Passion Week, to capitalize on a growing middle-class audience, which in 1736 earned him an official order to desist (Scouten xlv). In short, he made the theater a truly public venue, open to all classes at all times, full to the brim with the fare they most enjoyed: rollicking comedies and the popular tunes of Thomas D'Urfey and George Frideric Handel (Fielding, like most eighteenth-century composers, had no scruple in borrowing the music of others).

Joseph Andrews shows the consummate showman at work. Not content to weigh in on the question of words or music, Fielding applies the debate to every mode of entertainment in London—all of which modes are fit between the pages of his novel. As Luckless remarks in *The Author's Farce*, "since every-one has not Time or Opportunity to visit all the Diversions of the Town, I have brought most of them together in one" (258). Only in a novel could Fielding, now that he was deprived of the stage, offer all the pleasures of the town, at comparatively little expense, to draw the largest audience. More important, the novel was both a reading and an acting medium. After all, to read a novel is to act, as well as to become the director, stage manager, and opening night crowd. Similarly, when eighteenth-century readers read these novels, they recognized themselves as actors in a history—something recorded as a reading play for moral scrutiny—whereas many playwrights, when attempting to instruct the public, had their finely crafted lines mumbled by an incompetent actor and then never spoken again (as few plays survived the first performance). The combination of reading and acting must have been enormously attractive to Fielding the artist, as well as an enticing—and virtually untapped—venue for Fielding the impresario.

A particularly fascinating example of the reading/acting aspect of literature occurs early in book 1, chapter 8, when Lady Booby learns that Joseph values his virtue more than her attempts at seduction. The narrator, comically intruding on this intimate scene, remarks:

> You have seen the Faces in the Eighteen-penny Gallery, where through the Trap-Door, to soft or no Musick, Mr. *Bridgewater*, Mr. *William Mills*, or some other of ghostly Appearance, hath ascended with a Face all

> pale with Powder, and a Shirt all bloody with Ribbons; but from none of these . . . no, not from the inimitable Pencil of my Friend *Hogarth*, could you receive such an Idea of Surprize, as would have entered at your Eyes, had they beheld the Lady *Booby*, when those last Words issued out from the Lips of *Joseph*.—"Your Virtue!" (40–41)

In this passage, Salieri's dilemma is beside the point, as Fielding has it both ways. The effect of the scene is both read and staged, since the eighteenth-century reader would superimpose the celebrated performances of these famous actors over their own experiences at the "Eighteen-penny Gallery." The presence of both performances makes unnecessary the question of whether we are reading a play or acting one. Fielding even piles on the visual element of Hogarth's art as a third performance. There is a profound level of direction here, as the author withholds the actors' lines, merely evoking their shadows to support his own comic—and now mock-epic—description.

Of course, the twenty-first century reader needs footnotes to decipher these actors, and no student today has spent time in an "Eighteen-penny Gallery." Yet this loss of historical context is a hidden virtue of Fielding's technique, as the stage is no longer necessary. The performance heightens our enjoyment, but for Fielding it is the honey to catch the flies. To see Lady Booby as an actor portraying the ghost of Hamlet's father is ludicrous, hilarious, and entirely appropriate. Her sexual powers, wrapped up in her title and arrogance, have become a ghost to be exorcised by Andrews's morality. With that single word, "virtue," she is banished to the shades of old age and mockery. A similar moment occurs in book 2, chapter 13, when Mrs. Slipslop confronts Fanny, her rival for Joseph's affections: "[S]he flung herself in the Chaise, casting a Look at *Fanny* as she went, not unlike that which *Cleopatra* gives *Octavia* in the play" (159). Whether we see Shakespeare's or Dryden's version of this scene, the point is made: Slipslop is a Haymarket Cleopatra, losing herself in the playing of a role. Ironically, she would not have read the play in published form, which shows how much of Bookweight's "Wit and Meaning" resides in mere performance. As a member of an eighteenth-century audience, she embodies the roles of her time, which survive the translation of centuries. We may not read the same text as Fielding's readers, but we still know the mask—one that might fit on our own faces.

A work of art can never be reduced to one reading or one performance. Fielding makes this idea remarkably explicit in *Joseph Andrews*, a performance about performance. The music or the words, which ennobles us? which entertains? Parson Adams takes this question up early in the novel, exclaiming that "he was sorry to hear Sermons compared to Plays." The reply, conveniently by a bookseller, is, "'Not by me,' I assure you . . . though I don't know whether the licensing Act may not shortly bring them to the same footing.'" Adams is outraged by the very idea: "[I]s there no difference between conveying good or ill Instructions to Mankind?" (80 [bk. 1, ch. 17]). Thus we end with the eternal debate between reading and acting, though Adams is oblivious to his own role as a performer of sermons. The bookseller has no truck with sermons, as they do not sell—not like reading plays! In the end, the reader must decide what makes a sermon, a play, or a novel. Dare we laugh at the pretensions of others? Or does morality insist on the gravity of borrowed clothes? Only a playwright can negotiate the tricky business of reading and acting in a way that favors no one performance but allows the age—and a new generation of students—to examine themselves in the mirror of art.

Teaching Fielding's Idea of the Novel with *Joseph Andrews*

Stephen C. Behrendt

I teach *Joseph Andrews* in an undergraduate course in British fiction from 1700 to 1900. Students are a mix: as many as half may be English majors (a quarter to a third is more typical); others come from all academic areas. Most are juniors, and the rest are sophomores and seniors, usually in equal numbers. Because my department has few prerequisites for its courses, even the English majors have relatively little background in the history and culture of eighteenth- and nineteenth-century Britain; few have read any eighteenth-century novels other than *Robinson Crusoe* or indeed much fiction from before 1900. For most, Shakespeare (usually *Romeo and Juliet*) constitutes their acquaintance with what is called earlier British writing, and few arrive in my classroom with anything more than a high-school survey of British or American literature. I therefore select comparatively short novels and will assign no more than one long one, like *David Copperfield*; *Joseph Andrews*, of moderate length, my students can (and will) read relatively well.

Much of my class time goes into providing a framework of cultural and material history in which I encourage my students to assess our novels. I present this history through music, visual art, architecture, and costume and dress, an approach that students find more accessible than any straight account of dates and events. One aspect of eighteenth-century culture I stress is the playfulness that appears in all the arts. Having students listen to the first or final movement from Leopold Mozart's *Toy Symphony* (c. 1759) underscores the point, which I supplement by demonstrating some of the verbal-visual high jinks in Laurence Sterne's *Tristram Shandy* (blank pages, marbled pages, out-of-sequence chapters, extensive asterisks). Though Sterne is historically later, I suggest that Tristram's digressions and interruptions illustrate ideas about association (and therefore early ideas about how the mind works) that period writers like John Locke were examining. I also show how William Hogarth—especially since Fielding cites him often and admiringly—links visual humor with moral instruction in complex structures whose visual and verbal contents are heavily loaded with signification that we can read when we go beneath the surface (*The Enraged Musician* [1741], *Gin Lane* and *Beer Street* [1751]).

I also tell my students that many commentators see in *Joseph Andrews* signs of Horace's notion (from the *Ars Poetica* [*Art*]) that art should both delight and instruct, and I emphasize the novel's moral aspect by quoting Martin Battestin's claim that Fielding adopted this Horatian approach to offer his reader lessons "in the shaping of that greater artifact, the good man" (*Moral Basis* 151). Still, I find it best to approach Fielding's moral and aesthetic agenda indirectly: inviting my students to examine the play (and playfulness) in *Joseph Andrews* helps them discover that there is in fact a design in what they at first regard as a wandering and tangent-ridden novel. In this context I also mention Charles A. Knight's suggestion that Fielding deliberately undermined his own narrative authority by creating a sort of extratextual, or paratextual, compact between author (not narrator) and reader that is based on their shared recognition that the central characters are inherently good people ("*Joseph Andrews*"). The many ironic inconsistencies of the behavior of Joseph, Adams, and Fanny that the narrator presents reveal their essential moral goodness, unlike the behavior, particularly uncharitable behavior, of other characters. An illustration of this failure of charity is the episode where Joseph is robbed, beaten, and stripped (bk. 1, ch. 12), only to become the subject of the false moral horror and actual moral poverty of the coach passengers who encounter him in that condition. In Fielding's reprise of the Good Samaritan tale, only the poor postilion humanely covers Joseph's nakedness by offering his own coat (even though he rides outside the coach, exposed to the elements), for which charitable act he is reproved by the fastidious passengers, since he swore "a great Oath" (53) while doffing the coat.

Spending time on this episode (and on the events that follow at the Towwouses' inn) lets students explore the lessons about morality, humanity, charity, and hypocrisy that Fielding builds into this short narrative space. The discussion inevitably comes around to the relation of appearances to reality. When we finish the novel, I remind students that in the narrative's very first sentence the narrator tells us that Joseph "was esteemed to be the only son of Gaffar and Gammer Andrews" (20), and I ask them what the word "esteemed" means. Like Edgar Allan Poe's purloined letter, Joseph's true identity is concealed in plain sight by means of this deliberately misleading (because diversionary) word, which states the case fairly but in a way that most readers fail to understand. This is not the only place where we find that we cannot entirely trust the narrator, even when he explicitly warns us to take care: "[Book 1,] Chapter IX . . . in which we prophesy there are some Strokes which every one will not truly comprehend at the first Reading" (42). The prefatory inscription to book 1, chapter 8, announces that "[a]fter some very fine Writing, the History goes on" (37), as indeed it does following the narrator's purple prose in the first paragraph to describe evening's arrival. Later, after his "sarcastical Panegyrick" on vanity, the narrator admits, "I have introduced thee for no other Purpose than to lengthen out a short Chapter" (70).

Joseph Andrews is filled with invitations to the reader to participate in the novel's making. Jean-Paul Sartre wrote in *What Is Literature?* that "reading is directed creation" (53): when readers begin reading, they enter into a de facto compact with the author to realize or complete the work, whose kernel form is the printed text. Examining the interactive cues to readers that Fielding planted on virtually every page of *Joseph Andrews* helps students appreciate that he regards reading novels as an act of participation. Readers are not just spectators. In an early self-portrait, Joshua Reynolds peers out at us, shielding his eyes against a light that is implied to come from our viewing space. The portrait engages us by violating the supposed separation of the painter's subject and the viewer's space and forcing us to confront the painted image that overtly regards us. But Reynolds's image is a multistable representation of at least three alternatives: Reynolds looking at us, Reynolds looking into a mirror (a common practice in self-portraiture), the image of Reynolds in a mirror. As in Magritte's *This Is Not a Pipe* (1968), the painting is, of course, not Reynolds but an artistically mediated representation of him. A comparable multistability in *Joseph Andrews*, with all its metacommentary on how to read the novel, forces the reader to participate in the novel's making.

But, my students often object, isn't Fielding just playing with us? Yes, I tell them, but we need to understand why he takes that play so seriously and why we should too. J. Paul Hunter says that "Fielding seldom gives us what he leads us to expect or allows us what we think we want. . . . Invoking other literary contexts and playing to our vulnerable spots, Fielding manipulates our expectations mercilessly, and he often takes us to places we did not mean to go" (*Occasional Form* 95). Like Daniel Defoe's *Robinson Crusoe*, *Joseph Andrews* is advertised on its title page as a "history," a word that, while technically correct ("narrative of past events"["History"]) implies real persons and events. Like "esteemed," it's a semantic red herring. But if, as Fielding claims, confusing appearance and reality identifies the "Ridiculous" (7) as a source for comedy, elsewhere such confusion is deadly serious, as in *Paradise Lost* and an extensive body of sermonic literature that counsels against failing to recognize the deadly wiles of a disguised Satan. I point out John Milton's admonition in *Areopagitica*: "I cannot praise a fugitive and cloistered virtue, unexercised and unbreathed, that never sallies out and sees her adversary, but slinks out of the race where that immortal garland is to be run for, not without dust and heat." We must be purified by trial, he continues, "and trial is by what is contrary" (728). Reading, Fielding understood, involves a trial, to distinguish truth from appearance, for his readers no less than for the novel's characters. Even the narrator must be scrutinized, in fact, lest he mislead the unwary reader, as Fielding is not reluctant to have the narrator do.

My students always enjoy discussing the narrator—and the narrative voice—as a way of exploring Fielding's idea of the novel. I remind them that when *Joseph Andrews* was composed, the novel was still novel: authors were still experimenting with form and voice. We spend some time discussing what sort of individual the narrator is, on the basis of what he says and how he says it. Students note his chattiness and habit of commenting not just on the characters and events but also on the novel itself. Why this conspicuous self-reflexivity, I ask, and has anyone encountered this sort of storytelling before? Students recall tales told by friends and acquaintances who could not keep from interjecting extraneous personal commentary. They recall that, when they were given a gift, the giver, before it was unwrapped, offered surprise-quashing comments like "I hope it fits" or "I hope you like the color." Fielding's narrator frequently does something comparable, often in the guise of preparing the reader, as when he signals that what follows is a chapter "calculated for the Instruction and Improvement of the Reader" (264 [bk. 3, ch. 11]) or, more playfully, a chapter of "Adventures, which we hope will as much please as surprise the Reader" (267 [ch. 12]). Fielding even tells us at the start of book 2 that the predictive inscriptions preceding the chapters are "but so many Inscriptions over the Gates of Inns . . . informing the Reader what Entertainment he is to expect, which if he likes not, he may travel on to the next" (90). Hence the inscription to book 4, chapter 6: "Of which you are desired to read no more than you like" (294), unusual also for its second-person address to the reader, whom the narrator usually addresses in the third person (e.g., "to help our reader . . . we must inform him that . . . " [68 (bk. 1, ch. 15)]).

The more students talk about the narrator, the more they question the familiarity of his rhetoric and the appearance of his candor. Sometimes he declares that he knows his characters personally: "I have been often assured by both [Joseph and Fanny], that they spent these Hours in a most delightful Conversation; but, as I never could prevail on either to relate it, so I cannot communicate it to the Reader" (168 [bk. 2, ch. 15]). Earlier he professes similar ignorance about Adams's dining choice at the Tow-wouses' inn: "He accordingly [ate] either a Rabbit or a Fowl, I never could with any tolerable Certainty discover which" (68 [bk. 1, ch. 15]). This calculated evasiveness about details is in keeping with the narrator's early declaration about "the exact Rules of Biography" (21 [bk. 1, ch. 2]) that should apply to the sort of history (i.e., reality) that the narrator claims to be writing. Knowing that the novel is fiction, however, encourages students to examine other narratorial evasions, and they are surprised by the number of those evasions that accumulate. Eighteenth-century artists, thinkers, and early psychologists were fascinated by what we now call multistability, the ability of things to mean or to represent more than one thing without containing sufficient data to establish which meaning is the right one. The famous visual illusion of the Peter and Paul goblet, which depicts two facial silhouettes facing each other and, at the same time, an ornate goblet, depending on whether the viewer focuses on the figure or the ground, illustrates the principle. Sterne plays with multistability in *Tristram Shandy*, and Fielding does too in the final lines of *Joseph Andrews*, writing that Joseph, now living in happy retirement with Fanny, is determined not to "be prevailed upon by any Booksellers, or their Authors, to make his Appearance in *High-Life*" (344 [bk. 4, ch. 16]). Fielding's inside joke on the title of a hack writer's sequel to Richardson's *Pamela* notwithstanding, the refusal to appear in a book—which claim, of course, appears in a book—is sheer literary trompe l'oeil. Such textual and narratorial maneuvers epitomize Fielding's scheme for engaging his reader actively in the "directed creation" by which meaning is generated through repeated readerly acts of perception, cognition, and judgment.

I ask students to enumerate distinctive narratorial acts and strategies and to make notes about how they respond to these rhetorical events, both as they encounter them during their reading and later, when they reflect on that reading. Eventually—and predictably—they realize that the rhetorical model is predominantly a conversational one: not quite gossip but unquestionably interactive in its intent both to share and to implicate (in the sense of *entwine*). They begin to characterize that voice as witty, urbane, learned, sometimes prideful. Where, I ask, might such a voice be found? Students quickly identify Fielding's narrator's voice as that of a man addressing other men in a casual, congenial tone; it is a voice from a men's club or, perhaps more accurately, from a coffeehouse of the sort that was increasingly common in Fielding's London. This narrative voice assumes a shared store of knowledge and reference and a moral and social consciousness on the part of the reader-listener. Fielding addresses not the limited audience that a purely epistolary novel ostensibly presumes (letters are addressed to private individuals; reading them in a novel is a voyeuristic invasion of private space) but a broadly public audience that is part of the emerging "public sphere" that Jürgen Habermas associates in part with eighteenth-century coffeehouse culture. The convivial circle of relaxed but educated listeners inscribed by Fielding's narrator permits the apparent digressions (like the tales of Leonora, Dick Adams, and especially Mr. Wilson's memoir) as well as the offhand conversational manner. That female students often express an "Aha!" reaction shows their intuitive sense of this maleness and provides a wonderful opportunity for exploring issues of gender in narrative manner and the protocols of reading.

The novel's rhetorical framing involves a clearly governing structure. Each of the four books begins with a self-reflexive chapter about writing and reading, including the narrator's observations about readerly practices generally. Moreover, the preface's famous discussion of the novel as a "comic Romance" or "comic Epic-Poem in Prose" immediately introduces the epic genre (4), which subject is developed throughout by the naming of various epics, classical and recent. The four-book format recalls Milton's relatively recent *Paradise Regained* (1671), Vergil's four-book *Georgics*, and, intriguingly, the *Argonautica*, a third-century BCE four-book Greek epic that mixes the Homeric epic's high style with accounts of local customs and popular behaviors and beliefs. Familiar with the procedures of the modern Christian epic (Battestin, *Moral Basis* 41), including prose manifestations like John Bunyan's *Pilgrim's Progress* (1678), Fielding also appreciated the satirical tradition, which included the urbane Horace and more modern exemplars like the often cited Miguel de Cervantes of *Don Quixote* (1605 and 1615) and the never mentioned but unquestionably relevant Alexander Pope of *the Rape of the Lock* (1712, 1714) and *The Dunciad* (first published in three books, in 1728, and followed in 1742 with a, nota bene, fourth book whose new satirical object was the laureate Colley Cibber, whom Fielding targets throughout *Joseph Andrews*).

For me and my students, a particularly helpful indication of Fielding's idea of the novel comes near the end of the preface: "Having thus distinguished *Joseph Andrews* from the productions of Romance Writers on the one hand, and Burlesque Writers on the other, and given some very few short Hints (for I intended no more) of the Species of writing, . . . I shall leave my good-natur'd Reader to apply my Piece to my Observations . . ." (10). One could easily miss the unexpected and very significant order of the final words, which instruct the reader to apply the novel ("my Piece") to the "Observations" and not the other way around, as we usually do when we interpret fiction. When Fielding claims at the very beginning that *Joseph Andrews* is a "kind of Writing" that he does "not remember to have seen hitherto attempted in our Language" (3), he offers a valuable hint: all the name-dropping that follows helps the reader determine what *Joseph Andrews* is not, so that what it is becomes visible from the blank spaces that surround it, in a sort of multistable verbal optical illusion. Fielding's preface foregrounds what the novel is not, then, and also what it is not about, while stressing that it illustrates at every point the inherently comic nature of "the Ridiculous," which is rooted in "Affectation" (7). The novel is, in short, a representation of character in action and of virtue under the sort of trial "by what is contrary" that Milton alludes to in *Areopagitica*. By discussing narrative voice as a means of determining novelistic (and therefore both aesthetic and intellectual) intention, my students arrive at an appreciation of the coherence of what initially struck them as a wandering, puzzling, and unapproachable text. Along the way, they find themselves coming to regard Fielding's narrator—rather to their surprise—as an appealing, albeit garrulous and opinionated, grandfatherly teller of long and circuitous stories filled with surprises, revelations, twists and turns, and disarming humor.

Joseph Andrews and the European Novel

Adam Potkay

Not so long ago, teachers of the eighteenth-century English novel largely concurred that the novel originated in England and in the eighteenth century, either with Daniel Defoe's *Robinson Crusoe* (1719) or, for those who considered social interaction key to the novel form, with Samuel Richardson's *Pamela* (1740). The idea that *Pamela* is the first novel, distinct from all prose narratives that come before it, was argued by Ian Watt in his highly influential work *The Rise of the Novel* (130–31). Several generations of scholars were trained by Watt to think of the novel as defined by the formal realism—probability of events, realistic settings in time and space, and a central concern with dialogue and social relationships—that supposedly sets it apart from earlier genres, including romance and epic. Watt attributed to Fielding a "realism of assessment" (297) that made him, along with Richardson, one of the two fathers of the novel.[1]

However, Fielding never really fit the bill. He may or may not have been fathering something, but he was clearly the heir of an earlier, European tradition of prose fiction. *The History of the Adventures of Joseph Andrews, and His Friend Mr. Abraham Adams*, bears on its original title page the subtitle *Written in Imitation of the Manner of Cervantes, Author of Don Quixote*. *Don Quixote*, written in Spanish (1605, 1615) and translated into English from 1612 onward, is a candidate for the first modern novel. A striking part of its modernity lies in its critical relation to earlier prose narratives: its titular hero's head has been turned by reading chivalric romances—tales of ideal love, jealously guarded honor, and martial prowess—and in particular the multivolume romance *Amadis of Gaul*, written during the fourteenth century in Spanish and Portuguese and first printed in 1508. Don Quixote, seeing the world through chivalric lenses, makes a fool of himself in modern life, tilting at ordinary windmills as though they were giants and addressing common prostitutes as though they were damsels in distress. Yet Quixote is no despicable fool but rather God's fool, an ideal of service and moral simplicity against which the actual world may be judged. As such, he is the model for Parson Adams in *Joseph Andrews*, whom Fielding calls in his preface "the most glaring" character in the novel (10),[2] as well as for many later Quixote figures, from the protagonist of Charlotte Lennox's *Female Quixote* (1752) to Pierre Bezukhov in Leo Tolstoy's *War and Peace*. Fielding, in addition to introducing the Quixote figure to British literature, draws on other aspects of Cervantes's novel: its ironic gravity and its use of a narrator who self-consciously reflects on his novel's art, addressing his readers in varying tones of instruction, humility, and admonishment.

Yet Fielding does not categorize *Joseph Andrews* as a novel—a term that in the 1740s had neither a settled nor a favorable meaning. He calls it, rather, "a comic Romance" or a "comic Epic-Poem in Prose" (4). In this designation, he again borrows from *Don Quixote*, in which a clergyman from Toledo argues that

"Epicks may be as well writ in Prose as in Verse" and holds up the ancient epic as a model for modern romance writers (Fielding, *History of the Adventures* [ed. Potkay] 335). A proper modern romance, the clergyman claims, would reject the incredible events of chivalric romances and adhere instead to "probability" (334). In a probable or realistic narrative, the romance should present virtues, such as valor and friendship, that are worthy of admiration and vices, including treachery and boasting, that readers should know to avoid. It is a romance such as Cervantes's clergyman describes that Fielding saw himself writing, in a literary line stretching back to Homer, centered in *Don Quixote*, and extending through several French authors of the seventeenth and eighteenth centuries, authors who ought to be better known to students of the English novel. In the opening chapter of *Joseph Andrews*, book 3, Fielding situates his moral art (he describes virtuous or vicious character types, not specific individuals) in relation to a tradition that includes Paul Scarron's *Le roman comique*, written 1651–57 (the title may be translated as either "The Comic Romance" or "The Comic Novel"—French does not distinguish romance from novel), Alain-René Lesage's *Histoire de Gil Blas de Santillane* (1715–35; *History of Gil Blas*), and Pierre de Marivaux's *Le paysan parvenu* (1734–36; *The Upstart Peasant*).

In addition to these novels, Fielding likely knew, and was in any event influenced by, the *Aethiopica* (*Ethiopian Story*), an ancient Greek narrative attributed to Heliodorus (third or fourth century CE), rediscovered in the sixteenth century, greatly admired by Cervantes, and translated into English in 1717 as *The Adventures of Theagenes and Chariclia, a Romance*. In this work Heliodorus establishes the basic romance plot on which Fielding builds *Joseph Andrews* and later *Tom Jones*: a pair of lovers, repeatedly separated by misfortunes, undergo trials and sufferings, including attempts against the chastity each has vowed to maintain out of love and devotion to the other. In the end, the lovers are joyously and securely reunited. One lover has been brought up without knowing her or his true family and lineage—in *Aethiopica*, Chariclia discovers that she is the princess of Ethiopia. (In Fielding's novel, Joseph will turn out to be not a lowly Andrews but the abducted son of the genteel Wilsons.) The comic resolution of the romance plot involves the lovers' marriage and elevation to a social rank that both accords with and explains their virtues, virtues such as intelligence, courage, and loyalty, which in aristocratic cultures were held to be exclusive to genteel or noble-born persons. Heliodorus's romance plot—which essentially is also Fielding's—is tighter in construction and far more economical in its presentation than the vast and sprawling seventeenth-century chivalric romances, each containing many interconnected plots and subplots, that Fielding dismisses in the preface to *Joseph Andrews* (4). One of these, Madeline de Scudéry's *Artamène, ou le Grand Cyrus* (1649–53), consists of ten volumes and seven thousand pages.

Fielding's novelistic art thus takes us back to the prose narratives of Greek-speaking antiquity, if not directly then through French and Spanish novels of the seventeenth and earlier eighteenth centuries modeled on Heliodorus—notably

Cervantes's *Persiles and Sigismunda* (1617) and Scarron's *Le roman comique* (J. Lynch 15). These works can be called novels only if we adopt a more capacious definition of the form than Watt's. In *The True Story of the Novel*, Margaret Doody, addressing the history of the form from antiquity on, defines the novel as "*a representation of what it feels like to be alive* . . . as an individual in time" (282). Doody presents the novel as transhistorical, polyglot, and translational. Subsequent critical work that builds upon this more "global" conception of the novel—and that graduate students, in particular, might be directed toward—include collections edited by Franco Moretti (*The Novel*) and Jenny Mander (*Remapping the Rise of the European Novel*).

Fielding's debt to this tradition figures in two teaching editions of *Joseph Andrews*, both still in print, each of which features different but complementary selections from eighteenth-century English translations of the European novels on which Fielding drew: Homer Goldberg's 1987 Norton Critical edition and my 2007 Longman Cultural edition (*History of the Adventures*). Translations of the full novels are available through *ECCO* (Eighteenth Century Collection Online), for those teachers and students whose institutions have subscriptions; some translations are also available in inexpensive paperback editions—for example, Tobias Smollett's lively 1755 translation of *Don Quixote*.

Reading selections from the novels that influenced Fielding or reading one of these novels in its entirety puts students in touch with the matrix of narrative conventions and themes from which *Joseph Andrews* emerges. Much of what seems odd or artificial about Fielding's novel comes into better focus once we understand the tradition in which it operates. In modern fiction, the discovery of a character's true identity tends not to involve the recognition of bodily marks, certainly not marks or features imprinted by whatever a character's mother saw or imagined during conception. But this theory of maternal impression has an august lineage in ancient narratives, from Jacob's speckled sheep in the book of Genesis (30.25–43) to the *Aethiopica*, in which Chariclia is born with white skin because at the moment of her conception her black mother's "Eye chanced to be fixed upon the Picture of Andromeda naked" (Fielding, *History of the Adventures* 328). In *Joseph Andrews* the theory of maternal impression accounts for Joseph's identifying birthmark, which resembles a strawberry, "which his Mother had given him by longing for that Fruit" (225). Another element of Fielding's novel that looks back to tradition is the courtly-pastoral ballad that Joseph sings, at some length (and in a surprisingly bawdy vein), in book 2, chapter 13. Such ballads are a common feature of *Don Quixote* (e.g., vol. 1, bk. 3, chs. 12–13), as well as the long-eighteenth-century English stage.

Most significant is that modern novels tend to shy away from interpolated tales, lengthy narratives told by characters in the novel, such as, in *Joseph Andrews*, "The History of Leonora; or, The Unfortunate Jilt" in book 2, chapters 4–6, and "The History of Two Friends" (Paul and his married friend Leonard) in book 4, chapter 10. But interpolated tales, typically stories of love and marriage, are a staple of the earlier novel. An important example is "The Novel of the Curious Impertinent," told in *Don Quixote*, volume 1, book 4, chapters 6–8, in which Anselmo, having married the beautiful Camilla, unwisely asks his friend Lothario to test her virtue. (Fielding praises the instructive nature of these characters in book 3, chapter 1, of *Joseph Andrews* [186].) *Le roman comique* contains four interpolated tales, the most famous of which, "The Invisible Mistress," is reworked in Eliza Haywood's 1725 novel *Fantomina*. Examining how a given author makes use of such tales in the overall structure of a novel may provide topics for student essays. Cultivating a taste for tale telling per se attunes one to the aesthetic of the earlier novel as well as of prerealist narratives and tale collections such as Ovid's *Metamorphoses*, Boccaccio's *Decameron* (in which the story of Pinuccio and Adriano provides the ultimate source for the bedroom shenanigans of *Joseph Andrews* [bk. 4, ch. 14; "Night Adventures"]), and Chaucer's *Canterbury Tales*.

Another legacy of this narrative tradition is the figure of the sexually predatory older woman, vindictive when scorned. This character type extends back to the biblical story of Potiphar's wife, the Egyptian woman who, failing to seduce her Hebrew slave Joseph, falsely accuses him of treachery (Genesis 39). Fielding's Joseph undergoes a similar trial, albeit a comically elaborated one, at the hands of his employer, Lady Booby (bk. 1, chs. 5 and 8). But the dyad of predatory woman and chaste male protagonist is also a commonplace of the romance tradition. In book 1 of *Aethiopica*, Chariclia's caretaker tells his life story, the adventures of which stem from his persecution by his stepmother, who desired him and, repulsed, falsely accuses him of trying to kill his father. In books 7 and 8, Theagenes, a central character, is pursued by the lustful Persian queen Arsake, whose lady-gentlewoman warns him, "The best of women . . . are prone to Resentments . . . when provoked by Disappointments in their Love. In that Case, their Anger is implacable; they study nothing but Revenge" (2: 79).

Fielding gives to the story of unsuccessful seduction a comic twist, one anticipated in *Le roman comique*, chapter 10, in which the hefty Madame Bouvillon vainly attempts to seduce the novel's young hero, Destiny—devoted lover of the romance heroine, L'Etoile ("Star"). The comic artistry of Scarron's scene (reproduced in Fielding, *History of the Adventures* [ed. Potkay] 335–39) may be compared and contrasted with Fielding's presentation of Joseph's trials at the hands of Lady Booby, as well as at those of her gentlewoman, Mrs. Slipslop (bk. 1, ch. 6). Like Slipslop, Madame Bouvillon is a caricature or grotesque, but she is also, in her seduction attempt, more self-conflicted, and thus more human, than Fielding's predatory women: she blushes at her own designs on Destiny, a blush that causes Destiny to blush in turn. Mrs. Slipslop and Lady Booby are much more single-minded, and thus more purely comical, in their approaches to Joseph. The conflict of Lady Booby's emotions shows only in her post- or preseduction scenes of psychomachia, in which parts of her mind (desire, affection, sympathy) war with other parts (wounded pride, thirst for vengeance). These scenes of psychomachia (bk. 1, chs. 7 and 9; bk. 4, ch. 1) hark back not to Scarron but to scenes of psychological self-division in Marivaux's *The Upstart Peasant* (see, e.g., Fielding, *Joseph Andrews* [ed. Goldberg] 378).

In Fielding's novel, Lady Booby's carnal or concupiscent love finds a counterpoint in the brotherly love—or common charity—displayed by the stagecoach postilion who gives his coat to the naked and beaten Joseph in book 1, chapter 12. Fielding invites us to see this charitable love in opposition not only to concupiscence but also to an uncharitable English gentry and judicature—that is, to particular social ills in Georgian England. The postilion who takes pity on Joseph declares "that he would rather ride in his Shirt all his Life, than suffer a Fellow-Creature to lie in so miserable a Condition" (53). Fielding's model for this act of charity is the parable of the Good Samaritan, the social outsider who cares for a man who has been beaten and stripped by thieves and subsequently ignored and left to die by two men of high social and religious standing (Luke 10.29–37). But unlike the Gospel's Samaritan, Fielding's postilion is given a future. The narrator parenthetically remarks of the postilion—the lowest paid member of a stagecoach's staff—that he "hath since been transported for robbing a Hen-roost" (53). In the moral frame of *Joseph Andrews*, this aside may nod to the postilion's lack of prudence, the necessary counterweight to charity or good nature. But it also serves as a rapid-fire satire on an oppressive state system that banishes people to the colonies for what are in fact (if not in law) petty crimes. Recall that *Joseph Andrews* is a novel in which Joseph and Fanny are very nearly sent to jail by Lawyer Scout and Justice Frolic, at Lady Booby's vengeful pleasure, for the real or fabricated offense of snapping off a hazel twig (bk. 4, ch.5).[3]

As a critic of unjust institutions, as well as an ironist and self-reflexive craftsman, Fielding has been kept alive in Continental Europe during the twentieth century. His fine eye for the evils of Georgian legal and political institutions made him seem a forerunner of Karl Marx in the late Soviet Union—"the only nation," Martin Battestin notes, "to honor Fielding's memory on the bicentennial of his death [1954] by issuing a commemorative postal stamp" (*Henry Fielding: A Life* 545). Fielding also appears as a kindred spirit in Milan Kundera's intensely anti-Soviet novel concerning the Prague Spring and its aftermath, *The Unbearable Lightness of Being*: the protagonist, Tereza, immerses herself in a novel tradition that spans "from Fielding to Thomas Mann" (47). *Joseph Andrews*, along with *Tom Jones*, provides an opening into a wider European novel tradition, stretching both backward and forward from the 1740s. Fielding's self-reflexive and conversational storytelling, combined with his interweaving of physical comedy and social criticism, has considerable resonance in broader European and world fictions, especially in comedies considerably darker than his, from Fyodor Dostoevsky's *Notes from Underground* to Witold Gombrowicz's *Ferdydurke* and Salman Rushdie's *Midnight's Children*. Fielding's achievement, somewhat eccentric in English literary history, emerges as central to the novel form when we study that form in more global ways.

NOTES

[1] Watt argues that Fielding's work "serves as a perpetual reminder that if the new genre [of the novel] was to challenge older literary forms it had to find a way of conveying not only a convincing impression but a wise assessment of life, an assessment that could only come from taking a much wider view than Defoe or Richardson of the affairs of mankind" (288).

[2] I use the Wesleyan edition of *Joseph Andrews* except where I need to quote from the back matter of two teaching editions of the novel, designated as *History of the Adventures* (ed. Potkay) and *Joseph Andrews* (ed. Goldberg).

[3] On Fielding's sustained satire on English judicature in *Joseph Andrews*, see Potkay, *Story* 111–18.

Pulling the Anglican Thread: Using Parson Adams's Torn Cassock to Teach Fielding's Complicated Art

Christopher D. Johnson

Undergraduates in my satire seminar are a bit confused when Henry Fielding discusses religion. The doctrinal differences that defined eighteenth-century British Christianity have largely been lost, and Fielding's audience assumed connections between church and state that are absent from twenty-first-century American culture. As a result, students are puzzled by Fielding's harsh attacks on various Christian sects and miss important dimensions of his fiction. To aid recovery of the culture in which Fielding wrote, I ask students to consider the various functions of Parson Adams's ecclesiastical garments, particularly his cassock and gown, which are, with the exception of Jack's coat in Jonathan Swift's *A Tale of a Tub*, the most abused items of clothing in eighteenth-century fiction.

Focusing on Adams's clothing suits my pedagogical methodology, which emphasizes close reading and historical contextualization. As we work to interpret the garments through our class discussions, students discover not only how Fielding created meaning in his text but also how the novel interacts with his more overtly political writings and with the tensions that defined eighteenth-century Protestantism. These discussions, which define the text as both artistically coherent and culturally reflective, provide a useful model for the students' own writing.

Parson Adams's garments serve a variety of functions. They clearly have symbolic value, and Fielding's treatment of them is more complex than Swift's allegory of the three coats. By examining the garments' metonymic association to their owner and their metaphoric relation to the Anglican Church, we discover a range of interpretative possibilities, all of which help situate the novel in the world of eighteenth-century British Christianity.

As students begin reading *Joseph Andrews*, their attention immediately focuses on the jolly, avuncular Adams. As we begin discussing his appearance, I share pictures of the sorts of wigs, nightcaps, greatcoats, cassocks, and gowns that his character is likely to have worn, and we look at the eighteenth-century illustrations of Adams by James Hulett and Thomas Hearne, which are available in Adam Potkay's Longman Cultural Edition of *History of the Adventures of Joseph Andrews* and through the Web site for the British Museum. We also discuss the visual rhetoric of ecclesiastical garments. Since many of the students are members of congregations, I ask them to consider how ministers dress both in and outside church. Appearances, they assure me, are important, and a minister compromises his authority and ability to provide pastoral guidance by being poorly dressed.

In the novel, we discover, clothing is also important for communicating status and character. Early on, we learn that Sir Thomas was "too apt to estimate Men merely by their Dress" (25 [bk. 1, ch. 3]). Later, Parson Trulliber is so outraged by Adams's disheveled appearance that he proclaims that his fellow parson deserves to "have thy Gown stript over thy Shoulders, for running about the Country in such a manner" (167 [bk. 2, ch. 14]). We evaluate this judgment, looking at several passages where the appearance of Adams is comical, such as when he has a "Night-Cap drawn over his Wig, and a short great Coat, which half covered his Cassock" (73 [bk. 1, ch. 16]) or when he is running ahead of the coach and "his Cassock had just again fallen down below his great Coat, that is to say, it reached his Knees; whereas, the Skirts of his great Coat descended no lower than half way down his Thighs" (130 [bk. 2, ch. 7]). When I ask students if they would want Adams as a minister in their home churches, the responses are mixed. They agree that he would be a great chaplain for a fraternity, but many find him undignified and suggest that he lacks gravitas and judgment. He is a decent man, to be sure, but not an ideal minister. By the terms of the author's preface, he may not be ridiculous, since he seems to have little affectation (7), but he is certainly silly, and his clothing suggests an incongruity between his person and his vocation.

Exploring this incongruity, I suggest, helps us understand Fielding's complicated thoughts about the Anglican Church. Adams looks laughable because he is oblivious to the world around him and the social expectations that accompany his status as a clergyman. Equally important, his appearance reflects his humanity—he is inattentive to his clothing because he is thinking of others. Ironically, the characteristics that make him most suited for his vocation compromise his ability to look the part. How, then, is Fielding defining the role of the clergy? Are parsons spiritual and moral exemplars? Are they representatives of a powerful instrument of the state, having official ecclesiastical and legal authorities, or are they simply good, devout men who strive to serve those in need? Exploring these issues, we begin discussing the distinctions between the High Church and the Low Church, which are central to Fielding's idea of religion and which become important later when we examine Adams's comments on George Whitefield and Benjamin Hoadly.

To build further context, we turn to the anticlerical writings in the *Champion*, where Fielding, like other pamphlet writers, associates ecclesiastical clothing with corruption and political ambition (Lund, "Problem" 262). We pay particular attention to Fielding's description of "the black species of TRY [Tory]," who

> hath a particular Name, *viz*, a PRSN, and hath by some been mistaken for the Female, by a Covering which Nature hath bestowed on its Legs, like that which she hath given to the Female TRY; but, on examining several, I have found always that they are not in the least more deficient in their Formation, than the TRY of other Colours. (461–62)

Students easily differentiate this type of sycophantic parson, whose "usual Method of ascending . . . is, by Crawling" (461), from Adams, who has little desire to advance in the church. They also notice Fielding's condescending association of the clergy with the feminine. Adams, in contrast, bursts with specifically masculine strength, expressed not only in his many children but also in his frayed gown, which he tore many years earlier while jumping (boyishly, we suspect) "over a Stile" (164 [bk. 2, ch. 14]). Yet the squire persists in associating his cassocks with petticoats (247 [bk. 3, ch. 7]), and Adams confronts the stereotype again in a heated exchange with the captain: " '[The captain threatens][I]f you was not a Parson, I would not take these Words; but your Gown protects you.' . . . *Adams* replied, 'if he attempted any Rudeness to his Person, he would not find any Protection for himself in his Gown' " (249). Adams's ecclesiastical gown appears in opposition to his masculine strength. When we consider that the parson uses his strength for the wholesome and particularly Christian purpose of protecting the weak and vulnerable, the condition of his garments marks what is best about him and suggests a triumph over what is worst about his church.

The garments, then, serve as instruments, albeit complicated ones, of Fielding's anticlerical satire. With this idea established, students identify additional levels of significance. They notice, for example, that Adams's ecclesiastical clothing is more than sloppy; it is also shabby. As Adams starts his journey, his cassock has already been torn for about ten years. Parson Trulliber notes sardonically that Adams has "some Cassock; I will not venture to *caale* it a whole one" (164 [bk. 2, ch. 14]). So poor is Adams's clothing that Trulliber doubts his claim to be a parson, as does the justice of the peace in an earlier scene (146 [ch. 11]). In some ways, Adams's economic situation is of his own making: Adams has a larger family than his income of twenty-three pounds per year can support. His threadbare appearance, though, also reflects the treatment he receives from people who should ensure his well-being. His salary as a curate, for example, is determined by the absentee parson of the parish, who views Adams exactly as Sir Thomas and Lady Booby do, "as a kind of Domestic only" (25 [bk. 1, ch. 3]). When discussing this point, I share Samuel Johnson's telling definition for *curate*: "a clergyman hired to perform the duties of another." When Adams's clothing is stained in Parson Trulliber's pigsty, we again see his clerical status diminished: a fellow parson sees Adams as a potential customer rather than as an ecclesiastical peer, which is to say, in economic rather than spiritual terms.

Adams clothing, then, allows Fielding to criticize the low status of the lesser clergy and call attention to the indifference and greed of those in power. In this way, Adams's torn cassock and gown reinforce another point from the *Champion*:

> . . . without *being righteous over-much*, we may, I think, conclude, that if the Clergy are not to abandon all they have to their Ministry, neither are they to get immense Estates by it; and I would recommend it to the

> Consideration of those who do, whether they do not make a Trade of Divinity? Whether they are not those Buyers and Sellers who should be drove out of the Temple? Or lastly, Whether they do not in the Language of *Peter* to *Simon* sell the Gift of God for Money? (*Contributions* 271)

Despite his attempt to sell sermons, Adams could never be accused of making a trade of divinity. He is, instead, an honest parson committed to both his church and his parishioners, and he seems to pay a high price for his efforts. Differentiating him from his more worldly peers, his ragged clothing becomes both an ironic indication of his fitness for the clergy and a satirical symbol of episcopal corruption.

Exploring this idea further, we turn to book 3, chapters 6–7, where Adams's clothing receives its most sustained abuse. After the squire and his fellow hunters allow the dogs to tear off "a third Part of [Adams's] Cassock," they damage the garment further with firecrackers and then soak it, along with Adams, in a tub of water (237 [ch. 6]). The hunting party, to be sure, is a decadent mob of privileged scoundrels, and the squire, who reduces both Adams and Fanny to prey, is by far the worst of the lot. Living a life of pleasure, he abandons his obligations to the law, as evidenced in his attempted rape of Fanny, and to his faith, as evidenced in his huntsman's uncorrected comment that he "wondered his Master would encourage the Dogs to hunt *Christians*; that it was the surest way to spoil them, to make them follow Vermin instead of sticking to a Hare" (243).

To place the squire's destruction of the cassock and gown in a larger context, we return to *Tale of a Tub*. We look closely at Christopher Fox's compelling argument that the character Jack, who shreds his coat past usefulness and recognition, represents the Rabble Reformation of Scotland during the late seventeenth century, when radical Presbyterian dissenters attacked unwelcomed episcopal power. Gilbert Burnet, Fielding's favorite English historian (Battestin and Battestin, *Henry Fielding: A Life* 292), provides a succinct account of their actions: "They generally broke in upon the Episcopal Clergy with great insolence and much cruelty. They carried them about the parishes in a mock procession. They tore their gowns, and drove them from their Churches and houses" (804–05; qtd. in Fox 107). These activities, which started on Christmas Day, 1688, and continued for many months, were both terrifying and effective. As Fox notes, soon after the Rabblings, the Scottish episcopacy was abolished and Presbyterian governance restored to the Scottish Church (106–07).

Fielding certainly knew Burnet's *History of His Own Time*, the title of which he appropriates for *The True Patriot* (Battestin and Battestin, *Henry Fielding: A Life* 400–01), and there are interesting suggestions that he may have been thinking of the Rabblers as he was writing *Joseph Andrews*. Adams, for example, curiously associates Presbyterianism with atheism (230 [bk. 3, ch. 5]), and Trulliber seems to offer a reenactment of the Rabblers' ritualistic devestments when he threatens to strip Adams's gown "over thy Shoulders." More important for our purpose is the recognition that Fielding and the Rabblers, however theologically and ideologically divergent, associate the desecration of ecclesiastical garments with the destruction of the established church. The key difference is that the Rabblers were external threats to Anglicanism, as opposed to Trulliber, a fellow churchman, and to the squire, who is not only a nominal member of the Anglican Communion but also an aristocrat who should protect England's official church.

In his discussion with a gentleman, Adams recalls a time when "the *Church was in Danger*" (133 [bk. 2, ch. 8]). As Roger Lund explains, in so doing, he repeats a rallying cry that High-Church Tories used against those who sought greater tolerance for dissenters ("Problem" 260). The destruction of Adams's gown and cassock suggests the irony of his voicing this phrase. The church is indeed in danger but not from the forces that destroyed the Scottish episcopacy in the 1680s, nor from the dissenters, deists, and Socinianists of mid-century. The real danger for Adams's ministry is the worldliness of the clergymen like Trulliber and the indifference and profligacy of the aristocracy.

Once this danger is identified, we can move back to the discussion at the Tow-wouse inn between Adams and Barnabus. Adams's tattered clothing provides a useful way of exploring the parson's admiration for Bishop Hoadly's *A Plain Account of the Nature and End of the Sacrament*, which seeks to remove the mystery from the Eucharistic celebration. Once students understand a little about the Thirty-Nine Articles, Real Presence, and the authority those doctrines provide clergy, they easily equate clerical clothing with sacramentalism: both are manifestations of divinity and ecclesiastical power. Adams now appears as torn as his cassock. On the one hand, he is a defender of Anglicanism, as we see, for example, when he insists on the publishing of the banns before Joseph and Fanny's wedding (160 [bk. 2, ch. 13]). On the other hand, he seems unwilling to place ritual and status above the needs of the least of his parishioners. Putting the immediate and communal above the sacred and mysterious, he loses traditional clerical authority, as is represented in his deteriorating vestments, but he seems to gain a more authentic ethical authority, which can be readily seen in the contrast between him and Parsons Barnabus and Trulliber.

How, then, are we to understand Adams's admiration for Hoadly? Does Hoadly represent the salvation of the episcopacy, as Battestin seems to suggest *(Moral Basis* 14), or is he, as Lund argues, a dangerous radical (284)? We go back to the students' original thoughts on Adams's lack of appropriate seriousness and the importance of appearance for clergy members. His clothing reveals a paradox of his ministry: Adams cannot simultaneously act and look like an authentic parson. We search the novel for places where his torn clothing hinders his ability to serve Joseph and Fanny (when they appear before the justice of the peace [145 (bk. 2, ch. 11)]), and scenes in which he sacrifices the dignity of the cloth in order to protect them (when he runs into the brush with his crabstick to rescue Fanny [131 (bk. 2, ch. 7)]).

In the end, the cassock and gown may be as complicated as Adams himself, who occupies both the comic and moral centers of the novel. In the same way, it may be impossible to find in *Joseph Andrews* either a clear defense or specific attack on the Anglican Church. We can, though, be certain that thoughts of the episcopacy were close to Fielding's mind when Fielding wrote his first great novel. Through Parson Adams's tattered vestments, we catch a glimpse of the author's uneasy relation to a religious tradition that he found both essential and deeply flawed.

Finding the "Mark" of the Mother: The Feminized Birth Mystery and an Approach to Teaching Fielding

Brian McCrea

For many years, I taught *Joseph Andrews* and *Tom Jones* as Martin C. Battestin taught them to me. Emphasizing the moral basis of Fielding's art, I encouraged my students both to read closely (to attend carefully to the word *charity* in *Joseph Andrews*, to *prudence* in *Tom Jones*) and to find the grander and satisfying emblematic dimension of Fielding's characters and events—the significance of Adams's bad horsemanship in comparison with Joseph's success as a jockey, the reason why Fielding places Tom atop Mazard Hill at the center of his narrative (Battestin, "Fielding's Definition" 198–207). This approach worked particularly well for undergraduates because it helped them move more successfully than they typically do between the specifics of the text and their generalizations about it—that is, their interpretation. With Battestin as a strong presence in my classroom, my students seemed to do better with Fielding than with other eighteenth-century novelists, and they could replicate my own occasional successes as a Fielding critic.

Approximately fifteen years ago, I decided to change this formula. Not because I was dissatisfied with its results: the two teaching awards that I won in university-wide competitions had brought me institutional esteem and financial reward. Fittingly enough, at least for any scholar of eighteenth-century British literature, I changed how I taught Fielding because I changed how I taught Samuel Richardson. Despite my best efforts to help students admire Pamela's heroic and groundbreaking individualism (for which I used Ian Watt's ever-lucid chapter [208–38] and Nancy Armstrong's brilliant re-visioning of Watt to emphasize), I had suffered through too many classes in which my *Pamela*-weary students began to sound like the most benighted contemporary commentators on rape. "Can it really take that long to flower a waistcoat?" they would ask. "Her father has ordered her to come home immediately. Why doesn't she?" "Given all the time she spends looking at it in her mirror, why doesn't she admit that the country maid outfit is sexy?"

The last question was particularly disheartening because it came perilously close to showing that I, with all my learning and good intentions, had succeeded only in making my students—otherwise earnest, polite, and for the most part virtuous—blame the victim. With Angus Ross's fine paperback edition of the complete *Clarissa* available, I opted out of the *Pamela* cul-de-sac. Instead, I asked my students to read Ross's edition (roughly 125 pages a week) alongside their other reading; Wednesday would be our *Clarissa* day.

In its thorough unfolding of Robert Lovelace's villainy, *Clarissa* spared me those dark moments in which I feared that I was helping my students become moral reprobates. My change worked. But even in installments, the complete *Clarissa* can be a spirit-breaking not to mention a backbreaking assignment—my students' misshapen backpacks bore eloquent testimony to the latter. I realized that I needed to cut my students some slack. With *Clarissa* now on the reading list, *Tom Jones* would have to come off it. My students would encounter Fielding via *Joseph Andrews*.

In this redesigned course, I needed *Joseph Andrews* to do more than reveal a fine conflation of detail, diction, and emblem. It should look forward to *Tom Jones*; it should prompt discussion of the motifs and themes it shares with that later novel. I also needed to place *Joseph Andrews* in relation to fiction by the women writers (Haywood, Burney, Lennox, Inchbald) who, absent from the classes I had taken in the early 1970s, loomed large in the class that I now taught. My research at this time, which led to a book titled *Impotent Fathers: Patriarchy and Demographic Crisis in the Eighteenth-Century Novel*, suggested a solution. Rather than approach *Joseph Andrews* through the history of ideas (more specifically Battestin's Christian humanism), I would approach it through an idiosyncratic (some might say skewed) feminism. In my work on *Clarissa*, I was emphasizing that Clarissa is the victim of the absence rather than the presence of patriarchal power; recall her frequent and plangent requests to meet with her father, which her brother, James, cruelly and calculatedly thwarts. *Joseph Andrews* offers, albeit comically, a similar displacement of the patriarch.

In *Joseph Andrews*, as in *Tom Jones*, Fielding uses a "birth-mystery plot" (Frye 51). This plot, as Northrop Frye points out, goes back at least as far as the Pentateuch (Moses in the bulrushes) and the plays of Euripides. If we do not look closely at how Fielding sets up his birth mystery, we might consider him an old-fashioned writer, particularly by the standards Watt set over fifty years ago. Trained in the classics at Eton, Fielding does not fit well into Watt's "formal realism" (32), into Watt's account of the novel as a literary innovation. Fielding's diction not only is figurative, it is self-consciously so: "In vulgar Language, it was the Evening" (*Joseph Andrews* 38 [bk. 1, ch. 8]). Fielding stands against Watt's claim that novels use "descriptive and denotative . . . language" (29). His characters have names that are rich in symbolic possibilities—"*Joey*, whom for a good Reason we shall hereafter call JOSEPH" (29 [ch. 5])—not the "proper names" that according to Watt individualize characters in novels (18). Perhaps Fielding's greatest violation of Watt's version of the novel is his use of a "traditional plot" (13–14), perhaps even, as Frye suggests, the most traditional of plots.

Impotent Fathers, however, led me to see that, as early as *Joseph Andrews* and even more powerfully in *Tom Jones*, Fielding varies the birth mystery, in ways both significant and teachable, by displacing the father and emphasizing the mother. That variation informs my revised approach to his novels. Mr. Wilson tells Adams that the son who was taken from him by Gypsies—the son whose loss is almost the only blight (the squire's rude son is another) on his virtuous retirement—"had a Mark on his left Breast, of a Strawberry." And so, even though many years have passed, "he should know him among ten thousand" (225 [bk. 3, ch. 4]). Any reader with some background in traditional literature, particularly the romances of seventeenth-century French literature, will recognize that this detail is not gratuitous, that this missing son is going to be identified by his "Mark." Joseph, indeed, is when he shows it to his father (339 [bk. 4, ch. 16]). But I want my students to see that this mark is not of the father's making. Rather, it is given to Joseph by his mother, who during her pregnancy had a great "longing for that Fruit" (225 [bk. 3, ch. 4]). Homer Goldberg notes that Fielding here references a "folk belief . . . that failure to satisfy a pregnant woman's craving for a particular food (usually fruit out of season) would produce a representative birthmark on the infant" (Joseph Andrews *with* Shamela 176n).

I like to point out that Fielding, despite his training at Eton in the classics, also is in touch with the folk. But Joseph's mark has taken a central place in my teaching of Fielding because it originates in the mother's appetite, not in the lost child's patrimony. Although Watt has become less important in Fielding studies, it helps my students to read him and then see that Fielding's plot only seems traditional. Through his feminization of the birth mystery plot, Fielding has a strong claim to stand with Daniel Defoe and Richardson as innovators.

This feminization becomes even more notable and significant in *Tom Jones*. Bridget Allworthy holds the secret to Tom's birth and trusts it in her will (her writing) to Lawyer Dowling. Patrimony in *Tom Jones* is even more negligible than in *Joseph Andrews*. When we last see Joseph, he lives "in the same Parish with his Father" on a "little Estate . . . his Father . . . [has] stock'd for him" (*Joseph Andrews* 344 [bk. 4, ch. 16]). He apparently has become Joseph Wilson, although we do not hear him referred to as such; he is about to become a "Father," a word still capitalized. For all the happiness and goodwill that suffuses the conclusion of *Tom Jones*, the hero's name remains uncertain. He inherits great properties from Allworthy and Western (even though it remained a first principle of both common and chancery law that a bastard cannot inherit) and we now know that his father's surname was Summer. Does Tom Jones remain Tom Jones?

By focusing on the mother's mark, I help my students look forward to *Tom Jones*. Even more important, I help them make connections between the purportedly manly—in some accounts misogynistic (Prytula 178, 187, 192–93)—Fielding and the woman novelists of his era. In her *Betsy Thoughtless*, Eliza Haywood, Fielding's coadjutor and partner in theatrical productions, shows us a heroine who needs to acquire prudence, just as did Tom Jones. By emphasizing Fielding's feminization of the birth mystery, I can add formal corollaries to thematic. Frances Burney, for example, admired Fielding, as we know from the preface to *Evelina*, although we might have some trouble saying why (always a proper lady, Burney will give us no sex scenes).

In both her first novel, *Evelina*, which I teach, and her last, *The Wanderer*, which I don't, Burney feminizes the birth mystery in ways that build on the precedent set by Fielding. An obvious difference is that her birth mysteries involve female protagonists rather than male. A less obvious but more significant variation is that the birth mystery now (in the vein of Bridget Allworthy) resides in the purview of the female protagonist. Evelina is not confused or uncertain about who her father is, but until he acknowledges her, she remains a nobody. Burney's anagnorisis brilliantly combines two possibilities that Fielding opened for her. Evelina looks just like her mother, but she also has a letter from her mother that asserts her claim. Biology (the mother's appetite) and writing (the mother's will) are both on Evelina's side; only the deception under which her father labors (his impotence) prevents his recognizing her. That recognition, once achieved, brings joy to all except the father, whose pain at the memory of his mistreatment of the mother is intense and perhaps irremediable. In *The Wanderer*, Burney grants her heroine such powerful control of the birth mystery that readers need over six hundred pages to learn who she is—a knowledge that, nineteenth-century critics argued, comes too dear.

By basing my approach to Fielding on the mother's mark, I can refer in some detail to *Tom Jones* without imposing an unmanageable reading load on my students. I also can point them to that mark in fiction by women authors. Typically, as we talk about these eighteenth-century birth mysteries, my students need little prompting to compare them with the birth mystery most prominent in their culture—not Oedipus Rex or Moses in the bulrushes, certainly not Tom Jones (if that indeed is his name) or Evelina Anville (she knows that name is not hers). When Darth Vader and Luke Skywalker become part of our discussion, I take some pleasure in arguing, although many of my students disagree, that, in comparison with Fielding's birth mystery, George Lucas's is both masculinist and (no amount of special effects can hide this) elitist. I leave our *Star Wars* discussion not with a *Pamela*-induced sense of failure but with the gratifying knowledge that I have provoked (in the best sense of the word) my students. Who would have suspected that a commercially successful late-modern filmmaker and a creator of cultural icons is more of a traditionalist than the writer who, at least in Watt's account, comes a distant third to Richardson and Defoe in the "rise of the novel"?

Joseph Andrews as Travel Literature

Chloe Wigston Smith

The opening of book 2 of *Joseph Andrews* includes an extended comparison of the novel to a journey. The pauses between chapters "may be looked upon as an Inn or Resting-Place, where [the reader] may stop and take a Glass, or any other Refreshment" (89). Chapter summaries resemble "many Inscriptions over the Gates of Inns (to continue the same Metaphor), informing the Reader what Entertainment he is to expect, which if he likes not, he may travel on to the next" (90)—though, of course, these summaries do not always align with the actual contents, just as signs can sometimes be misleading. This analogy suits a novel that plots the travels of Joseph Andrews, Parson Adams, and Fanny Goodwill, but it also raises questions about the value of books and the relation between reading and consumption. The narrator imagines that thoughtful readers will benefit from the blank pages between the novel's four books, which "are to be regarded as those Stages, where, in long Journeys, the Traveller stays some time to repose himself, and consider of what he hath seen in the Parts he hath already passed through" (89–90). Such resting points offer travelers and readers an opportunity to reflect on the value of their transportation, whether physical or imaginative. The narrator cautions his audience not "to travel through these Pages too fast" for fear of missing "some curious Productions of Nature which will be observed by the slower and more accurate reader" (90). Reading, like traveling, turns on the experiences of memory, narrative, and entertainment. Progress on these literal and figurative roads depends on pleasure but also on a commercial world flush with inns, food, drink, and print.

Fielding's first long novel regularly features in my upper-division course for English majors that is focused on travel literature in the global eighteenth century. *Joseph Andrews* finds its place in the course's section on domestic travel and tourism. Our focus allows for a full contemplation of Fielding's turn to the picaresque tradition as well as of how this turn capitalizes on *Don Quixote*'s popularity in the literary marketplace. Above all, this approach provokes discussions that are engaged less with *Joseph Andrews*'s satirical reworkings of *Pamela* than with its treatment of genre, commodity culture, the country and the city, and the road.

The course as a whole looks at travel in nonfiction prose and novels, including depictions of real geographic settings, invented ones, and purely imaginary places. We begin by contemplating fabricated worlds, for which we read two texts: Margaret Cavendish's science fiction *The Blazing World* and John Bunyan's conversion narrative *The Pilgrim's Progress*. These texts foreground the relations among travel, science, religion, autobiographical prose, and individualism. The next module addresses domestic travel and tourism in Britain and considers excerpts from the nonfiction travel prose of Celia Fiennes (*Through*

England on a Side-Saddle) and Daniel Defoe (*A Tour through the Whole Isle of Great Britain*).[1] We pair these guides with *Joseph Andrews*, after which the syllabus shifts beyond British shores, moving outward to early America and the West Indies, in readings such as *Oroonoko*, *Robinson Crusoe*, *The Female American*, *The History of the Life and Adventures of Mr. Anderson* (Kimber), *Obi; or, The History of Three-Fingered Jack* (Earle), and *The Woman of Colour*. We then study texts that feature the Middle East, Turkey, and India, such as *The Arabian Nights' Entertainments*, Frances Sheridan's *The History of Nourjahad*, Lady Mary Wortley Montagu's *The Turkish Embassy Letters*, Elizabeth Hamilton's *Translation of the Letters of a Hindoo Rajah*, and Sydney Owenson's *The Missionary*. Throughout, novels are supplemented with selections from journals and letters penned by travelers to these geographic regions.

Our discussions are informed by scholarship on race, religion, national identity, and postcolonial readings of the eighteenth-century novel, including the work of Srinivas Aravamudan, Rosalind Ballaster, Eve Tavor Bannet, Lynn Festa, Suvir Kaul, Felicity Nussbaum, and Roxann Wheeler. These perspectives, which I tend to summarize or excerpt but which could be integrated into a graduate course, prompt students to eye the vertical rise of the novel with skepticism and to consider instead its emergence in more lateral and spatial terms. Aravamudan, for instance, reads fictions as "provisional translations linked to fictional elsewheres," an approach that positions the English novel in a rich, varied, and geographically eclectic space. For him, novels function as "cultural transportation devices that carry something over from afar" (75). Such critical insights cast an international light on the novel's aesthetic influences and encourage students to question the national identity of the British novel.

We examine the expansiveness of space, too, in the material culture of the novel. In many eighteenth-century novels, the acts of purchasing and reading fiction are coupled with the consumption of domestic and international goods; thus buying a book is akin to furnishing a house with the latest ceramics, cabinetry, and textiles from France, India, and China. Our conversations pair the expansion of the literary marketplace with the period's growing tourist industry, country-house building, and modes of transportation. Mark Girouard's study of the English country house fills in the contours of Fielding's attention to the hierarchies of service and to the hallways, bedrooms, and kitchens of taverns, inns, and eventually Booby Hall. Cynthia Wall's discussions of domestic tourism's link to novelistic detail illuminate *Joseph Andrews*'s dynamic engagement with the practice and epistemology of travel. According to Wall, domestic tourism (and the travel journals and guidebooks that supported it) stressed the importance of knowing one's country, its "manufactures, roadways, waterways, mines, local produce, and gardens" (*Prose* 191). Paul Fussell ties period interest in travelogues to the Lockean philosophy of mind, which emphasizes the sequential accumulation of experience. Lockean psychology "furnishes the context for the flourishing of the travel book as one of the most vigorous of the contemporary kinds" (263). It is through a knowable landscape that Fielding's jovial, omniscient narrator leads—sometimes astray—his main characters, to whom he frequently refers as travelers.

From this introduction, which absorbs our first meeting, we turn to the nexus of travel, narrative structure, and commodity culture in *Joseph Andrews*, which often hinges on the conflict between firsthand experience and knowledge culled from books. Parson Adams, for instance, is "entirely ignorant of the Ways of this World, as an Infant just entered into it could possibly be" (23 [bk. 1, ch. 3]). By contrast, Mrs. Slipslop "always insisted on a Deference to be paid to her Understanding, as she had been frequently at *London*, and knew more of the World than a Country Parson could pretend to" (25). The tensions between experience and knowledge come into even sharper focus toward the end of book 2, when Adams insists that armchair travel can substitute for actual experience: "[T]he travelling I mean is in Books, the only way of travelling by which any Knowledge is to be acquired" (182 [ch. 17]). He promises the innkeeper, "I can go farther in an Afternoon, than you in a Twelve-Month" (181). His claim provokes his listener to anger, but the conversation elicits a number of guiding questions about the novel's representation of travel: What kinds of experience and knowledge do Adams, Joseph, and Fanny acquire? And, by contrast, what forms of knowledge elude them?

We return periodically to these questions in parsing how the novel deploys its characters as moving parts across a narrative landscape. Although the novel opens with Joseph's journey to London, where Joseph adopts some cosmopolitan fashions and customs, the plot eventually settles into a movement away from the city to the country. In his first letter to his sister, Pamela, he confides, "*London* is a bad Place" (32 [bk. 1, ch. 6]). Indeed, the city presents few attractions after his dismissal from Lady Booby's service. Martin C. Battestin frames his hasty retreat in spiritual terms, describing it as "a moral pilgrimage from the vanity and corruption of the Great City to the *relative* naturalness and simplicity of the country" (*Moral Basis* 89). This pilgrimage, however moral, is still defined through the tangible world of the road, one marked by vehicles and pit stops, from the stagecoach to the saddle, tavern, and country house. A violent storm forces Joseph to take shelter at an inn early in his journey (50 [bk. 1, ch. 11]). This natural event is soon followed by human calamity when pistol-bearing thieves steal his money and clothes, leaving him shivering and groaning in a ditch (52–53 [ch. 12]). Fielding returns repeatedly to the corporeal suffering endured by his hero, relating how his journey is as much physical as moral.

At this point and throughout the novel, Joseph's progress pivots on his class status, which suggests how travel is contingent on social factors. Joseph is rescued from the ditch by the driver of a stagecoach but not before his servant status casts doubt on this rescue. The coach's passengers argue over whether or not to help the destitute and naked Joseph before the young postilion offers his own coat (52–53); the passengers' varied responses to Joseph's predicament inaugurate the novel's interest in the relation between class and travel. The theme reappears when Miss Grave-Airs balks at the idea of sitting alongside Joseph in a coach: "[S]he would not demean herself to ride with a Footman" (123 [bk. 2, ch. 5]). Mrs. Slipslop emulates Miss Grave-Airs when she denies Fanny a place in a coach (159 [ch. 13]). The economics of travel produce different experiences for the novel's range of travelers, dividing mobility by class lines.

Class-inflected modes of transportation also shape the narrative's pace and our knowledge of characters. Fielding's travel analogy, as J. Paul Hunter observes, "operates implicitly, and the reader's acquisition of experience derives from his movement through book-space, a movement that, while paralleling and depending upon Joseph's movement through space to experience, is by no means equivalent" (*Occasional Form* 143). The movements of Parson Adams, in particular, meddle with our access to Joseph's travels, often with comic results. For instance, Fielding relates the details of the "*ride and tie*" method used by Adams and Joseph to share a horse (94 [bk. 2, ch. 2]); the method results in the friends' being separated. Later Adams gets lost when he strives to outpace a coach: "[F]or the faster [the Coachman] drove, the faster ran the Parson, often crying out, *Aye, aye, catch me if you can.*" Instead of lingering, the narrator follows the more dynamic Parson Adams: "[L]eaving the Coach and its Company to pursue their Journey, we will carry our Reader on after Parson *Adams*, who stretched forwards without once looking behind him" (130 [ch. 7]). Thus Adams bends our attention to his route as he proceeds on foot.

Modes of transportation can function as narrative vehicles (here one could include illustrations of coaches and taverns from the digital collections of the British Museum and Lewis Walpole Library). Will McMorran argues that the stagecoach is a "mobile version of the inn" (127). In book 2, for instance, we are privy to the interpolated story of Leonora, as told by a lady who introduces her history as the stagecoach passes by Leonora's estate (102 [ch. 3]). This tale of amatory fiction enters the coach by way of the moving landscape outside its windows. For Hunter, such "interpolations are places of rest and refreshment" (*Occasional Form* 160). The novel's rhythm of stasis and movement, with interpolated tales that introduce pauses, silences, and parodies, demonstrates book 2's analogy between travel and reading. Parson Adams listens with rapt attention to a romance grounded in love at first sight of a coach: "[A] Coach and Six passed by: which [Leonora] declared the completest, genteelest, prettiest Equipage she ever saw; adding these remarkable Words, *O I am in love with that Equipage!*" (108 [ch. 4]). Leonora falls in love with the luxurious equipage before meeting its owner, and the telling of her story depends on the movement of the coach in which it unfolds. In linking her tale so squarely to several examples of horse-drawn vehicles, the novel shows how that tale depends on moving objects. To Adams's dismay—for his "Ears were the most hungry Part about him" (118)—the story is interrupted when the coach reaches an inn. His ravenous ears underscore his position as a consumer of Leonora's story, but the slippage of listener (and reader) into consumer is undercut by the fact that Adams never hears the conclusion to the tale in chapter 6, because by this point, he is traveling on foot. The episode reminds us that narrative is the handmaiden to chance, as tales start, stall, and proceed no matter what the composition of the coach's passengers.

The novel's interest in modes of travel is matched by its descriptions of the range of inns and taverns that lodge Joseph, Parson Adams, and Fanny, as Fielding riffs on Don Quixote's travels and travails in *Don Quixote*. Our examination of these interior spaces highlights the inn as a narrative realm that gives travelers opportunities to connect with one another (such connections later enable Joseph and Fanny's marriage). Joseph happens on Adams at the Tow-wouse inn (64 [bk. 1, ch. 14]). Of course, the innkeepers possess their own plotlines, which disrupt the main narrative of Joseph, Parson Adams, and Fanny, thereby delaying their progress. One such disruption is the marital dispute of the Tow-wouses. Inns and taverns foreground the problem of money and competing economic values. At the Tow-wouse inn, Joseph is unable to pay the hostler's bill, although he does possess a gold piece (one that is stolen and returned to him). He views the piece not in monetary terms but in sentimental ones. His "dear Piece" connects him to Fanny, and his refusal to part with it provokes Mrs. Tow-wouse to deny him credit. The narrator quips, "As we cannot therefore at present get Mr. *Joseph* out of the Inn, we shall leave him in it" (95 [bk. 2, ch. 2]). Students often enjoy seeing how the logistics of travel underscore the curious unreliability of our narrator-judge.

If stagecoaches introduce obstacles to travel (too fast here, too crowded there) and the narrative, inns also obstruct the telling of the story. Throughout the novel, narrative progress is blocked by exacting, unsympathetic innkeepers brandishing their bills. These bills bleed onto the very page, as when Fielding inserts a bill for lodging and ale into the prose, beneath which he tallies the meager funds in his characters' pockets (161 [bk. 2, ch. 13]). True, Parson Adams is a hungry traveler, having a ravenous stomach as well as ravenous ears. He arrives at an inn and "as was his Custom, made directly to the Kitchin" (118 [ch. 5]). But the novel revisits the difficulty of settling bills and accounts with such regularity that James Cruise compares the travelers' financial struggles to the exodus from Egypt: Fielding's wanderers eventually triumph over the "bondage brought about by a string of commercial establishments met on the long road to the promised land—home" (259). The presence of bills reminds us of the interconnections among travel, commerce, and the novel.

While bills and receipts function as the commercial tokens of travel and the literary marketplace, the failure to pay raises questions about the role of community and kin on the road. A lack of funds prompts Parson Adams's unsuccessful visit to Parson Trulliber. Adams describes his fellow clergyman as a "Brother in the Parish" (161 [bk. 2, ch. 13]), but this claim of kinship—kinship through shared spiritual identity rather than through blood ties—is rejected by Trulliber with verbal and physical force. The episode encourages students to consider how travel yokes knowledge to kinship: How does *Joseph Andrews* stage the problem of missed connections—and absent families—on the road? Just after meeting Trulliber, the travelers stumble on a false squire who promises them lodging, money, a coach, servant, horses, and a sizable parish living for Adams (172–73 [ch. 16]). Together, these episodes of unmet expectations are in sharp contrast with Mr. Wilson's bucolic homestead, a domestic (noncommercial) setting that raises again the possibility of forging familial ties through travel.

Travel both impedes and sustains family structures, but the novel also conveys that femininity constitutes a special travail for Fanny, whose experiences, both alone and in the company of Parson Adams and Joseph, manifest the gendered risks of travel. We meet her first as a failed traveler, whose naïveté leads her to trust a stranger who claims to be bound for London. Soon he "laid violent hands on her, and was attempting to execute his wicked Will" (139 [bk. 2, ch. 9]), when Adams prevents him. Fanny encounters more threats at the house of the Roasting Squire, whose minions kidnap her, confiding that "the 'Squire will be much kinder to you if he enjoys you willingly than by force" (268 [bk. 3, ch. 12]). Fanny must appeal to more than one traveler for help. Our discussion returns to the role of community when she crosses paths with Peter Pounce, servant to Lady Booby, who recognizes and rescues her (though Pounce proves far from virtuous elsewhere). Although Fanny is delivered from all these dangers, their repetition conveys how strangers view her body as an object—and indeed the narrator renders her body desirable not only to other travelers but also to readers through a vivid blazon (152–53 [bk. 2, ch. 12]). The attacks convey the violent undertone of much of the novel's comedy but also illustrate how gender and class produce special risks for women on the road.

Toward the end, our travelers catch up with Lady Booby's coach and six as the group crosses into the parish. Lady Booby retreats to Booby-Hall, and Parsons Adams "carried his Fellow-Travellers home to his House" (278 [bk. 4, ch. 1]). Despite this emphasis on houses, both the grand and the humble, the plot is resolved by outsiders, those who arrive from elsewhere. Adams believes that his youngest son has drowned but finds instead that a poor peddler has rescued him (309 [ch. 8]). This turn of events reinforces the importance of chance encounters on the road, for this same peddler earlier helped settle our travelers' bill at an alehouse (170 [bk. 2, ch. 15]). Strangers become family when the peddler shares his own tale of travel as a drummer in an Irish foot regiment. He solves the puzzles of Fanny's and Joseph's origins, and his knowledge paves the way to marital resolution. That both Joseph and Fanny were kidnapped by Gypsies as children shows how the source of their mistaken identities is located in travel. Wanderers disrupt family and parish structures, but this disruption is mended by other travelers, who knit together couples and kin. Coincidence on the road turns to consequence, as a flurry of coaches and country walks unite Fielding's itinerant characters in domesticity. This burst of physical and narrative movement in the novel's final pages brings us back to the domestic tourists that took to Britain's roads, stagecoaches, inns, and great houses, yearning to deepen their knowledge and experience of the nation. In *Joseph Andrews*, travel from the city outward to the country brings our characters home, but this domestic return—and indeed the knowledge of personal identity—depends on the activity, entertainment, and commerce of the road that bond travelers and readers through the merits and marketplace of the page.

NOTE

[1] The class's nonfiction readings are all drawn from *Travel Writing, 1700–1830: An Anthology* (ed. Bohls and Duncan).

Fielding, Print Culture, and the *Pamela* Media Event

Lisa Maruca

The eighteenth century provides rich material for studying the history of its media cultures. Books and other print texts circulated as material objects in coteries of readers; provided one source of entertainment among many (competing with Vauxhall Gardens, Drury Lane, or a Handel concerto); and functioned as a marker of class and other forms of status, whether displayed in a personal collection, offered through a circulating library, or available for purchase in a bookshop. Whenever I teach the eighteenth century, be it in a novel course, in a survey (of the century itself or of British literature from 1700 to the present), as background for the study of Jane Austen, or at the graduate level, I always emphasize the themes of textual materiality, authorship, and the print marketplace. Eighteenth-century readers and writers were as obsessed with their means of literary production as we today are with our own technologies of writing, and observing this past fascination helps students grapple with what can otherwise be a difficult and foreign period.

Studying Fielding in this context yields a number of useful insights into his works as well as into his contribution to the debate about which texts were proper for which readers. Most germane here is his participation, through the publication of *Shamela* and *Joseph Andrews*, in what has become known as the "*Pamela* media event" (Warner, *Licensing* xv). Before students can take on these texts, however, they must learn more about the print culture of eighteenth-century England. We study the history through secondary works as well as through such primary texts as treatises and legal documents, read the statements of printers and booksellers of the period, and consider the references to print in the literature of writers both canonical and less studied.[1] We expand the often cited yet frequently criticized notion of the Habermasian public sphere, looking at the rise of coffeehouses as just one instance of the rapid emergence of sites devoted to the mediation and circulation of ideas.[2] Over the course of the term we cover a variety of related issues: the business of print; its transition from a medieval guild to a capital-intensive endeavor; the development of copyright and changing notions of authorship, originality, and collaboration; and other forms of dissemination, such as subscription publication and circulating libraries.

We also analyze the many references to this newly consolidated culture of print in our syllabus of literary works of the period. For example, when we read Jonathan Swift's "Battle of the Books," we discuss both its conceptual background as well as Swift's deployment of the concrete images of the tools of writing, from ink to printed page, in his depiction of learned argument as warfare. Alexander Pope's *The Dunciad* is another source for both material references and attitudes about the trade, as is his shockingly hilarious "A Full and True

Account of a Horrid and Barbarous Revenge by Poison: On the Body of Mr. Edmund Curll, Bookseller; With a Faithful Copy of His Last Will and Testament" (if there is anything that will rid students of their assumption that the eighteenth century is staid and boring, it's this). The material technologies of writing were understood, even by their detractors, as inevitable yet open to manipulation and modification. The stage, too, can be seen as part of a literary-commodity culture that participated in multiple networks in the creation and dissemination of its entertainments. For example, in my classes we study John Gay's *The Beggar's Opera* as a media event in its own right by thinking about its origins in the collaborative coterie of writers who inspired it, about how the play is embedded in satires of popular Italian opera in the periodical press of Joseph Addison and Richard Steele, about the structure and technologies of the stage, about the play's embodiment by actors, and about how the play relies on oral folk music traditions. The print market encourages and shapes the production and circulation of broadsheet scores, the circulation of playbills, the printed play itself, and the many responses to it, outraged or thrilled. Finally, there are the commodity spin-offs such as Polly figurines and playing cards.[3] Fielding saw this rampant commercialization as both a frustrating problem and an opportunity. As early as *The Author's Farce*, he railed against the lack of appreciation for learned writers. That play highlights the problem of a print market that allows new readers, uneducated yet authorized by virtue of their purchasing power, to make judgments.

All this preparation readies us to consider what is for most students a more familiar form: the novel. Because of this genre's immersive qualities, its ability to seduce readers into identification, and its emphasis on interiority—all of which do their work now as they did in Fielding's time—it can be easy to forget that the novel was also a material print product. It is precisely this materiality that made the novel controversial in the eighteenth century. Students light up visibly when I tell them that the disputes over the role, value, and use of novels then parallel today's heated debates over the suitability of video games. In both cases, critics focus on the vulnerability of young people, the discussion is explicitly gendered (young women were of more concern in the eighteenth century, young men in the twentieth and twenty-first), and the link between fictional representation and real life behavior is scrutinized.

The Pamela *Media Event: Richardson*

By the time we reach the *Pamela* media event in the syllabus, the students have developed a background in the print culture of England in this period, are ready to notice representations of the materiality of writing, and can understand literature as a commercial as well as aesthetic phenomenon. Warner defines a media event as beginning with a media production that does not necessarily reflect an earlier, outside event, such as a political scandal or famous battle. The intense interest in the event, demonstrated by further production, "feeds upon itself, producing a sense that this media event has become an ambient, pervasive phenomenon" (*Licensing* 178). The event eventually becomes a locus of criticism and commentary. To fully understand this event, one must study more than a novel or two. We thus read not only Samuel Richardson's *Pamela* and Fielding's *Shamela* but also *Joseph Andrews*, Eliza Haywood's *Anti-Pamela*, short sections from the anonymous *Pamela Censured,* and even Sarah Fielding's *Remarks on* Clarissa, which might be seen as a belated entry into the fray, as can her *Governess*. We look at paintings and book illustrations, and students learn about the famous fan and waxworks (Keymer and Sabor 127, 143–45). For a course focusing on the eighteenth century through the lens of print culture, this section is central; if a course tells a story, the *Pamela* media event is our climax. "A defining moment in the history of print and consumer culture as well as that of genre," as Thomas Keymer and Peter Sabor put so succinctly, "the controversy gives special insight into the agility, responsiveness and entrepreneurial vigor of eighteenth-century Grubstreet . . ." (5).

I'm not sure if it is this approach, their twenty-first-century cynicism, their outrage that a fifteen-year-old would marry her would-be rapist, or all of the above, but most of my students are resolute Shamelists, unconvinced by Pamela's all-too-frequent protests of goodness. As a result, I often find myself defending the novel. We discuss its boldness in constructing a deep interiority for a servant girl who stands up to her upper-class employer, Richardson's "generic breakthrough" (Keymer and Sabor 4) in transforming the amatory fiction of the 1720s into something more centered on the individual experience of romance and relationship building (Haywood's *Love in Excess* makes a terrific contrast), and his explicit purpose of teaching morality through narrative pleasure—a risky venture not fully supported by his peers. In line with our class themes, we also discuss Pamela as an embodied writer, noticing her reliance on, even obsession with, her writing tools, her "forty sheets of paper, and a dozen pens, and a little phial of ink; which last I wrapped in paper, and put in my pocket; and some wax and wafers" (100).

But it is the culture of the spin-off engendered by the novel that most resonates for this generation of students, who have grown up with the international merchandizing of culture—Harry Potter, Disney, Pokémon—through book series, TV shows, fast-food toys, collectible figures and cards, video games, and theme parks. Although we discuss how the prominence of Richardson in print culture allowed him to promote his novel, I stress that his marketing savvy alone cannot account for the novel's popularity. The novel hit a cultural nerve. The phenomenon of *Pamela*'s interaction with its fans, adapters, and critics exceeds any one position in the fraught ideologies of gender and class of the time. *Pamela* became a cultural lightening rod because it encapsulated so many issues of its day. Yet this media event could take place only in a culture that relied on the mediated nature of dispute. As Keymer and Sabor make clear, we must think of "controversy in a way that was second nature to many in the eighteenth-century book trade: not only, and perhaps even not primarily, as a forum of urgent debate, but as a mechanism for generating and selling print, in which contentiousness itself had a commodity value" (11). Looking at the debate in this way helps students reflect on the marketing regimes of twenty-first-century infotainment. Does a Hollywood adaptation of a favorite novel underline or undermine the original's artistic and political stances? Should a work's popularity exclude the work from the canon of worthy cultural expression? Can a blog or online news venue that sells ads be counted on for reliable reporting?

Part of the event was Richardson's textual revisions, the inclusion of new and extensive paratextual material for the second edition, and ultimately his penning of a "continuation" (or what modern readers would call a sequel) of the *Pamela* narrative in what has come to be called *Pamela II.* Richardson made these changes in response not just to the market as an economic force but also to individual readers and their opinions. Reference to these materials, even if we cannot go over them in depth in most classes, highlights to students the differences between Fielding's time and ours in copyright law (Richardson had no control over the use of the name of his character or the idea for the novel), in ideas of authorship (the eighteenth century's idea was more collaborative than ours), and in the concepts of what a work was (in the eighteenth century, a work was more open than it is now to revision and additions in later editions).[4] It also makes clear how concerned he was with reading. He includes in the front matter a letter from his friend and fan Aaron Hill that shows how the novel could be used to fulfill John Locke's imperative to instruct with delight (see *Educational Writings*): the story of an uneducated foster child who, upon hearing *Pamela* read aloud, not only mimics its language and memorizes its passages but is inspired to attend to his lessons so that he can read the novel himself. Hill goes on to discuss the emotional power of the text when the same boy listens in on a group reading the novel aloud: "[W]e heard a Succession of heart-heaving Sobs; . . . his little Sides swell'd as though they wou'd burst. . . .[He] is, perhaps, the youngest of *Pamela's Converts*" (*Pamela* 515). It is notable that Hill uses the language of religion—the boy is converted by *Pamela*—for novels were considered attractive and seductive forms that could lead readers into right thinking. Yet our reading of a few excerpts from the anonymous *Pamela Censured* (1741) sees that seduction as literal and dangerous, though, as students point out, this diatribe against the warm scenes does a perfect job of packaging the naughty bits for consumers not willing to wade through Richardson's protracted prose.[5] We also notice how the concern that young people will imitate Mr. B's bad behavior closely parallels the anxiety today, intermittently resurrected over the last few decades, about a connection between video games and school shootings.

The Shamela *Response*

Fielding, too, worried about the seductive power of fiction. Like so many of my students, he believed that Pamela was manipulating her readers (or, rather, that

Richardson was manipulating his) and resented it. Students seize on *Shamela* and need little of the political background to grasp the satire, though the sexual puns, the "Fanny" and "&c" of the dedication, once explicated, add to the fun (231). To find that Fielding has anticipated their objections to Pamela and used them so thoroughly is a surprise and a delight to my students. Richardson would have been dismayed to learn that many of them find the character of Shamela more frank and honest than that of her predecessor.

Fielding's prefatory letter "The Editor to Himself" damningly spells out Richardson's self-promotion in *Pamela*'s second edition. That *Pamela Censured*, published barely three weeks after *Shamela*, devotes quite a bit of space to this same criticism shows students that Fielding was not alone in finding overt reader manipulation distasteful. Parson Tickletext, in his nearly orgasmic rhapsody, is barely distinguishable from the readers Richardson quotes:

> For my own Part (and, I believe, I may say the same of all the Clergy of my Acquaintance) "I have done nothing but read it to others, and hear others again read it to me, *ever* since it came into my Hands; and I find I am like to do nothing else, for I know not how long yet to come: because if I lay the Book down *it comes after me*. When it has dwelt all Day long upon the Ear, it takes Possession all Night of the Fancy. It hath Witchcraft in every Page of it." ——Oh! I feel an Emotion even while I am relating this: Methinks I see *Pamela* at this Instant, with all the Pride of Ornament cast off. (155)

Tickletext is moved sexually as well as sensibly—Fielding seems to suggest a slippery slope of invoked emotion and titillation. In the satirical layering characteristic of him, though, he also uses the parson's immoderate fervor to castigate Methodist enthusiasm, revealing his mistrust for the inward-looking discovery of God's grace that parallels the novelistic interiority he disdains. In an age when even religion was spread by celebrity authors, it is no accident that Shamela's mother is a fan of Whitefield's sermons. Part of Fielding's concern is that novel reading was replacing the study of the older, more explicitly religious texts that made up the ethical underpinning of his day. Tickletext's continued comment makes this danger clear: "Happy would it be for Mankind, if all Other Books were burnt, that we might do nothing but read thee. . . . Thou alone art sufficient to teach us as much Morality as we want. Dost thou not teach us to pray, to sing Psalms, and to honour the Clergy? Are these not the whole Duty of Man?" (155).

Joseph Andrews

To emphasize to students the inexorable appetite of Grub Street, it is worth pointing out that *Shamela* became part of its own minimedia event, spinning off *Joseph Andrews* and *Anti-Pamela*.[6] When students read *Joseph Andrews*, it doesn't take them long to see that what might have started as a satire soon proceeds under its own steam. In fact, during much of the novel it is easy to forget that Pamela exists at all, until she puts in an appearance at the end. In that appearance, she is vain, haughty, and supercilious, concerned that her brother's marriage to Fanny will lower the newly risen Andrews family, but this passage seems more a criticism of arriviste pretensions than a specific send-up of Richardson's character. If anything, we might borrow a term for what Fielding is doing here from a twenty-first-century form familiar to students, many of whom have dabbled in it themselves: fan fiction. Though *fan* implies a certain respect, if not adulation, the word does not apply to Fielding's work in that sense; fan fiction is any work taking place in the fictional universe created by another writer. As Henry Jenkins, a media theorist, explains, "Fan fiction can be seen as an unauthorized expansion . . . which reflects the reader's desire to 'fill in the gaps' they have discovered in the commercially produced material."[7] It's useful to have students think about what those gaps might be and how Fielding is trying to fill them.

In *Joseph Andrews*, as in *Shamela*, Fielding takes a skeptical attitude to the construction of an interiority based on and fed by the reading of texts. Even epistolarity is short-circuited by the simple fact that Fanny, like many in her social strata, cannot read (49 [bk. 1, ch. 11]). Pamela might be accused of the twenty-first-century sin of oversharing, but Fanny's delicacy at discussing her feelings with an amanuensis forestalls the voyeuristic impulse of readers to peer deep into her psyche. Fielding questions not just the reading of private letters but other sorts of reading as well. When Joseph is sick in the Tow-wouses' inn, a debate is staged between a well-read gentleman and a well-practiced surgeon, both of whom claim the most knowledge; the plot distracts us, though, and the tension between education and experience is never resolved (59–60 [ch. 14]). The same surgeon a few pages later, armed with a law textbook, argues criminal justice with the town parson, armed with a different one (62–63 [ch. 13]). Swift's battle between ancient and modern has expanded to a competition between modern book-based claims for truth: Fielding reveals that increased literacy and market expansion have spawned an epistemological crisis. Similarly, Adams and the host discuss whether reading counts as travel (180–84 [bk. 2, ch. 17]). Later, Wilson's story parallels Fielding's own life in its attempt and failure to write for the press and stage in London, yet Wilson retires, a choice not made by Fielding (213–25 [bk. 3, ch. 3]). Once we notice the frequent references to reading and the book trade, we realize that Fielding has expanded the repertoire of problems he pinpointed in *The Author's Farce* and is now discussing them with more complexity. Because Fielding eschews the pat solution, reading and the workings of the press remain a problematic to be explored.

To illustrate that reading and books were an ongoing social concern not limited to Fielding, I have my students read Samuel Johnson, who, almost a decade after the publication of *Pamela*, expostulates in the *Rambler* about the promises and perils of the novel. He explains:

> [W]hen an adventurer is levelled with the rest of the world, and acts in such scenes of the universal drama, as may be the lot of any other man; young spectators fix their eyes upon him with closer attention, and hope, by observing his behaviour and success, to regulate their own practices, when they shall be engaged in the like part.
>
> For this reason these familiar histories may perhaps be made of greater use than the solemnities of professed morality, and convey the knowledge of vice and virtue with more efficacy than axioms and definitions. But if the power of example is so great as to *take possession of the memory by a kind of violence, and produce effects almost without the intervention of the will*, care ought to be taken, that, when the choice is unrestrained, the best examples only should be exhibited; and that which is likely to operate so strongly, should not be mischievous or uncertain in its effects.
>
> (my emphasis)

That a a bound collection of folded sheets impressed with ink could violently take over one's will is frightening indeed. It is little wonder that the activity of reading was open to scrutiny, surveillance, and regulation at every level. In some classes, following *Joseph Andrews* with Sarah Fielding's *The Governess* and Charlotte Lennox's *The Female Quixote* illustrates the variety of ways contemporary writers envisioned and tried to resolve this problem.

Tools and Assignments

In courses that stress the new media of the eighteenth century, it only makes sense to have students experiment with the tools and technologies that have emerged in their own lifetime. I require students to create blogs and post weekly about the reading. We discuss the dangers inherent in writing in such a public forum, and a few choose to adopt pen names—as did many eighteenth-century writers. Students are also encouraged (though usually not required) to collaborate to create Web sites instead of writing single-authored papers.[8] While some still choose the safe route—after all, many in the millennial generation do not feel like digital natives and prefer the familiarity of the traditional essay—the resulting Web projects have been delightful. Students in a Jane Austen course created a Web site devoted to exploring filmic adaptations and spin-offs. Two students teamed to pen a fictional travel blog authored by Lady Mary Wortley Montagu (who of course used *Twitter* to promote her posts). One Web site was devoted to showing the links among a network of children's publishers and writers in the period, another exhibited the clothing of the period and explained its importance in novels, and a third annotated a book of the *Dunciad*.

None of these projects required intensive technological training. They do not employ the latest in data visualization or create a new database that will reinvigorate the discipline, yet for most students, who are new to online authoring and not quite ready for an NEH grant, these baby steps into academic technology are an achievement. Creating content-oriented Web sites provides a useful bridge into the digital humanities because students can utilize lots of text—English majors feel comfortable with text—and even a simple Web site demands many skills beyond textual analysis. Students must articulate and convey a real-life purpose; must decide why a site needs to exist in the world; must reflect on an actual, not an imagined, audience beyond just a single professor; must organize information, think about functionality, and make decisions about visual design, such as choices regarding color, typography, and images. Using images requires that they learn about copyright, Creative Commons, and the ethics of Internet borrowing and citation practices. As they develop these projects, I point out how many of the tasks they face were present also in the authoring, designing, and marketing of eighteenth-century print.

In undergraduate courses, the creation and sharing of the Web projects lead to discussions about the importance of media writing skills for future careers. In graduate courses, the digital humanities is part of a broader range of professionalization discussions. I also bring to the attention of students the problems and potential of various research tools now at their disposal. The *Reading Experience Database* is an exciting resource collecting real readers' responses to texts, but for the eighteenth century the material is still sparse. *Eighteenth Century Collections Online* (*ECCO*) has been the most significant resource in the last decade, but I like to point out its challenges along with the possibilities it provides. When discussing the ways title page layout, typography, chapter headings, and *mise-en-page* affect interpretation, we must look at the texts as eighteenth-century readers saw them. The richness of *ECCO* helps us in this study, but there are issues that limit *ECCO*'s usefulness—its price, for example. My own library could not purchase the database for many years. *ECCO* does not contain every eighteenth-century text that has survived, because it is a curated collection. Searching it also can be difficult for students (and for many scholars!) who don't know a few tricks about negotiating the period's typographical idiosyncrasies.[9]

The most important point I make about *ECCO* is that what we see in this database are not originals but a representation of photographic images taken for another, distant purpose, *ESTC* (*English Short Title Catalogue*) microfilming, now recontextualized among thousands of artifacts and then scanned and sent as bytes and displayed on a screen. The original readers, of course, did not encounter these texts electronically. Thus one of the chief tasks in my classes is to imaginatively recreate the setting of bookshops and circulating libraries, the many sites and practices of reading—in addition to the many ideas about that mysterious and sometimes frightening process that circulated in and became the *Pamela* media event.

NOTES

[1] Besides the works by Gay, Swift, and Pope discussed below, primary sources include Addison and Steele (in Erin Mackie's usefully thematized edition); published, unpublished, and pedagogical letters by Montagu, Richardson, and Chesterfield; Johnson's "Plan of an English Dictionary," "Preface to the Dictionary," and famous letter to Chesterfield; selections from booksellers such as Francis Kirkman and John Dunton; excerpts from Locke on property; the 1710 Statute of Anne (other copyright texts are optional and can be found in the online archive *Primary Sources on Copyright, 1450–1900* [http://copyrighthistory.org], funded by the UK Arts and Humanities Research Council); and Edward Young's "Conjecture on Original Composition." Works from the period focused on novel reading can be found in Cheryl Nixon's *Novel Definitions: An Anthology of Commentary on the Novel, 1688–1815*, esp. part 3: "Cultural Commentary."

[2] Siskin and Warner list the plethora of new, interconnected mediations in this period: infrastructures, genres and formats, associational practices, and protocols ("This Is Enlightenment" 12–14). For their critique of Habermas's vagueness of "public," see 22–23. Paula McDowell's insistence of the role of women in political print is also useful in this context (*Women*).

[3] The Beggar's Opera*: Original Songs and Airs*, by the Broadside Band, contains both the original version (sometimes versions) of the folk songs followed by *The Beggar's Opera* and linear notes with lyrics, which I copy and pass around. Students can view playing cards at Simon Wintle's The Beggar's Opera *Playing Cards, 1728*. Other *Beggar's Opera* paraphernalia can be seen in the film *Sense and Sensation: English Culture in the Eighteenth Century*, written and narrated by John Brewer and based on his book *The Pleasures of the Imagination*. The film is an invaluable resource for introducing students to debates about the arts of the period. An underused (as far as I can tell) resource for viewing *The Beggar's Opera* as part of print culture is Guerinot and Jilg.

[4] I discuss these ideas in more depth, analyzing Richardson's notion of paternal authorship and gendered copyright, in my *Work of Print*.

[5] Keymer and Sabor, against the long tradition in Richardson studies of seeing *Pamela Censured* as the work of a fusty, overwrought prude, believe that it is likely a satire—or, more intriguingly, actually penned by Richardson or a friend as a gambit to attract "a new market of libertine readers" (35; for the entire discussion of this option and others, see 32–37). Whether or not *Pamela Censured* was intended as a satire, such a strategy perfectly fits the logic of print culture that Richardson relied on.

[6] For this reason I prefer the Broadview edition of *Anti-Pamela* that includes *Shamela* (Fielding, *Shamela* [ed. Ingrassia]).

[7] Jenkins's comments are part of a discussion of the broader phenomena of transmedia storytelling: "The encyclopedic ambitions of transmedia texts often result in what might be seen as gaps or excesses in the unfolding of the story: that is, they introduce potential plots which cannot be fully told or extra details which hint at more than can be revealed. Readers, thus, have a strong incentive to continue to elaborate on these story elements, working them over through their speculations, until they take on a life of their own."

[8] Examples of my assignments and some sample student projects can be found at my class blogs, Novel(ties) (http://18cnovelties.wordpress.com/) and Mechanick Exercises (http://lmaruca.wordpress.com/syllabus/).

[9] For more details on the problems of *ECCO*, as well as some tips and tricks, see Battigelli; Spedding. For teaching with *ECCO*, see Greenfield; Mace, "Using"; and Shevlin, "Exploring." Another useful but still developing field-specific site is *18thConnect*, which allows users to search both the *ESTC* and peer-reviewed Web resources, as well as save searches and create exhibits. Ambitious students can work at the intersection of the print and digital realms by editing the dirty OCR behind the page images using the *TypeWright* tools, then receiving in return the text for online publication or analysis.

TOM JONES

Tom Jones as the Cornerstone in the Course The English Novel through Austen

Pamela S. Bromberg

The usual structure for an undergraduate English majors' course on the eighteenth-century novel is chronological, tracing a story of generic development and innovations in style and narrative technique. My class The English Novel through Austen disrupts that teleological narrative for both practical and substantive reasons. In a course that combines formalist focus on the novel as a genre with attention to historical constructions of authorship, gender, class, and the family and that will later include early fiction by Aphra Behn, Jane Barker, and Eliza Haywood, *Tom Jones* serves as both starting point and cornerstone. I position *Tom Jones* at the beginning of the semester, as foundation rather than destination, for two reasons: Fielding's eighteen introductory chapters on the art of the novel articulate ideas about the emerging genre that we use throughout the semester; the novel's panoramic view of mid-eighteenth-century England provides a rich historical context for the course. I assign *Tom Jones* as the first novel also because it works wonderfully to build students' reading muscles for the semester. At the beginning of the term, the demand in students' other courses is often not as high as it will be, so I sneak in this very long book then. I deal with its stylistic challenges by acknowledging them in class, by reading passages aloud, and by doing careful textual analysis. I assure students that after they've read *Tom Jones*, the other novels will seem easy. I discuss the educated (primarily male) audience that Fielding addresses, stressing the background in the classics that twenty-first-century readers generally lack, and encouraging students to rely on the annotations in the Norton Critical Edition to supply missing information.

I teach *Tom Jones*, the central text in the course, as a kind of high-water mark in terms of style, plot, and design; the development of the omniscient authorial voice; the representation of a panoramic and detailed view of English society that includes a wide diversity of regional and class voices; and the self-conscious articulation of a theoretical view of the novel's potential as a literary form. We read *Tom Jones* as a novel that carefully makes the case for its own excellence, and we pay close attention to Fielding's arguments, in the introductory chapters on the novel, that he is the "Founder of a new Province of Writing" (77 [bk. 2, ch. 1]). At the same time, I point out limitations in the work's narrative technique—that is, in its representation of thought and feeling. In addition, I contextualize Fielding's portrait of mid-century English society in comparison with competing narratives about gender, politics, and socioeconomic change.

After we read *Tom Jones,* we move backward to read Behn's *Oroonoko* (1688) and early-eighteenth-century selections by Behn, Haywood, and Barker from Paula R. Backscheider and John J. Richetti's *Popular Fiction by Women: 1660–1730*. These earlier works of fiction share a frank eroticism and celebration of female emotional intensity that students find surprising. The existence of these works, along with their variety and evident narrative interest, challenges Fielding's self-proclamation as the sire of a new literary genre and prepares students for William Warner's essay "The Elevation of the Novel in England" later in the semester. Warner argues that both Fielding and Samuel Richardson polemicize to give their novels a "higher cultural calling" in relation to the popular fiction written by an earlier generation of women authors such as Behn, Delarivier Manley, and Haywood and that their "elevation of the novel in the 1740s operates like a vortex within every subsequent effort to read the early novel in England" (582, 589). I wait until midpoint in the semester, after students have had a chance to read both the early-eighteenth-century fiction by women and Sarah Scott's mid-century bluestocking novel *Millenium Hall* to assign Warner's essay. But from the beginning of the semester we focus on gender: men and women writers, representations of women and of marriage, norms of masculinity and femininity, and male and female readers.

Our reading of *Tom Jones* introduces central historical subject matter for the semester, including the debate on dynastic versus companionate marriage, the relation between social class and female sexuality, rising tensions about land ownership and wealth, and changing concepts of masculinity. These themes continue to resonate as we read later eighteenth-century fiction, such as Scott's feminist country house utopia, Horace Walpole's groundbreaking gothic romance *The Castle of Otranto*, and Frances Burney's brilliant satiric epistolary debut *Evelina*. The course culminates with two novels by Jane Austen, *Northanger Abbey* and *Mansfield Park*, that synthesize much of the thematic content and narrative technique from the earlier fiction. Throughout the semester we refer back to Fielding's text both for its technical achievements and for its presentation of rules for the emerging genre of the novel.

In the first class meeting, before the students have begun to read the text, I explain how Fielding's book is structured and alert them to the importance of its introductory chapters. I project the title page of the first edition, inviting the class to reflect on what the plot might be of a novel that presents itself as a "History" and defines its protagonist as a "foundling." We discuss the meaning of *foundling*, consider what pressures might lead women to abandon newborn infants, and note the central mystery of identity and social class posed at the novel's outset. I draw attention to the motto that Fielding has taken from Horace, which introduces the mock-heroic style and subject and point out that this Latin text assumes a reader who is masculine and educated in the classics. I then read aloud the first couple of paragraphs, pausing to define a few unfamiliar words and to give students a chance to ask questions and comment on the author's voice and style. Before students begin their reading of the novel, it is helpful for them to hear Fielding's cadences and note the dramatic persona of the "Author as Innkeeper" engaging in a witty commercial transaction with the reader who expects to be entertained. We discuss the extended metaphors of taste, cookery, and dining, as well as Fielding's promise to provide the full range of "human nature," from country to city and court, from "the vilest Stall in Town" to "the Table of a Duke" (32–33).

I allot two and a half weeks to *Tom Jones*, a brisk pace that puts pressure on students to do the reading. I supply them with an annotated outline of the novel and direct their attention to Frederick Hilles's graphic representation of the "pattern" of *Tom Jones* as a neoclassical edifice: the novel's symmetrical, three-part division into sections that take place in Somerset, on the open road, and in London ("Art" [ed. Baker] 789). I find that weekly quizzes motivate students to keep up with their reading and reward them for their knowledge of plot and character.

As students work through the novel, we talk about Fielding's authorial persona, a man of the world with extensive knowledge of human nature high and low, of rural and urban life, and of English and classical literature. We consider the relation between authorship and gender, comparing the authoritative masculine voice of Fielding's narrator with the less confident self-presentation of women writers, such as Behn, who apologizes for the limitations of her "female pen" in *Oroonoko* (69), or Burney, who begs forgiveness for her "weak pow'rs" as she apologetically inserts herself into a masculine pantheon of eighteenth-century fiction writers in the poem of dedication to her father and the preface to *Evelina* (3). Fielding's essays on the art of fiction become key documents in our discussion throughout the semester as we compare his assertion of the importance and excellence of his literary production with the variety of narrative techniques employed by his predecessors and successors. We look at his introductory chapters on the treatment of time (bk. 2), style (bk. 4), credibility and realistic fiction (bk. 8), and the development of morally nuanced characters (bk. 10). I find the introductory chapter to book 5, "Of the SERIOUS in Writing, and for what Purpose it is introduced," to be particularly useful in its articulation of the "Art of Contrast" as a formal principle ordering this novel (209 [bk. 5, ch. 1]). We identify pairs of characters who are foils to each other and think about how they define each other, and I list the opposed traits on the board. Later in the semester, we continue to explore the importance of foils as a technique of characterization in fiction by Burney and Austen.

In the first chapter of book 9, a central essay on the emerging genre of the novel, Fielding makes his strongest case for the superiority of his work and criticizes the mass of "foolish Novels, and monstrous Romances" (487), arguing that his "historic Kind of writing" is set apart, or "elevated," to use Warner's term, by the very inclusion of these introductory chapters and by his qualifications as author, which he enumerates: "Invention and Judgment"; "a good Share of Learning," including a "competent Knowledge of History and of the *Belles Lettres*"; universal "Conversation . . . with all Ranks and Degrees of Men," from the high to the low; and finally "a good Heart" (491–94). When we read the earlier fiction written by women, we ask whether women writers could possibly meet those qualifications, given that gender norms excluded them from formal education and discouraged them from gaining wide experience. We discuss the different kinds of knowledge and experience that inform the works of writers such as Behn and Haywood, comparing their representations of female characters with those of Fielding. For instance, Galesia, the young heroine of Barker's *Love Intrigues* (1713), and the group of female protagonists in Scott's *Millenium Hall* (1762) present compelling alternatives to Fielding's broadly satiric and unflattering portrait of Mrs. Western as a prototypical educated woman. Galesia controls the turmoil of her romantic passion with the disciplines of academic study and writing and with the successful management of her father's "Servants and Labourers" (102), work that distracts her from amorous confusion and promotes healthy self-esteem. Likewise, Scott's novel expands on Barker's defense of the value of education for women (109) with many portraits of educated, competent women who work together as exemplary landowners and estate managers.

In recent years I introduced students to Mikhail Bakhtin's concepts of heteroglossia and double-voiced discourse as useful tools for understanding the intersection of narrative technique with Fielding's representation of mid-eighteenth-century English gender codes, social class, and political factions. I give a couple of examples of heteroglossia from book 6 and do a careful reading of a double-voiced passage from its chapter 9 ("I wull have Satisfaction o' thee . . ." [302]). Fielding transitions rapidly from the speech of Squire Western to direct authorial narration; he employs his own high style, with Latinate diction and complex syntax, to describe the squire's very low speech that he is too polite to include in his novel in its entirety. Fielding manages in this passage to capture the comic energy of Western's transgressive "kiss your A—" while maintaining decorum (303). On the preceding page Fielding uses the same double-voiced technique to poke fun at his hero and heroine (and at pastoral conventions) with exaggerated epic similes.

Book 6 also furnishes rich material for discussion of the novel's dramatization of contested concepts of marriage, a debate that is central both to *Tom Jones* and to the course as a whole. The discourse of the Westerns reflects their understanding of marriage as dynastic and economic alliance. Mr. Allworthy serves as a contrasting father figure to Squire Western; the latter is concerned more with his patriarchal power and the inheritance of the estate, the former with the more modern view of marriage as an institution supporting the happiness of children as individuals instead of furthering the interests of their parents. *Tom Jones* dramatizes this debate with authorial commentary on the true nature of love in the introductory chapter to book 6 and with numerous, sometimes digressive, subplots and minor and major characters who enact the full array of courtship and marriage models, from the low comedy of Partridge and his wife to the melodramatic story of Harriet Fitzpatrick's escape from imprisonment in her husband's Irish country house.

Early in the novel, Bridget Allworthy and Captain Blifil marry, respectively, for the "solid Satisfaction" of sexual pleasure and the "solid Enjoyments" of Mr. Allworthy's estate (66–67 [bk. 1, ch. 11]); Fielding's judgment on their motives is rendered through the evil nature of their offspring. We learn in book 7, chapter 4, that Squire Western's own "heartily hated" wife "had been married against her Will, by a fond Father, the Match having been rather advantageous on her Side" (339). Fielding presents Squire Western and his father-in-law as foils to Mr. Allworthy, in an exploration of emerging models of fatherhood, a subject that Fielding develops in subsequent episodes, with additional examples of tyrannical fathers who seek to arrange their children's marriages for financial motives.

Discussion of the marriage debate introduces students to another central focus of the course: the intersection of sexuality, gender, and social class. We debate whether Fielding entirely succeeds in presenting Tom as a reformed rake, and we note the dangers to well-born young women, as well as lower-class women, of seduction and abandonment. Students are surprised at the sexual freedom of Molly Seagrim and Lady Bellaston, women at opposite poles of the social hierarchy. As the semester progresses, we contrast the male writer's view of women's sexuality in *Tom Jones* with those of the women writers of early-eighteenth-century amatory fiction and with the more conservative views of the later authors, and these comparisons illuminate the socially constructed, class-contingent, and changing norms of female identity. Haywood's *Fantomina* subversively has a young well-born woman, the counterpart of Sophia, express sexual desire through a series of disguises that allow her to occupy different positions in the social hierarchy, each with its distinctive norm of female sexual behavior. Burney's *Evelina*, with its diverse cast of characters and satiric view of a cross section of British society, affords a rich comparison with *Tom Jones* and the earlier amatory fiction. For instance, Fielding's narrative of Sophia's courageous and rebellious escape from patriarchal tyranny and the dangers of dynastic alliance imagines an almost masculine agency for the heroine, unlike

Burney's view of the dangers that beset Evelina, who is vulnerable because of her desirability and her ambiguous status as a female bastard, the counterpart of Tom Jones. Juxtaposing the novels raises many subjects for discussion, including how gender across social classes is represented in different ways.

After we have finished reading and discussing Fielding's novel, I arrange for a class screening of the 1963 Tony Richardson movie version, and we discuss it as an adaptation of the book. By this time students have become partisans of *Tom Jones* and find the film to be an inadequate reduction of the novel. They particularly miss the voice of the author. I ask them to focus on how the movie employs music, visual elements, and pacing to convey Fielding's voice and style and to think about the movie's own historical and cultural contexts as they consider what material from the novel is included and emphasized. In recent years I have highlighted the historical contexts of *Tom Jones* by projecting visual material during class, including portraits of writers and historical figures, images of settings and places, background material on eighteenth-century neoclassical and gothic architecture, and eighteenth-century satirical art by William Hogarth and others. I show the class the Hogarth engravings specifically mentioned by Fielding in books 1 through 3 of *Tom Jones* as well as *The Four Times of Day* and *Southwark Fair*. Together, the text of *Tom Jones*, the visual contexts, and the twentieth-century cinematic adaptation offer a rich set of representations for our semester-long journey into the world of eighteenth-century England.

Narrative Voice in *Tom Jones*

Anthony J. Hassall

Tom Jones and *Paradise Lost* are my desert island books and the ones I most enjoy teaching, but both present so many difficulties to twenty-first-century students that making them accessible is a real but rewarding challenge. In C. S. Lewis's phrase, therefore, I set out to "hinder hindrances" (129), to enable and encourage students to read these two enduring masterworks as they deserve to be read and appreciated.

Among the difficulties both works present for students is their unfamiliar form. John Milton, expecting contemporary readers of *Paradise Lost* to know the epics of Homer and Vergil, did not have to explain its form, though nowadays we as teachers face that task. The situation for Fielding was more complex: he could also expect his more serious readers to know the classical epics, but he was attempting something different, a comic epic in prose. The only classical model he could refer to was the lost comic epic *Margites*, so, unlike Milton, he needed to familiarize his readers with the new/lost genre he was inventing.

Students approach *Tom Jones* expecting a novel, which is not exactly what they find. Important elements of its form are unfamiliar, one of the most unfamiliar being its prominent narrative voice, and so I begin by talking about that. Students are surprised to find extended discussions of the art of fiction embedded in the narrative. Accustomed to mainstream novels, and to film and television dramas, they expect their authors to be covert, not overt; to show, not tell; to keep comments on their art for promotional tours and writers' festivals. Knowingly or not, students have absorbed the modern critical dogma that a story should be left to speak for itself: "Never trust the artist. Trust the tale," as D. H. Lawrence famously observed (14). The teller of *Tom Jones* does not observe this rule: he is ever present, talking incessantly to his readers and guiding their responses.

Irritated by this constant intrusion of the author, students often skip the introductory chapters, and as much of the commentary as they can, to concentrate on the love story of Tom and Sophia. No less a figure than W. Somerset Maugham endorsed this practice by publishing in 1948 an abridged version of *Tom Jones* that edited out most of the narrative voice. I counsel students to avoid this approach, which is the least rewarding way to read the book. The narrative commentary is not a questionable extra; on the contrary, its interaction with the narrative is fundamental to what *Tom Jones* offers its reader. The story of Tom and Sophia, I suggest, is unremarkable when stripped of its commentary.

For students to understand why Fielding employed so prominent and self-conscious a narrative voice, *Tom Jones* needs to be viewed in its historical context, which I outline in lectures. Storytelling may be as old as mankind, but the novel is not. It did not exist for Fielding in the 1740s. He is, he said, "the Founder of a new Province of Writing" (77 [bk. 2, ch. 1]), one he famously describes in *Joseph Andrews* as the "comic Epic-Poem in Prose" (4 [bk. 1, ch. 1]). Because this is a new province of writing, a new fictional genre, he needs to explain it to his readers.

Fielding uses the term "History" to describe the genre, but it is not history as we know it either, because it is fictional, not factual, though it half pretends to be factual. So what is it? That question is progressively answered in the eighteen introductory chapters explaining the thoughts about fiction on which *Tom Jones* is based and in the frequent comments in the narrative chapters telling readers what the author is doing and how he expects them to respond. I urge my students to pay attention to the narrative voice's commentary while they enjoy the more familiar novelistic pleasures of the story of Tom and Sophia.

Students who do this learn that Fielding situates his new genre in the long tradition of fictional writing that includes the epic, dating back to Homer in the eighth century B.C., and the romance, dating back at least to the *Aethiopica* of Heliodorus in the third century A.D. As his copious quotations and parodies attest, Fielding was well read in this tradition and acknowledges his debts to it. Later readers need to remember, however, that while he knew what preceded his new venture, he did not, could not, know how the genre would develop after him. Unlike him, they do, and so they come to *Tom Jones* expecting a more modern kind of novel. Students have to put this expectation on hold and try to think of themselves instead as mid-eighteenth-century readers.

This adjustment can be easier for students if they are reading *Tom Jones* alongside *Robinson Crusoe*, *Gulliver's Travels*, and *Pamela* or *Clarissa*, protonovels that contribute to the context in which Fielding was writing. Like him, the writers of these fictions were not constrained by our modern critical orthodoxies. They were familiar with prenovel, prerealist fiction, which was often more self-conscious than the later mainstream novel, but even these contemporary fictions do not prepare readers for the narrative voice they encounter in *Tom Jones*.

The narrator in *Robinson Crusoe* is covert, hiding behind the ostensible first-person telling of his character Crusoe, and it is often difficult to determine the narrator's own views, particularly in potentially ironic situations. In *Gulliver's Travels*, the narrator seems covert but is in fact overt: we can hear his voice overriding the voice of Gulliver and often ironically reversing what Gulliver says. In *Pamela* and *Clarissa*, the narrator is covert, masked by the letters his characters write. The narrator of *Tom Jones* is not only overt but also self-consciously telling a story that he has clearly invented, though at times he pretends, as *Robinson Crusoe* and *Gulliver's Travels* do, that it is a history.

Because Fielding knew that his readers would find *Tom Jones* unlike anything they had encountered before, he includes in it advice on how to read it. His introductory chapter to book 2, for example, is entitled, "*Shewing what Kind of a History this is; what it is like, and what it is not like*" (75). One couldn't have a blunter statement that the author will tell readers, as they go along, what to expect and what not to expect. Reading the book thus becomes a continuing process of learning how to read it.

Readers who ignore this user-friendly instruction manual make *Tom Jones* unnecessarily difficult for themselves. They should, instead, take the advice of Fielding's contemporary, Alexander Pope:

> A perfect judge will read each work of wit
> With the same spirit that its author writ. ("Essay" 151)

I acknowledge that this is not a popular approach with current critics, who resist novels and their authors, read against the grain, and argue that it is impossible to recover the original author's spirit. But it is sound eighteenth-century advice, and if students want to read *Tom Jones* in the spirit in which Fielding wrote it, they will not skip the commentary. It is their one sure guide to reading a book that is as out of the common run for a twenty-first-century reader as it was for Fielding's contemporaries, though for different reasons. *Tom Jones* stands at a unique point in the history of fiction, a point at which the epic and the romance feed into the novel, and it has affinities with, and differences from, all three genres. It is therefore very much sui generis, as so many great works are. It stands alone, like Joyce's *Ulysses*, Sterne's *Tristram Shandy*, or Swift's *Gulliver's Travels*, and like those highly idiosyncratic works, it takes some getting used to, and some getting into, before it can be enjoyed and appreciated.

At this point I cite the twentieth-century novelist E. M. Forster, who reads Jane Austen with "the mouth open and the mind closed . . . while criticism slumbers" (140–41). Some novels may be best read this way, but *Tom Jones* is emphatically not one of them: we need to read it with our minds open. When Fielding was writing, the fictional options were many and the intertextual influence of other novels was minimal or nonexistent. To see what he made of that heady situation, readers need to be attentive.

The narrator of *Tom Jones* talks to his readers about the genre he is creating, his qualifications for the task, and the qualities he looks for in his readers. Trying to read this novel like Forster would involve surrendering to the narrative illusion while ignoring the narrative voice. Fielding's critical account of human nature, the stated subject of *Tom Jones*, requires repeated reflection on the accuracy and perception with which the characters and their actions mirror extrafictional human nature.

Fielding prefers this second kind of reading and invites the first so it can lead to the second. He wants readers who are critical, who reflect on what they read, who do not allow the narrative illusion to submerge their critical intelligence or awareness that they are reading a work of art, not a slice of life. The narrative voice continually reminds them to remain critically alert, to judge and evaluate, even as they are amused and sympathetically involved.

Fielding tries to do something more complex than maintain a steady level of illusion and defer reflection to times outside the reading experience, as later novelists did. In his narrative he seeks a degree of engagement; in his commentary he invites reflection on that narrative. If he had simply wanted to explain his theory of fiction, he could have done so in the usual manner with a single preface, leaving the narrative illusion intact; but by interrupting the illusion, he moves readers from illusion to reflection and back again throughout the book. As C. J. Rawson points out, "The authorial command of *Tom Jones* . . . has to be earned . . . by a continuous and vital plasticity of relationship between moral urgency and urbane detachment" (*Henry Fielding and the Augustan Ideal* 245). Whether or not readers think this shuttling is successful, they need to see how it operates and what Fielding is trying to accomplish with it.

This unfamiliar method makes responding to the narrator a fundamental part of reading *Tom Jones*. When the book is finished, we remember its narrator more than its characters. Henry James perceptively, if somewhat patronizingly, notes this unusual balance:

> It is very true that Fielding's hero in *Tom Jones* . . . has so much "life" that it amounts, for the effect of comedy and application of satire, almost to his having a mind, that is to his having reactions and a full consciousness; besides which his author—*he* handsomely possessed of a mind—has such an amplitude of reflexion for him and round him that we see him through the mellow air of Fielding's fine old moralism, fine old humour and fine old style, which somehow really enlarge, make every one and every thing important. (68)

I ask my students to reflect on this statement. Are Fielding's characters simpler than their creator? Do we remember the narrator as much as, or more than, the characters? To what extent are the author's humor, moralism, and style essential to this kind of narrative? What does James suggest by repeating the adjective "old"? Finally, do readers need to suspend disbelief in the concept of a common human nature? How comfortably can they accompany an eighteenth-century Christian humanist as he expounds his "old" reading of that nature?

Having used lectures to mount this explanation and defense of the self-conscious narrative voice, and the complex mode of reading it requires, I turn to more interactive discussion of that reading, drawing examples from the early, first-read chapters of the book. We explore some introductory chapters, then some intranarrative commentary.

In his first introductory chapter, the narrator announces that his subject "is no other than Human Nature" (32) and that his skill will be in "well dressing it up" (33). It is clear that his take on human nature will be comic, not tragic. To start a discussion of the nature of that comedy, I cite the truism of Horace Walpole, another eighteenth-century novelist: "*[T]his world is a comedy to those that think, a tragedy to those that feel*" (7: 166). I also cite Maynard Mack's more recent explanation of Fielding's comedy:

> The point of view that ours must be continuous with in comedy is not the character's but the author's . . . the comic artist subordinates the presentation of life as experience, where the relationship between ourselves and the characters experiencing it is the primary one, to the presentation of life as spectacle, where the primary relationship is between himself and us as onlookers. (58)

As Walpole observes, tragedy is predicated on engagement, whereas comedy requires detachment. As a result, as Mack points out, the primary relationship in the comedy of *Tom Jones* is between the author-narrator and the readers, not between the characters and the readers. We do empathize with the characters, but they come to us accompanied by the author's narrating voice, which invites us to judge their actions as we watch them and to reflect on the traits of human nature they exemplify.

I compare Fielding with the twentieth-century German dramatist Bertolt Brecht, who alienates his audience from immersion in the illusion of his plays. Brecht believed that his audience needed to be periodically alienated, or distanced, or disengaged from the action, if its members were to view the action thoughtfully and to apply it to life outside the theater. Fielding did the same thing in many of his plays. How similar is this strategy to that of *Tom Jones*? What other examples of this practice in recent, postmodern fiction come to mind?

Throughout *Tom Jones*, the narrator is conscious of the need to justify his presence and to assert the credentials of "*those who lawfully may, and of those who may not write such Histories as this*" (487 [bk. 9, ch. 1]). The "very rare Talents" needed "[t]o invent good Stories, and to tell them well" (488) are, he says, possessed only by those endowed with "Genius" (490), "a good Share of Learning" (491), and "Conversation . . . with all Ranks and Degrees of Men" (494). He sets the bar high, aspiring to equal the epics of Homer and Milton, "Historians of our Order" and "Masters of all the Learning of their Times" (492). Later under the "Genius" of comedy he cites Aristophanes, Lucian, Cervantes, Rabelais, Molière, Shakespeare, Swift, and Marivaux as distinguished predecessors he hopes to emulate (686 [bk. 13, ch. 1]).

Few writers can hope to attain such heights, and not all readers, he suggests, are able to respond to such narratives appropriately: "Reader, it is impossible we should know what Sort of Person thou wilt be: For, perhaps, thou may'st be as learned in Human Nature as *Shakespear* himself was, and, perhaps, thou may'st be no wiser than some of his Editors" (523 [bk. 10, ch. 1]). I use these quotations to prompt a discussion of the validity of Fielding's definitions of who is qualified to write and who to read such fiction.

We compare and contrast two more introductory chapters. I find that students have difficulty unpacking the ironies of the narrator in the first chapter of book 5, "*Of* The SERIOUS *in writing; and for what purpose it is introduced*" (209). Its subject may be serious, but the narrator's tone is playful, ironic, and at times self-contradictory, as this concluding passage illustrates:

> In this Light then, or rather in this Darkness, I would have the Reader to consider these initial Essays. And after this Warning, if he shall be of Opinion, that he can find enough of Serious in other Parts of this History, he may pass over these, in which we profess to be laboriously dull, and begin the following Books, at the second Chapter. (215)

The introductory chapter to book 6, which in contrast is unironically serious, ends with another invitation to unsatisfied readers not only to skip the introductory chapters but even abandon the book as a whole:

> Examine your Heart, my good Reader, and resolve whether you do believe these Matters with me. If you do, you may now proceed to their Exemplification in the following Pages; if you do not, you have, I assure you, already read more than you have understood; and it would be wiser to pursue your Business, or your Pleasures (such as they are) than to throw away any more of your Time in reading what you can neither taste nor comprehend. (271)

Only readers who pass these tests and continue reading are judged capable of appreciating *Tom Jones*: they understand love, relish multiple ironies, and enjoy learning how to read "Prosai-comi-epic Writing" (209 [bk. 5, ch. 1]). I ask my students if they think they qualify.

Moving to the intranarrative commentary, I invite them to unpack the multiple ironies in the two paragraphs introducing the Inn at Upton, which begin with this passage: "Our Travellers had happened to take up their Residence at a House of exceeding good Repute, whither *Irish* Ladies of strict Virtue, and many Northern Lasses of the same Predicament, were accustomed to resort in their Way to *Bath*" (500 [bk. 9, ch. 3]). It is a challenge for students to negotiate and appreciate the rich complexity of the narrator's blend of irony, humor, and satire. I remind them of his remark, "[S]urely a Man may speak Truth with a smiling Countenance" (569 [bk. 11, ch. 1]), which indicates that *Tom Jones* is intended to be at once a profoundly serious and a seriously funny book.

In a written assignment, students must compare and contrast three examples of narratorial commentary: the range of opinions expressed about Blifil's freeing of Sophia's pet bird and Tom's attempt to recapture it (159–61 [bk. 4, ch. 3]); the extended commentary on the behavior of Black George Seagrim after he finds and keeps Tom's £500 (319–20 [bk. 6, ch. 13], 325–29 [bk. 7, ch. 1]); and the commentary on Tom's behavior when his emerging love for Sophia conflicts with his impoverished state and his expulsion from Allworthy's favor (309–19 [bk. 6, chs. 12–13]).

Finally I encourage students to discuss and reflect on the intriguing passage in which the ever voluble narrator, never short of an opinion or a judgment, declines to tell us what "the great, useful and uncommon Doctrine which it is the whole purpose of this whole Work to inculcate, and which we must not fill up our Pages by frequently repeating," is (652 [bk. 12, ch. 8]). William Empson describes the passage as an example of Fielding's "double irony" (126), but I think of it as a triple irony. Can my students work out what those ironies are and what that doctrine is? Why does the narrator tease us by not stating it?

As a parting thought, I suggest that we might borrow the title of Sterne's novel and retitle Fielding's original, highly intelligent, and marvelously engaging book *The Life of Tom Jones and the Opinions of Henry Fielding*. Isn't that ultimately what every novel, every fiction, is? Isn't that why we read novels?

Fielding's Style

Jill Campbell

> . . . but surely a Man may speak Truth with a smiling Countenance.
>
> —*Tom Jones*

Diction, Heteroglossia

As early as the second line of *Tom Jones*, a reader is alerted that Fielding intends in his novel to take advantage of the entire range of English words, including ones that reside in fairly obscure corners of the lexicon: stumbling on the long and peculiar-looking word "eleemosynary" (31; meaning "charitable," from a Medieval Latin term, derived from Greek, for alms), the reader is forewarned that this novel will require some stretching of her vocabulary, perhaps even repeated dives into the dictionary, as well as frequent and nimble movements among levels of diction—at the very time that the author, ushering the reader into his novel, assures her that he regards her not as a guest at a private entertainment, dependent on her host's will, but rather as the equivalent of a paying customer, who has a right to review in advance and accept or reject the "Bill of Fare." The short opening chapter of *Tom Jones*, labeled "*The Introduction to the Work, or Bill of Fare to the Feast*," announces inclusiveness and comprehensiveness as the novel's values, promising that the "Provision" it offers "is no other than HUMAN NATURE." This provision, it asserts, includes as many different dishes under the name of "one Article" as a tortoise, with its many edible parts, does for the knowledgeable cook (32).

As it develops this odd culinary trope, the novel's opening chapter also makes it clear that the manner of preparation and presentation is what makes all the difference in the experience of consumption, whether of eating or of reading: "[T]he Difference between the Food of the Nobleman and the Porter" is "in the seasoning, the dressing, the garnishing, and the setting forth" (33). With its flamboyantly eccentric mix of word choices—specialized or foreign terms such as "*Calibash*," "*Calipee*," and "ragoo," elegant words such as "exquisite Viands" and "Quintessence," learned references such as to "*Heliogabalus*," alongside common, monosyllabic words of Old or Middle English origin such as "Fare," "Stall," "Ox," "plain," and even "d—n"—this opening chapter calls attention to the author's command over a great verbal range, from high to low diction and around the globe, and highlights the audaciously performative quality of his prose (31–34). It also immediately focuses attention on the relationship between the author and his reader and on the act of free choice with which a reader embarks on reading his long novel. Students setting out on this difficult but rewarding project must be encouraged to enter into the spirit of Fielding's verbal enterprise, beginning on the simple, atomistic scale of word choice: the frequent unfamiliarity of his vocabulary and the variegation of his lexicon should be acknowledged, celebrated, wondered at, and puzzled over, in whatever way is appropriate for a particular group of students. A basic activity might be the collective pooling of dictionary searches or the listing of favorite words. (My own first copy of *Tom Jones*, read when I was a senior in college, contains dozens of "vocabulary words" handwritten in the inside of its back cover. Some of those words are now familiar to me, but a number remain rare sights in my reading over the years.) The exuberance with which Fielding seizes on words common and uncommon—as do, for instance, the best artists in rap music today—should be savored in itself as a form of verbal energy. But the question should also be posed early on: What, if anything, is achieved by placing such unlike words side by side and by making us stumble over a surprising word, or even stop reading and take the time to look it up? Why does Fielding, sometimes distractingly, direct our eyes and minds to the surface of the written medium, to the words through which he tells his story?

In a course devoted to sustained study of the novel, *Tom Jones* provides a particularly rich opportunity to introduce the concept of heteroglossia and, with that concept, some key elements from Mikhail Bakhtin's understanding of what distinguishes the novel from other kinds of literary work. Even in simplified explication, Bakhtin's account of the novel as essentially distinguished by its capacious inclusion of the many sublanguages that exist within one national language is confirmed by the striking, prismatic display of the distinct "languages" as well as kinds of diction that comprise *Tom Jones*. The almost riotous profusion of forms of speech in this novel—regional dialects (219 [bk. 5, ch. 2]), lower-class idioms (185–86 [bk. 4, ch. 9]), pedantic philosophical and religious harangues (161–64 [ch. 4]), ludicrously earnest and formal romantic utterances (200–01 [ch. 13], 256 [bk. 5, ch. 10], 313 [bk. 6, ch. 12]), lawyers' jargon (164 [bk. 4, ch. 4]), medical terms (380–82 [bk. 7, ch. 13]), gamblers' cant (463–64 [bk. 8, ch. 12]), political buzzwords and rallying cries (335–37 [bk. 7, ch. 3]), vulgar malapropisms (185–86 [bk. 4, ch. 9]), Irish "bulls" (528–32 [bk. 10, ch. 2])—can be traced as intertwining threads in the complex fabric of the text and can be highlighted figuratively by spoken identifications, or even literally with differently colored pens in students' texts or with different fonts in a slide. Fielding's enthusiastic incorporation in his novel of the characterizing voices of many different groups of English people illustrates in an easily recognizable form the following excerpt from Bakhtin's "Discourse in the Novel," which can go far as a stand-alone paragraph introducing the fundamentals of his approach:

> The internal stratification of any single national language into social dialects, characteristic group behaviors, professional jargons, generic languages, languages of generations and age groups, tendentious languages, languages of the authorities, of various circles and of passing fashions,

> languages that serve the specific sociopolitical purposes of the day, even of the hour (each day has its own slogan, its own vocabulary, its own emphases)—this internal stratification present in every language at any given moment of its historical existence is the indispensable prerequisite for the novel as a genre. The novel orchestrates all its themes, the totality of the world of objects and ideas depicted and expressed in it, by means of the social diversity of speech types and by the differing individual voices that flourish under such conditions. (262–63)

Of course, Fielding's interest in incorporating different spoken idioms in quoted dialogue from a wide range of characters in *Tom Jones* is only the beginning of the ways in which his novel is profoundly and philosophically "heteroglossic." The recognition of how exuberantly Fielding portrays the great variety of his characters' forms of speech must lead into discussion of the much broader and more subtle heteroglossia in the narrator's voice, which constitutes the text of the whole novel. The unquoted sentences of the narrative themselves contain flickering elements—individual words, kinds of phrasings, syntactic structures, generic conventions, allusions, learned or professional references, tonalities, modes of address—that derive from many different discourses and that therefore "bespeak," side by side, the different social positions and postures, and the often conflicting assumptions and points of view, associated with those modes of expression.

In a course on the eighteenth-century novel that culminates in the study of Jane Austen or in a more general course on the novel that passes through Austen in a longer arc, this remarkable aspect of Fielding's prose in *Tom Jones* in some ways anticipates what students will learn to call free indirect discourse, a crucial feature of Austen's innovation in the novel form. Whereas Austen's use of free indirect discourse often involves the unannounced and sometimes ironized incorporation into her narrator's prose of the thought processes and (self-justifying, self-deluding, or simply expressive) verbal formulations of a particular character's inner life, Fielding's prose is forever miming, dramatizing, incorporating, and fluidly juxtaposing a variety of broadly representative social forms of thought and conventions of expression. Even as the extraordinary "voice" or style of the narrator of *Tom Jones* is constantly present to us, speaking in such a distinctive manner and tone that readers have declared him the most important "character" in the novel, the sentences pronounced by that voice demonstrate what Bakhtin means by "hybrid construction": they display vividly how any utterance appropriates the words of others, how many systems of expression exist in a language one thinks of as unified, and how tightly those systems are tied to different points of view (304–05). As authoritative and even imperious as Fielding's narrator appears, Fielding's book is a novel, in Bakhtin's terms, because its orchestration of "a diversity of speech types" refrains from subordinating one system of expression stably to another or ordering them all hierarchically within one "authoritative" language (262).

This principle of shifting juxtaposition and mutual refraction, traceable in the different elements of Fielding's narrator's prose, is closely related to the seemingly ineffable effects of irony, indeed of double irony, that I discuss below. It is essential to such effects that they are experienced by the reader dynamically, in reading time; Fielding's characteristically long sentences, with their syntactic complexities that dilate the period of suspended resolution, provide the infrastructure that makes this experience possible on the small scale of the individual sentence's unfolding, at every point along the way.

Periphrasis, Mock-Epic, Syntactic Suspension

Alongside a theoretically resonant approach to the many and various verbal somethings that can be found coexisting in Fielding's sentences, which Bakhtin's account may provide, one needs some ways to talk about the deliberate gaps, the absences or deferrals of obviously pertinent words, that also insistently, sometimes seemingly perversely, characterize the style of *Tom Jones*. In the several indecorous knock-down, drag-out fights that constitute *Tom Jones*'s scenes of epic combat, for example, damage is often inflicted by a lowly bodily weapon, the fingernails; but Fielding refrains from using that straightforward term. In Partridge's battle with his enraged wife, we learn of her use of fingernails in her attack when the narrator observes that "from [Partridge's] Face descended five Streams of Blood, denoting the Number of Claws with which Nature had unhappily armed the Enemy"; eventually, by "getting Possession of her Arms [note Fielding's pun, by the way, on this last word]," Partridge is able to render useless "those Weapons, which she wore at the Ends of her Fingers" (89 [bk. 2, ch. 4]). The rhetorical term *periphrasis* provides a starting point for identifying the inventive, sometimes spectacular circumlocutions with which Fielding makes reference to both abstract and concrete entities without directly naming them. Students should be encouraged to relish the playfulness, the stubborn creativity, even the audacity with which Fielding sets about generating unprecedented ways to refer to familiar objects or ideas rather than seizing on the closest term that comes to hand.

One kind of recurrent set piece in which Fielding makes particular use of periphrasis is the mock-epic episode, which is often formally set off from the narrative as a special performance by the narrator, perhaps even requiring the invocation of a muse. Fielding's elevated style announces the aspiration to reach even greater heights in these passages, heights that are then played to comical effect against the base materials and motives that accompany them. Most famously, in book 4, chapter 8, headed as "*A Battle sung by the Muse in the* Homerican *Stile*," the "Muses then, whoever ye are, who love to sing Battles," recount a no-holds-barred fight in a country churchyard in which women pelt Molly "with Dirt and Rubbish" and she responds by throwing skulls and battering her opponents with a thigh bone found lying by a new-dug grave. In this scene, outrageously mixed diction, the blending of burlesque physical actions with learned allusions and periphrases for sexual infidelity, cuckoldry, and (once more) faces scratched by a wife's fingernails through elaborately formal and witty locutions—a bloody face "denot[ing] Talents (or rather Talons) of a different Kind" (181)—induce what Fielding's Shamela would term "violent" laughter (166), worthy both of enjoyment and serious analysis in class. Fielding's interest in dramatizing the distance between epic heroism and his contemporary world has obvious connections to the mock-epic poetry of Alexander Pope, Jonathan Swift, and John Gay, and any course in which *Tom Jones* follows study of the Augustans or Scriblerians sets up particularly rich discussions of these episodes.

Yet Fielding's periphrases and elaborate syntactic constructions are not designed only to provoke laughter. Particularly in an age of writing instruction long dominated, as Richard Ohmann has observed, by the often echoed, decisive injunctions of Strunk and White—"Use definite, specific, concrete language," "Omit needless words!" (241–51)—not to mention in our digital communications age, which so privileges brevity that a tweet cannot exceed 140 characters—it is worth considering closely Fielding's choice, for example, to employ a series of phrases and attached clauses consisting of 74 words or 440 characters to make reference to what could be named by a word of three letters:

> In fact, the good Squire [Western] was a little too apt to indulge that Kind of Pleasantry which is generally called *Rodomontade*; but which may, with as much Propriety, be expressed by a much shorter Word; and perhaps we too often supply the Use of this little Monosyllable by others; since very much of what frequently passes in the World for Wit and Humour, should, in the strictest Purity of Language, receive that short Appellation which, in Conformity to the well-bred Laws of Custom, I here suppress. (194 [bk. 4, ch. 11])

Why does Fielding's narrator refrain from labeling a lie Western's confident assertion that he knows Allworthy to have been a womanizer at college (although Allworthy in fact never attended college, much less was known to be a womanizer there), when he insinuates strongly that the label applies? At the center of this long and syntactically complicated sentence are two references to the short, common word of Old English origin, *lie*, that the sentence never utters and that it concludes by acknowledging that it has "suppress[ed]." In the context both of this sentence and of its narrative occasion, the withheld word (that "much shorter Word," that "little Monosyllable," tantalizingly held just out of view) seems refreshingly direct—willing, as it is, unlike the fanciful, euphonious foreign term *rodomontade*, to offer a blunt designation of a moral lapse. The action of Fielding's sentence is to call that word into any alert reader's mind while withholding it from his sight (though at least one heavy-handed editor supplies the word in a footnote to this sentence, overriding the effect that

Fielding thus elaborately arranged). Through the dramatization of this suppression of *lie* as the proper description of Western's damaging social babble, the sentence creates a parallel between the falseness of what is said in this and many like cases and the equally insidious falseness of what so often goes unsaid. Silence as well as speech—or the cooperation of the two, when voluble speech allows the obvious to be passed over—may carry untruths, Fielding's periphrasis here pointedly suggests.

At first reading, this sentence may seem an instance of uncharacteristically loose or incompletely integrated syntax. Its initial main clause ("the . . . Squire was . . . apt to indulge that Kind of Pleasantry") is followed by two parallel subordinate clauses that both modify "that Kind of Pleasantry," providing two contrasting ways in which the phenomenon might be named and thus differently understood ("which is generally called . . . ; but which may, with as much Propriety, be expressed by . . ."). Since a semicolon separates these two adjectival clauses, we might expect what comes after the next semicolon (". . . Word; and . . .") to follow the same construction, attaching itself too back to "that Kind of Pleasantry," the real topic, if not the grammatical subject, of the sentence. Instead, what follows this further semicolon introduces a new independent clause with a different grammatical subject (now a generalized "we" rather than "the Squire"), elaborating on the pervasive social tendency to steer clear of "the little Monosyllable," though it applies perfectly well to so much that we encounter in social speech. My charting of the syntax and punctuation of this sentence is labored, but simply in moving through this sample sentence's unforeseeable syntactical turns, the reader must "discover" rather than be shown a disorienting parallel between the disciplined, polite, and cosmopolitan tones of the narrator's language use and the unthinking, baseless assertions of the Jacobite country squire. An unspoken word floats over Fielding's prose from mid-sentence on; it is only at the sentence's close that the author marks the spot of that word's burial ("here") to localize our awareness of how a word—and the moral or social perspective it encapsulates—may be present and absent at the same time.

Double Irony

Both dramatic and verbal irony appear in such episodes as the accidental revelation of the philosopher Square, that great proponent of "the unalterable Rule of Right, and the eternal Fitness of Things" (128 [bk. 3, ch. 3]), squatting ignominiously among various "female Utensils," Molly's nightcap atop his head, in the makeshift closet at the end of her bed, where he has hastily concealed himself when Tom unexpectedly appears (229–30 [bk. 5, ch. 5]). The satiric effect of the stripping away or exposure of hypocrisy's false front that is literalized in this scene, like the mock-epic passages in the novel, connects Fielding's verbal and narrative project with Scriblerian critique. What is most extraordinary and most elusive, however, about the effects of irony in Fielding's prose is what William Empson long ago identified as its "doubleness": the way that in the unfolding sentences of *Tom Jones* the ironizing of one constructed worldview—the look that Fielding allows his reader through or behind the customary phrases and reified forms of speech covering up that worldview's denials and lies—is constantly played against an ironizing of that very perspective from which the first is revealed to be wanting and false. Such double or mutual (or multiple) effects of irony can be achieved only in the medium of time, in the dynamic shifts and unsettling series of reorientations that Fielding's extraordinary style induces in a reader as she moves through his sentences in successive syntactic waves. Thus a close attention to the "surface" of Fielding's style is the only way to catch him in the act. That is, to glimpse the means by which he elicits the cognitive, emotional, moral process in which he wants us to engage: the "great, useful and uncommon Doctrine" of his novel, which "it is the Purpose of this whole Work to inculcate" and which he refuses to name (652 [bk. 12, ch. 8]).

Formalism, Historicism, and *The Author's Farce*: Making the Modern Author in *Tom Jones*

Rivka Swenson

Tom Jones is hard to teach, not because of its length but because of its narrator, "Fielding," arguably the element of the novel most likely to be glossed over by students.[1] The narrator's character is difficult. Moreover, the significance of his presence is difficult—even for seasoned students of the novel—to figure out. Indeed, Patricia Meyer Spacks attests to the ongoing "puzzlement" over "the novel's conspicuous narrator and his relation to the novelistic action" (*On Rereading* 171–72). If "Fielding" turns readers into skeptics, exposing our failures of foresight, what then?

Students, like other readers, tend to read for the plot (see Brooks); doubting that the narrator's intrusions have any real connection to, or effect on, the progress of the story, irritated by his didacticism, students tend to pass "Fielding" by.[2] Some student readers, interested in metafiction, may be moved to investigate how "Fielding" empowers himself by creating and then frustrating our expectations; their interest may make them eager to broaden their readerly lexicon with concepts such as implied author and career-author, implied reader, paratext and focalization, authorial intention, intentional fallacy, death of the author, author function, breaking the fourth wall (and fifth wall), and more.[3] But "Fielding" offers much more to classrooms than a vehicle for literary-critical terminology, and real gains may be achieved by repeatedly asking students to consider how the novel's meaning is affected by this pushy narrator with his paratexts and in-chapter interruptions. First, if the narrator's intrusions are "interventions" (Bender, Introduction x), in what way are his "instructions" instructive? (523 [bk. 10, ch. 1]). Second, how do the novel's themes of anxious paternity relate to the narrator's themes of anxious authorship? Third, how does the narrator's repeated rug pulling potentially destabilize the happy ending?

Such questions, requiring students to reread and rethink instead of just reading for plot, are designed to help teachers and students engage the puzzle (following Spacks's word "puzzlement") of narrator and plot. They also provide an excellent opportunity to bring formalism and historicism together, illuminating both the form of *Tom Jones* and its resonance with the context of Grub Street and eighteenth-century authorship and print culture.[4] Positioning *Tom Jones* and "Fielding" as the result of contexts that include the emergence of modern authorship (the lapsing of the Licensing of the Press Act; the Statute of Anne; the Actor Rebellion; the Stage Licensing Act), I offer a strategy for approaching key scenes and elements: the Molly Seagrim debacle, the narrator's character (resonant with the fraught author Luckless in Fielding's earlier play *The Author's Farce*), and Tom's status as foundling and as father at novel's end. Between the history of authorship and *The History of Tom Jones,* students can develop answers to the questions I pose that may just satisfy our long-standing desire to connect the narrator to the action.

The Molly Seagrim Debacle

The scene in Molly Seagrim's bedroom, like the lead-up and aftermath, merits close in-class scrutiny. This material appears early in the book, which means it can be revisited later as both a heuristic and a hermeneutic device. If *Tom Jones* has a "main Design" (524 [bk. 10, ch. 1]), how are individual episodes emblematic of the whole and of each other?

Consider the Seagrim debacle: Molly is pregnant, and Tom believes he is "the Author" of her condition (227 [bk. 5, ch. 5]). He intends to offer her money, then retreat. But Molly gains the upper hand in their competitive discourse, until the exchange is interrupted when a little closet of sorts behind her bed yields a big surprise: an "old Rug" covering the "Hole . . . got loose . . . , and discovered . . . Square," Tom's tutor, like a failed puppet master, wearing only Molly's bedcap (229). "Fielding" intrudes, "the Surprize of the Reader will be here equal to that of Jones; as the Suspicions which must arise . . . may seem so inconsistent with that Character which [Square] hath, doubtless, maintained" (230). This moment offers a vantage point from which to reread: could we in fact have guessed at this development? Or at what happens next, when the narrator tells us that the "Author" of Molly's child is neither Tom nor Square but Will Barnes, a character we have not met before?

A larger question looms: To what extent do such farces (the novel is full of false steps) problematize the novel's happy ending? The resolution seems tidy: Tom's mother is Bridget Allworthy, and his father is Mr. Summer; Tom marries Sophia; Sophia "produce[s] him two fine Children" (981 [bk. 18, ch. 13]). And yet. When students reach the final book of the novel, I ask them how this happily-ever-after moment becomes more complicated, potentially, in the light of the book's patterns throughout. J. Paul Hunter, considering *Tom Jones* as a whole, observes, "The better the reader, the more easy the rug-pulling victimization" (*Before Novels* 50). If Hunter is right, how does the ending fit within "the formal accomplishments of *Tom Jones*" ("Re-thinking Form" 310)? Working individually or in groups to test the hypothesis that the Seagrim debacle is emblematic, students may be enabled to articulate how Fielding's "Design" expresses, as I suggest, a fractal narrative poetics of uncertainty—a reiteration of gaps that stand for the anxious whole.

The Narrator's Character

The narrator-patriarch's authority over his interpolated reader has been much written about.[5] He interrupts our experience and exposes his artifice, breaking the equivalent of the dramatic fourth wall by addressing us directly, and breaking the fifth wall, too, by reducing us all to a single implied reader who is under his thumb. "Fielding" is "Founder of a new Province of Writing, . . . at liberty to make what Laws . . . my Readers, whom I consider as my Subjects, are bound to believe in and to obey" (77 [bk. 2, ch. 1]). He is superior to "Criticks," to "every Reader in the World" (396 [bk. 8, ch. 1]). It is useful to ask students to track, or to go back and trace, the surprises, about-faces, and instances in which the "Instructions very necessary" are insufficient, even misleading (523 [bk. 10, ch. 1]). Scrutinizing such gaps, we can come to the historical crisis of authorship as idea and practice.

To better elucidate the historical dimension of the dynamic between the *Tom Jones* narrator and the implied reader, it is worthwhile to preface the novel with a class period devoted to Fielding's play *The Author's Farce* (1730, 1733–34), a metadrama that exemplifies, as Lisa Freeman explains, his irregular "plays about plays" (53).[6] Allegedly written by "Scriberlus Secundus," this play is the brainchild of the self-proclaimed heir of Martinus Scriblerus, that emblematic Scribbler forged by Alexander Pope, Jonathan Swift, *et al.* It shares with early Scriblerian texts its paradoxes, antecedent to the paradoxical and self-reflexive *Tom Jones* narrator.[7] Here is dystopia, caused partly by popular culture's accessibility and rise: "Learning is decried, Wit not understood," and "the Theatres are Puppet-Shows" (234 [act 1, sc. 5]).[8] In a world upside down (optional reading: Bakhtin on the carnivalesque [*Rabelais*]), playwrights are at the mercy of audiences (optional reading: both Barthes ["Death"] and Foucault on authors and readers). Adding insult to irony, audiences allegedly want "farce," a slippery genre that Fielding uses coterminously (and derogatorily) with "puppet show" and "Nonsense." In an age of degraded aesthetics, Harry Luckless, protagonist-poet-playwright, suggestive of Fielding himself (Lockwood, Introduction 285), cannot get his noble, nonfarcical drama produced. Starving, demoralized, he stoops to write a farce in which people play puppets: *The Pleasures of the Town: A Puppet Show*.[9]

If acts 1 and 2 of *The Author's Farce* pillory modern authorship (see Freeman 58–63), in act 3, a performance of Luckless's farce, we see modern authorship in action. The characters in this act are facets of the modern author, Duncical avatars that include Don Tragedio, Mrs. Novel, Seignior Opera, Sir Farcical Comic, Bookseller, Poet, Dr. Orator, Monsieur Pantomime. They "are all Authors" (262 [sc. 1]). The action of *The Pleasures of the Town* is supposed to be a (mock-epic) competition: the dunces meet to compete for the honor of becoming mate to the Goddess Nonsense (reminiscent of Pope's Dulness in *The Dunciad* and Swift's "Criticism" in *The Battle of the Books*).[10] The action *is* supposed to be a competition, but suddenly the performance of the play within the play is interrupted: Constable and Murdertext arrive to arrest the play's author, Luckless, for "abusing *Nonsense*" (282). The arrest is *also* interrupted, when yet another new character, Bantomite, arrives, melding the play with the play within the play when he announces that the King of Bantam has died. Luckless is now king—"Henry I"! His lineage is proved by way of a jewel that was tied around his wrist when he was an infant (shades of Odysseus, and of Fielding's earlier hero, Joseph Andrews). Like the infant Tom Jones, who was found at Allworthy's in a box filled with rainwater, the infant Luckless is, we learn, a Moses-like foundling for his times: falling from a ship, washing up along the Thames, Luckless was raised by a London waterman and oysterwench, only to prove a king's son. Witmore says with a shrug, "[I]t is very common in this Country for a Man not to know his Father" (285). Henry I—attentive students will notice Fielding's own first name—leads his people (Mrs. Novel, Don Tragedio, and the others) as a Moses, giving them all titles (attentive students will notice the bookish pun on *titles*) in Bantam. He declares:

> Taught by my Fate, let never Bard despair,
> Tho' long he drudge, and feed on *Grub-street* Air.
> Since him (at last) 'tis possible to see
> As happy and as great a King as me. (289)

With this silly ending, "Nonsense" wins. No wonder Albert Rivero supposes that the success of the play "must have confirmed [Fielding's] worst fears" (*Plays* 31).

At the same time, if "Nonsense" wins, so does Henry I, legitimated as both author and authority. Arguably, it is this very quest for authority, in the context of modern authorship, that drives "Fielding" in *Tom Jones.* With a play like *The Author's Farce* in mind, students are primed to watch for statements by "Fielding" in *Tom Jones* that suggest the novel genre can empower authors in a way that the modern playhouse did not.[11] The dystopia of *The Author's Farce* depicts *auctors* at the mercy of actors. Bookweight opines, "[Y]our Acting Play is entirely supported by the Merit of the Actor, without any Regard to the Author" (237 [act. 1, sc. 6]). Luckless's actors do not simply perform badly; they revolt against direction. But Luckless revises the conclusion of the real-life Actor Rebellion of 1733: he succeeds in asserting control. That rebellion, to which the 1733–34 production responded, was a gain for actors (Hume, *London Theatre World* 173–79), so when the Stage Licensing Act of 1737 sent Fielding, and "Fielding," offstage, an opportunity presented itself: the novel. On the one hand, if the genre gives "Fielding" access to readers, those same readers are "critics" who, in closets, behind curtains, dare "assume a Dictatorial Power" (*History* 210 [bk. 5, ch. 1]).[12] On the other hand, novel spaces give "Fielding" the vexed chance to assert or reassert the "Laws of Writing" (211): a certain amount of amiable bullying is "necessary to this kind of Writing, of which we have set ourselves at the Head" (209).

But, of course, the modern rebel-reader was only one element in the historical transformation of the idea of author and the reality of authorship. Students may benefit from a brief lecture on the broad historical tension between competing ideas about "originality" and worth: in an older tradition, legitimacy derives from tracing a work to its origins;[13] in a nascent modern tradition, value and authenticity derive in part from newness. Making students aware of these two kinds of originary anxiety enables one to introduce them to moments in the contemporary history of authorship that informed and were informed by the tension between those anxieties. The lapsing of the Licensing of the Press Act (1695), for instance, led to a democratizing, destabilizing explosion of authors, texts, hybrid genres, monstrous forms, ephemerae, rip-offs, misattributions, piracies, and compromised Foucauldian "author function." In *The Author's Farce,* Scarecrow "translates" the *Aeneid* "out of Dryden" and is "obliged to translate Books . . . never Printed in any Language." Bookweight says with a shrug, "[W]e give a Foreign Name to our own Labour—and sometimes we put our own Names to the Labour of others" (250 [act 2, sc. 6]). Moreover, the Statute of Anne (1710), instead of confirming authors as natural owners of literary productions, merely vested them with ownership of copies.[14] "Fielding" is in a difficult position. Time permitting, it may be worthwhile to bring in selections from a range of Fielding's metadramas and other novels (before and after *Tom Jones*) to get a sense of how "Fielding" manifests (develops?) across texts as a narratorial presence in line with Wayne C. Booth's theory of the "career-author" (*Rhetoric* 431).

Having considered these historical and literary contexts, students should be ready to see in *Tom Jones* a fascinating allegory of paternity as authorship and authorship as paternity that includes the narrator's self-advocacy as implied author-owner (implied author and narrator are one in *Tom Jones*). The key is to look for instances in *Tom Jones* where "Fielding" discusses his relations with his muse or muses, with his literary works, and with other authors. In these accumulated passages lie ambivalence, paradox, and a thematic connection to plot.

Tom as Foundling and Father

As the novel comes to a close, the question is, Can "Fielding" be trusted? Or will there be one last pull of the rug? Or, even, will he suggest that his muse might have misled him? After all, the muse of *The Author's Farce* turns out to be a cat, and thus she is a *quean* in two ways (a female cat and an impudent, ill-behaved, bawdy woman). Played by the same actress who plays Mrs. Novel, Cat speaks the epilogue, giving a happy ending geared to "pleas[e]": "For as a Whore is lik'd, for being tawdry, / So is an Epilogue for [being bawdry]" (291). Is the *Tom Jones* muse also a *quean?* Can she be trusted?

Examine with students the description of "Fielding's" novel's muses and ask them to consider for themselves. One of his muses is a classical muse: a Sophia figure, a Platonic emblem of wisdom. The other, described at length, is a modern Grub Street Molly who recalls Swift's Criticism, Pope's Dulness, Fielding's Nonsense. She "produces" for the author, the "tender father" (568–69 [bk. 11, ch. 1]), but who really fathers the goddess's "prattling Babes" (685 [bk. 13, ch. 1])?[15] If authors were traditionally the superiors of muses (Hunter, "Manliness" 178), the *Tom Jones* narrator/ implied author is an exception: he says he cannot reveal the muse's "secrets" (e.g., whether or not Partridge is Tom's father) until she reveals them to him and then not "till she shall give me leave" (101 [bk. 2, ch. 6]). At the same time, "Fielding" complains that other men's "writings" have been "fathered upon him" (914 [bk. 18, ch. 1]). He is an insecure author. Sandra Gilbert and Susan Gubar observe that the idea of "author" as "paternalistic ruler" cannot bespeak security: "[T]hat his child is *his* is in a sense a tale" (5). If the ending of *Tom Jones* is suspect, perhaps "Fielding" (in the book's conceit about tricky muses) is not lying but being lied to. Janet Lembke observes that the classical Homeric muse had devolved by Hesiod's time into a muse who mixed falsehood with truth: thus "[t]he poet's task was in part to separate golden words from gilded ones" (22). Can we trust "Fielding"? Can he, can we, trust his muse?

If Fielding demands obedience, he also encourages skepticism. Because paradoxical authors deserve paradoxical readers, we *should* ask questions even as "Fielding" wraps up. Assuming the Mr. Summer story is deemed plausible, what of the larger happy ending? Will Tom be faithful to Sophia? "Fielding" assures us that he will "now" be constant (871 [bk. 16, ch. 9]), but Sophia doubts Tom's future fidelity even as Tom, patronizing and flattering by turns, wavers among prevaricating, rationalizing, and making big promises. Students should close-read this exchange, which constitutes the entirety of the second-to-last chapter. More crucial to the novel's resolution is Sophia, she with whom everyone is "in Love" (149 [bk. 3, ch. 10])—is she nevertheless a *quean*? If the narrator's early comparison of his book to a public tavern amounts to a "parodying" of "the language of the marketplace" (Richetti, *English Novel* 137), is the ending a parody too? Or, if the happy ending is not quite as absurd as the happy ending of *The Author's Farce*,[16] does it resolve all the uncertainties of what John Bender calls a "conversation with the reader about the complexities involved in knowing and judging" (Introduction x)? If uncertainties persist, things come down to a question of faith: Do we choose to believe in the fidelity of Tom's muse, Sophia, who "produced him two fine children" (981 [bk. 18, ch. 13])? Yes, probably, despite all previous rug pullings. And we probably believe that Mr. Summer is Tom's father. Of course, much earlier, we accepted Molly's claim about Will Barnes—the muse, according to the novel's general conceit, told "Fielding" so . . . but can Molly herself, intimate with both Tom and Square, be sure of that claim? We took her word for it. We believe in Fielding, despite his compromised position and his misdirections; my point is not actually that Sophia is a *quean* or that Tom's parentage is unknown but that Fielding achieves brilliantly his primacy as (modern) *auctor.* Working with students to expose the aporias that "Fielding" constructs and contains, we can get both to the heart of *Tom Jones* and to the contexts of the modern author.

NOTES

I would like to thank John Richetti, J. Paul Hunter, Jennifer Wilson, and Elizabeth Kraft for advice as I was writing this essay. And I want to thank my teachers: John O'Brien for introducing me to *The Author's Farce,* and Patricia Meyer Spacks, Paul Hunter, and Gregory G. Colomb for hearing me out when I first started thinking things about *Tom Jones.*

[1] John Bender explains in his introduction to *Tom Jones,* "This narrator is usually called 'Fielding,' both for the sake of convenience and because the voice rings true as the historical author's self-depiction" (x). My quotation marks around "Fielding" differentiate narratorial "Fielding" from historical Fielding.

[2] J. Paul Hunter remarks in *Before Novels* that the aspect of early novels "that has most often embarrassed" modern readers is "didacticism" (54).

[3] From Booth, we get the concepts of implied author and career-author (*Rhetoric*). From Wolfgang Iser, we get the concept of implied reader. Paratext, like focalization, comes from Gérard Genette (*Paratexts*). Students interested in narrative theory will want to follow complications of Booth's concept (Genette's schema of "focalization" in *Narrative Discourse: An Essay* [64–66], Mieke Bal's differentiation between narrator and implied author). E. D. Hirsch defends readings that expose "the author's intention" (8), whereas W. K. Wimsatt and Monroe Beardsley complain about "intentional fallacy" (1). The death of the author is articulated by Roland Barthes. Michel Foucault gives us, among other things, the term "author function" (107). Lastly, from Denis Diderot we get the concept of the fourth wall or "grand mur" (269); theories of a dramatic or cinematic fifth wall can be found in Davenport, Agamanolis, Barry, Bradley, and Brooks; Hunter and Lichtenfels.

[4] Other kinds of formalist-historicist approaches to *Tom Jones* can be found in Battestin, "Tom Jones"; Leith Davis; Schmidgen; Schonhorn; and Stevenson, *Real History*.

[5] The narrator's manipulations have been described in detail by numerous critics. See, for instance, Spacks's *Desire* and *Privacy*.

[6] See also Hunter, *Occasional Form* 48–75 ("Fielding's Reflexive Plays and the Rhetoric of Discovery"), for analysis of *The Author's Farce* and Fielding's other metadramas; Rivero, who covers *The Author's Farce* among other Fielding plays (*Plays* 31–52); Keymer on Fielding as dramatist ("Fielding's Theatrical Career"); and Hume's larger study of Fielding's playwriting career (Henry Fielding).

[7] Hunter (*Occasional Form* 48–54), Claude Rawson ("Some Considerations"), and Anthony J. Hassall ("Authorial Dimension") make useful connections between *The Author's Farce* and *Tom Jones*. See also Rawson, *Order* 261–310 ["Dialogue and Authorial Presence in Fielding's Novels and Plays"]).

[8] Throughout, I cite the 1730 version of *The Author's Farce*, although none of the lines differ from those of the 1733–34 version. I cite by act, scene, page number. Lockwood's introduction in the Wesleyan edition serves as a fine preface to the play, its contexts, and its history on stage and page.

[9] Students curious about the hybridity and variety of the eighteenth-century stage and of plays like *The Author's Farce* will be enlightened by John O'Brien's *Harlequin Britain*.

[10] George Sherburn ("Dunciad") and Aubrey Williams connect Dulness and Nonsense. Nonsense owes much to the Dulness of Pope's *Dunciad* (1728) and *Dunciad Variorum* (1729), while the Dulness of book 4 in *The New Dunciad* (1742) owes much to Nonsense

(Erskine-Hill). For commentary on the gendered significance of Nonsense's choice of Seignor Opera, a eunuch, send students to Jill Campbell's *Natural Masques*.

11 Hunter remarks that, in some sense, "Fielding's separation from the theater was a forced one, but the expulsion was fortunate" (*Occasional Form* 69). Students who are curious about how this transition figured practically in the course of Fielding's life and career should consult biographies by Pat Rogers (*Henry Fielding*), Ronald Paulson (*Life*), and Harold Pagliaro. Also see Lockwood, "Fielding."

12 For an illuminating discussion of the stage-closet dynamic in the period's literature, see Hunter, "World."

13 Homer O. Brown's theory of Tom Jones as a "bastard" novel will be helpful (82–115).

14 There is rich material on authorship in eighteenth-century England—for example, J. Greene; Rose; Temple. Students who desire a more comprehensive sense of authorship's legal and cultural status over time may wish to consult Johns, *Nature* and *Piracy*; Loewenstein.

15 On the uncontrollable reproductive capacities of Dulness and Criticism, see Gubar; Francus; and Ingrassia 40–76.

16 Valerie C. Rumbold gets at the fundamental absurdity of Luckless's surprise reclamation of a lost identity, what Hume describes as "Fielding's parody of recognition scenes" (*Henry Fielding* 65).

Sophia's Smile: Reading Jenny Cameron in the Margins of *Tom Jones*

Eric Leuschner

When Sophia Western, in book 11 of *Tom Jones,* is mistaken for Jenny Cameron, students may turn to the footnotes and discover that Jenny Cameron is a fictionalized version of Jean Cameron, who reportedly raised and led three hundred men in the 1745 Jacobite rebellion in support of Charles Stuart. Critics usually examine the parallels between the novel and the '45 in the light of Fielding's overt anti-Jacobitism, which is best evidenced by his papers *The True Patriot* and the satiric *Jacobite's Journal*. They read the novel as a criticism of the Young Pretender's cause and would have us believe that the reference to Jenny Cameron is negative. In his recent political biography of Fielding, J. A. Downie continues the argument that Fielding is "unequivocal in his support for the Hanoverian Succession" (*Political Biography* 184) and that this support is expressed in *Tom Jones*. John Allen Stevenson counters this view, suggesting a "more playful and more ambiguous" use of the historical materials relating to the '45. In particular, he claims that Fielding concedes the public "appeal of Charles Stuart" and refuses to "demonize the Stuarts or their followers" in the novel, recognizing that "the Stuart's stories were better than the tales Hanoverians told" ("*Tom Jones*" 576). Thus Fielding appropriates the story of Charles Stuart for his hero.

A footnote in the Norton edition adds that Cameron, "in her late forties, was present among her father's clansmen when Prince Charles raised his flag at Glenfinnan, and later was among the company when he held court in Edinburgh, but had virtually no personal acquaintance with him." "Nevertheless," the note continues, "Whig pamphleteers pictured her as his Amazonian mistress and companion at arms" (Fielding, *Tom Jones* [ed. Baker] 372n4). The Wesleyan edition footnote concurs that "the spirited, witty daughter of a Highland laird was popularly supposed to be the Young Pretender's mistress and to have attended him in battle, leading the clan against the British at Prestonpans" but concludes that "most of the stories about her were, however, fabrications. At the time of the rebellion she was a faded beauty in her mid-forties" (*History* 578n3 [bk. 11, ch. 3]). Should Jenny Cameron then simply be dismissed as a sign of Fielding's acrimony toward the Jacobite cause? Twenty-first-century students may be quick to overlook the reference, but for Fielding's contemporary readers, Jenny Cameron (or Jean, Jeanie, Jane) existed as a legendary if somewhat historical—and ambiguous—figure, celebrated (and vilified) in everything from ballads, songs, and reels to engravings. Devoting classroom time to unpacking this reference forces students not only to expand their knowledge of the political and historical context of the novel but also to rethink their image of Sophia, in particular her own rebellion against her father. Identifying her with Jenny

Cameron works to counter any idealistic portrayal ("the Somersetshire Angel") that readers may have.

In considering Jenny Cameron, students may think of a Marilyn Monroe mixed with Lady Gaga because she is identified both as a mistress of Bonnie Prince Charlie and a cross-dressing Amazonian warrior leading the troops into battle. Indeed, there were at least three Jenny Camerons: the in-your-face promiscuous mistress, the cross-dressing military leader, and the demure Romantic heroine. Many examples of her image are available to bring into the classroom or have students explore outside class to reconstruct her. Students can download at least four versions from Amazon.com of the still-popular ballad "Bonnie Jeanie Cameron," for instance, where she is cast as the heroine:

> Yell a' ha'e heard tell o' Bonnie Jeanie Cameron,
> How she fell sick, and she was like to dee
> And a' that they could recommend her
> Was ae blithe blink o' the Young Pretender.
> Rare, oh rare, Bonnie Jeanie Cameron!
> Rare, oh rare, Jeanie Cameron!
>
> To Charlie she wrote a very long letter,
> Stating who were his friends and who were his foes;
> And a' her words were sweet and tender,
> To win the heart of the Young Pretender.
> Rare, oh rare, Bonnie Jeanie Cameron!
> Rare, oh rare, Jeanie Cameron!
>
> Scarcely had she sealed the letter wi' a ring,
> When up flew the door, and in cam' her king;
> She prayed to the saints, and bade angels defend her,
> And sank in the arms o' the Young pretender.
> Rare, oh rare, Bonnie Jeanie Cameron!
> Rare, oh rare, Jeanie Cameron!

This ballad portrays her as an innocent, sickly Scottish lass, and her romanticized rescue (sinking in the arms of the Young Pretender) positions her as the willing victim of the gallant Charles. Students may recall Sophia's swooning in the presence of Tom, as in book 5, chapter 12:

> Jones, who had hitherto held this lovely Burthen in his Arms, now relinquished his Hold; but gave her at the same Instant a tender Caress, which, had her Senses been then perfectly restored, could not have escaped her Observation. As she expressed, therefore, no Displeasure at this Freedom, we suppose she was not sufficiently recovered from her Swoon at the Time. (264–65)

Jenny is also incidentally the intelligence of the Jacobites, being the source of identities of allies and enemies. Even her name, with Bonnie, recalls the prince's appellation.

This romanticized view contrasts with the sexualized depiction that appeared in many sources. The image of her as Charles's mistress was especially popular in anti-Jacobite propaganda, supporting as it did the idea of Charles's immoral behavior. Students with access to *ECCO* can find "An Excellent New Song on the Battle of Culloden," where she is associated with Charles in the poem's attack on his sexual dalliances, including those with Anne Mackintosh:

> Such prudence always had his race;
> and he's his father's son
> tho modesty doth bid me hush,
> the muse still bids me on,
> to sing his feats with M'Intosh
> and Jenny Cameron. (Teacle)

The lyrics of the song, which turns to a celebration of the victory at Culloden, hint at certain salubrious details, but in other popular songs Jenny's scandalous behavior was clearly described.

James Ray, the source of much of the fictionalized biography of Jenny Cameron in his *Compleat History of the Rebellion* (1749), also wrote of her in his *Acts of the Rebels, Written by an Egyptian*, where, in parodic biblical style, the encounter of Charles and Jenny is given in detail:

> And it came to pass, that when JANE the Daughter of one of the *Camerons* heard that CHARLES was come, she adorn'd herself with clean Linen and gay attire, with Frankincence and Perfumes was her Garments sprinkled nay nothing was left undone to make her person seem lovely before him. / And JANE carried gifts unto CHARLES and when she had got into his Appartment, she said unto him, Oh! Prince I have yet greater riches in store for thee which Eye hath not seen. (7)

The sexual titillation increases as Ray tells how Charles "fell down on his Face, and took of what seemed best unto him, and said verily the Lips of thy mouth are sweeter than the Honey or the Honey Comb" (7–8). Several historical accounts, now available through *Google Books*, including Ray's *Compleat History*, A *Brief Account of the Life and Family of Miss Jenny Cameron, the Reputed Mistress of the Pretenders Eldest Son, Containing Many Singular Incidents*, which was popular enough to warrant a second edition in 1746, and, *The Memoirs of the Remarkable Life and Surprising Adventures of Miss Jenny Cameron* (also 1746) add to the intrigue of Jenny by providing extensive details on her sexual appetite as a young woman, including her cross-dressing exploits and being impregnated by her great-aunt's footman, among other encounters. Bringing these narratives to the attention of students may cause them to rethink Fielding's intent in some of his running jokes in the novel, such as the continued reference to Sophia's muff. Fielding's own comments seem prescient in relation to the reference to Jenny Cameron:

> Though this Incident will probably appear of little Consequence to many of our Readers, yet, trifling as it was, it had so violent an Effect on poor *Jones*, that we thought it our Duty to relate it. In reality, there are many little Circumstances too often omitted by injudicious Historians, from which Events of the utmost Importance arise. The World may indeed be considered as a vast Machine, in which the great Wheels are originally set in Motion by those which are very minute, and almost imperceptible to any but the strongest eyes. (225 [bk. 5, ch. 4])

Observing the muff, akin to the sexualized image of Jenny Cameron, and Tom's response to it, like Sophia's smile here and later at the Upton Inn, rewards the careful reader.

A final image of Jenny is that of Amazonian warrior who not only raised the Cameron standard at Glenfinnan but also led the clan into battle. The National Library of Scotland (www.nls.uk) digital gallery contains a substantial repository of Jacobite images, including an engraving of Jenny dressed in male Highland attire, two pistols tucked into her belt and bearing a rifle at ready. Another illustration shows her wearing a military-style hat, holding a miniature of Prince Charles, and brandishing a naked sword. These portraits convey a positive picture for the Jacobite cause, providing a Joan of Arc for the clans. But they were also used to demonize Jenny, especially when combined with the sexualized version of her. In Ray's *Compleat History*, Jenny in male dress rides up to Charles at Glenfinnan "without least Concern, and gave him a Soldier-like Salute." She announces to him that she has brought the men of the Cameron clan and, although commanded by a woman, hopes "they had nothing womanish about them; for she found that so glorious a Cause, had rais'd in her Breast every manly Thought, and quite extinguish'd the Woman" (37). Similarly, a letter published in the *Gentleman's Magazine* and *General Evening Post* recounts how Jenny, on meeting Charles,

> jump'd off her Horse, and told him with great Frankness, that she came like the Queen of Sheba, to partake of the Wisdom of Solomon: He answered, and thou shalt, my Dear, partake of all that Solomon is Master of.—He took her in his Arms, and retired with her into his Tent, and were there some Time alone. ("Extract")

Students can debate on how these descriptions can be interpreted.

Which is the real Jenny Cameron, the "warlike Amazon" or the "shameless hussy" (Craig 46)? Maggie Craig notes that the fictionalized biographies and propaganda got it completely wrong; other than a few basic facts (Jenny did lead a group of men at Glenfinnan), everything else was made up and "nobody knew anything about [her]" (45). Craig suggests that not only are there many images but also many historical figures who may lay claim to the name Jenny Cameron: the widow of Archibald Cameron, a Jacobite martyr; an Edinburgh milliner (who in the end capitalized on the association with Jenny for her business); and a Jenny of Glendessary, who may have been arrested by the duke of Cumberland in 1746 (46–49). But the historical facts are not what is important about Jenny Cameron in *Tom Jones*, and for this reason her existence in its footnotes is marginal and problematic.

Students can explore how the rumors about and ambiguous identity of Jenny in the minds of British readers destabilize the equating of Jenny and Sophia through one particular text in the Jenny Cameron debate. *The Memoirs of the Remarkable Life and Surprising Adventures of Miss Jenny Cameron,* first published in 1746 attributed to Archibald Arbuthnot, appears to be an anti-Jacobite-driven biography detailing Jenny's scandalous youth and subsequent activity during the '45. While praising her military skills, Arbuthnot or the narrator declaims:

> [H]ad she not been so violently prejudic'd in Favour of a bad Cause, she wou'ld have appear'd in the first Class of the Female Worthies of the present Age. Had she happen'd to have took the right side of the Question, her Praises wou'd have been sung and said, both in Prose and Rhime, by all the Loyal Wits in England. (259)

Jill Campbell summarizes a similar work, the shorter *A Brief Account of the Life and Family of Miss Jenny Cameron,* concluding that the sixty-three-page pamphlet "vilifies the Jacobite cause by associating it with the overturning of proper gender roles," emphasizing the "specifically sexual transgressions of Jacobite women," and arguing for a "proper feminine education" (*Natural Masques* 154). While seeming to be an expansion of the *Brief Account*, the 269-page *Memoirs* is framed by a preface that ultimately upends the *Memoirs* argument that follows.

The first part of the preface is a facetious rant on the female sex, concluding, "There is scarce one Women in ten Thousand but what is a Hypocrite" and "Woman, from her Cradle to her Grave, is the constant Fatigue and Vexation of a Family" (iii–vi). Arbuthnot then commences a narrative: "I had here, I thought, concluded my Preface, and accordingly laid down my Pen, it being Nine o'Clock in the Evening, and went to a neighbouring Coffee-House to smoke my Pipe, and read the News" (viii). While he is absent, his sister Bel ("a pert Hussy [who] passes for a Wit") happens into his study ("to amuse herself among my Books"), sees the preface he has just composed, reads it, and, "not a little nettled at the Freedom I had taken with her Sex" (ix), responds by writing a defense of women immediately following the close of Arbuthnot's original preface. "What an unsufferable Coxcomb is my Brother!" Arbuthnot's sister begins and addresses the absence of equal female education as one reason for his claim of women's ignorance. As Bel prepares to turn to the subject of Jenny Cameron, the preface is broken off by a long dash as Arbuthnot returns. He relates how she must have heard him enter, cough, and call for my "lin'd slippers and double Night-cap" (xii).

Arbuthnot decides to "punish" Bel by publishing "what the saucy Baggage says" alongside his preface in order to show how woman "has no more Reason than a Horse, nor Docility than a Hog" (ix). What began as an attempt to justify the current status of the public sphere (i.e., that women are unfit to be members of it) becomes an actual debate between the sexes. Although Arbuthnot has the last word in the preface and claims that "whatever my pert Sister has advanc'd in Contradiction thereto, is merely Fruit of her own Invention," his sister emerges as the more rational person, and he becomes a clown, literally figured with "his lin'd slippers and double Night-cap." Readers of the preface never learn what Bel thinks of Jenny Cameron, but we can assume, on the basis of the ensuing memoirs, that her opinion would be opposed to Arbuthnot's. In the preface, Arbuthnot maintains the position of power, and we are left with only the trace of Bel in her impertinent scribble. But his attempt to marginalize Bel backfires, and the memoirs, read in the light of the preface, ironically valorize Jenny, essentially bringing her back from the margins.

Understanding the context of the Jenny Cameron debate helps us better appreciate Mrs. Honour's defense of Sophia and Sophia's response to that defense in book 11:

> What doth your Ladyship think? Would you imagine, that this impudent Villain, the Master of this House, hath had the Impudence to tell me, nay, to stand it out to my Face, that your Ladyship is that nasty, stinking Wh—re, (*Jenny Cameron* they call her) that runs about the Country with the Pretender? Nay, the lying, saucy Villain, had the Assurance to tell me, that your Ladyship had owned yourself to be so: But I have clawed the Rascal; I have left the Marks of my Nails in his impudent Face. ["]My Lady!" says I, "you saucy Scoundrel: My Lady is Meat for no Pretenders. She is a young Lady of as good Fashion, and Family, and Fortune, as any in *Somersetshire*. Did you never hear of the great Squire *Western*, Sirrah? She is his only Daughter; she is,—and Heiress to all his great Estate.["] My Lady to be called a nasty *Scotch* Wh—re by such a Varlet.—To be sure, I wish I had knocked his Brains out with the Punch-bowl.
>
> (603–04 [ch. 8])

Mrs. Honour acts the role of loyal Whig supporter, while Sophia, more concerned that her true identity is out but finally understanding the landlord's behavior, cannot keep from smiling ("nor could she, upon the whole, forbear smiling" [604]), which earns yet another reproof from Mrs. Honour. Mrs. Honour's anti-Jacobite sympathies are unsurprising, but Sophia's smile is, particularly in the light of Fielding's own feelings. Why would Sophia appear to approve of being mistaken for Jenny Cameron? That she is the daughter of Squire Western, a Tory, perhaps explains her amusement, but her position as rebelling against her father undermines that explanation. In a novel of apparently stark party divisions, Sophia breaks down easy allegiances.

Most if not all critics writing on the Upton Inn section of the novel remark on the misidentification of Sophia as Jenny but read it simply as a comic diversion. Anthony Kearney, for instance, attributes it to what he describes as "a comic working of the anxieties which disturbed Fielding between 1745 and 1749" (69). Leo Braudy dismisses the scene as having "little 'reality' or 'meaning' beyond that imposed upon it by characters for their own interests" (177). But the allusion is too resonant not to merit more attention. Stevenson does not mention the Jenny Cameron episode, but it seems to me that just as Fielding appropriates the story of Charles for Tom, he also appropriates the story of Jenny Cameron for Sophia. After all, Jenny's story is as good as any other—when students hear it, they may think it better. This episode is further evidence for, as Stevenson puts it, Fielding's "being playful with those fraught issues that so divided Britain and left so many scars" ("*Tom Jones*" 584), which brings into question the adamant political attitude ascribed to Fielding. Conflating Jenny and Sophia conflates nation and home, and the political tensions in the air are partially allayed as Sophia, fearing her father has discovered her, is relieved that it is only "several hundred thousand" French come to murder and ravish:

> So Sophia, than whom none was more capable of tenderly feeling the general Calamity of her Country, found such immediate Satisfaction from the Relief of those Terrors she had of being overtaken by her Father, that the Arrival of the French scarce made any Impression on her. She gently chid her Maid for the Fright into which she had thrown her; and said, "she was glad it was not worse; for that she had feared somebody else was come."
> (593 [bk. 11, ch. 6])

Sophia is undoubtedly not a closet Jacobite like Partridge, but much as Stevenson argues that Fielding situates Partridge as the focal character in the theater episode of book 16—as opposed to the actor David Garrick's playing Hamlet—to "suggest that Fielding's attitude toward the Stuarts was more nuanced, even ambivalent, than we have assumed" ("Fielding's Mousetrap" 555), the offhand reference to Sophia's smile suggests that she is the true focus of book 11.

We are tempted to look at Mrs. Honour's histrionics but rather should watch Sophia respond to the chaos at the inn. If we follow Fielding's cue, her surreptitious smile evokes sympathy for Jenny Cameron, particularly given the contested discourse surrounding her, and leads us to reconsider, as Stevenson suggests, the "potent . . . appeal" ("Fielding's Mousetrap" 565) of the Stuarts during the 1740s along with the ideal image of Sophia. Certainly, contextualizing Jenny Cameron, for whatever reason Fielding chose to dramatize her, encourages students to view Sophia differently and to shed any simplistic political reading of the novel.

Tom Jones and the Comic Tradition

James Evans

Beginning book 13 of *Tom Jones* with a chapter simply called "*An Invocation*," Fielding addresses Genius as follows: "Come thou, that hast inspired thy *Aristophanes*, thy *Lucian*, thy *Cervantes*, thy *Rabelais*, thy *Molière*, thy *Shakespear*, thy *Swift*, thy *Marivaux*, fill my Pages with Humour; till Mankind learn the Good-Nature to laugh only at the Follies of others, and the Humility to grieve at their own" (686). Several years ago this invocation led me to develop an undergraduate course that included texts by four of these predecessors and culminated with Fielding's novel. Now I'm modifying this design and adding four writers who came after Fielding and could list him as one of their precursors. My revised plan, which would be appropriate for a topics course or a senior seminar, situates Fielding's novel as the midpoint of a tradition that extends from Aristophanes to Martin Amis. I want students to explore the many strands of comedy incorporated in the dialogic fiction that is *Tom Jones*, which can serve, for pedagogical purposes, as a practical encyclopedia of comic forms, among which are festive comedy, social comedy, manners comedy, intrigue comedy, humors comedy, romantic comedy, sex comedy, farce, parody, and burlesque. To accomplish this goal, I include pairs of representative texts from the classical era (Aristophanes's *Lysistrata* and Plautus's *Pseudolus*) and the early modern period (Shakespeare's *A Midsummer Night's Dream* and Molière's *Tartuffe*) and three later comic texts (Byron's *Don Juan* [canto 1], Shaw's *Pygmalion*, and Amis's *Money*). I conclude with the recent adaptation of an Italian farce contemporary with *Tom Jones*, Richard Bean's astonishingly funny *One Man, Two Guvnors*, still on stage in London as I write.

Two critics lead us to see Fielding's relation to comic tradition in very productive ways. J. Paul Hunter reminds us what "a very bookish book" *Tom Jones* is. He finds in Fielding's narrative "a tendency to reach outward eclectically toward other texts, and to draw into his own text the implications of reading he imagines his readers to have previously done," a strategy that "counts on previous reading or a working knowledge of previous texts, even where there is no direct reference" ("Rethinking" 315–16). This process is as true of comic texts as the more serious ones Hunter discusses. His statement complements M. M. Bakhtin's earlier assertion about the comic novel's "classic representatives in England," including Fielding, whose texts evidence "a comic-parodic reprocessing of almost all the levels of literary language, both conversational and written, that were current at the time" ("Discourse" 301). In this course I want students to apply such ideas about Fielding's novel to their critical reading and subsequent writing. They should connect *Tom Jones* to the earlier comedies by discovering his adaptations, parodies, and rewritings of situations, characters, and languages. They should explore the subsequent texts from a similar perspective, even when the links may be less explicit or unacknowledged by their authors. Student essays, both take-home exams and a longer paper, have this comparative focus.

Inspired by the laughter of a London audience at *One Man, Two Guvnors* (based on Carlo Goldoni's *Il servitore di due padroni* [*A Servant of Two Masters*]), I make one emphasis of the course the carnivalesque or festive comedy. Bean's play, set at a seaside resort in the 1960s, performed to the accompaniment of a skiffle band, demonstrates that what we used to call the comic spirit often comes attached to material bodies, a connection that begins with the Dionysian festivals associated with Aristophanes and the Saturnalian contexts of Plautus. (Richard Lester's 1966 film *A Funny Thing Happened on the Way to the Forum* captures this spirit in the performance of the irrepressible Zero Mostel as Pseudolus.) Perhaps my students will define a new category—comedy of appetites—to identify a strand of characterization that extends from Pseudolus to Bean's Francis Henshall and Amis's John Self. While pointing out that "reveling is both unrespectable and disrespectful by nature," Harry Levin observes that theorists of the comic long paid "much less attention . . . to the ludic and festive than to the didactic and satirical" (21). My course is a serious one, but it does not ask students to search for high purpose in the comic.

As students will discover, appetites provide the comic core of most of their texts. *Tom Jones* begins with the welcoming "*Bill of Fare to the Feast*" (31 [bk. 1, ch. 1]) and at its midpoint offers "An *Apology for all Heroes who have good Stomachs*," in which the narrator wonders "whether *Ulysses* . . . in that eating Poem of the Odyssey, ever made a better Meal" than Tom with Mrs. Waters (509 [bk. 9, ch. 5]). Their feast, memorably represented in Tony Richardson's 1963 film *Tom Jones*, also offers a variation on Fielding's definition of love in book 6, where the narrator allows that even love's purer form can be "heightened and sweetened by the Assistance of amorous Desires," described as "satisfying a voracious Appetite with a certain Quantity of delicate white human Flesh" (270 [bk. 6, ch.1]). The power of sexual appetites and their comic potential for characterization extend throughout the course, whether as sexuality withheld in *Lysistrata*, first enjoyed in *Don Juan*, or ridiculously exemplified in the coupling of the Queen of the Fairies with the transformed Bottom in *A Midsummer Night's Dream*. Tom's pastoral frolic with Molly Seagrim in book 5, just after he vocalizes his devotion to Sophia, exposes the folly of that devotion in a way that recalls the narrator's mock anxiety about the likelihood that Tom's "*Insensibility*" will "*lower his Character in the Estimation of those Men of Wit and Gallantry, who approve the Heroes in most of our modern Comedies*" (171 [bk. 4, ch. 6]). That's exactly what I want students to see about comedy: it lowers.

My course includes two plays distinct from the more festive ones, *Tartuffe* and *Pygmalion*, so that students will recognize Fielding's interest in plays that represent manners and morality, dress and language in the city—high comedy, if you will. Fielding claims to find "the Manners of upper Life" dull and asserts that "lower Spheres produce the great Variety of humorous Characters"; he judges "Knowledge of upper Life . . . no very great Resource to a Writer whose Province is Comedy, or that Kind of Novels, which, like this I am writing, is of the comic Class" (741–43 [bk. 14, ch.1]). Nevertheless, the last third of *Tom Jones*, beginning with Tom's meeting Lady Bellaston at a masquerade, immerses the hero in urban folly. After financing Tom's being "genteelly drest," the lady declares that "the Fellow hath Words" when Sophia praises "an Elegance in his Discourse" (737 [bk. 13, ch. 12]). A male Galatea to a decadent female Pygmalion, Tom reverses the gender roles that George Bernard Shaw more traditionally represents through Eliza Doolittle's treatment by Henry Higgins, which causes Eliza and her father to express anxiety about her becoming a kept woman. Another nobody like Tom, Eliza learns to appear and sound like a lady, which leads to her triumphant performance at the embassy in act 3. On the other hand, after reading *Tartuffe*, students will see that Fielding's novel incorporates a version of Molière's character in Blifil, whose hypocrisy is aided and abetted by Thwackum and Square. Like the seemingly pious Tartuffe desiring Orgon's estate, his wife, and his daughter, Blifil, in a country-house version of this plot, uses his reputation for rectitude against a credulous Allworthy. Fielding even includes a passage much like the preface to *Tartuffe*, identified as "*a necessary Apology for the Author*," to defend his ridicule of Blifil's tutors: "Upon the whole, it is not Religion or Virtue, but the Want of them which is here exposed" (128–29 [bk. 3, ch. 4]).

The endings of *Tartuffe* and *Pygmalion* should also problematize for students another prominent aspect of comedy high and low: the happy ending. Orgon requires extraordinary intervention from King Louis XIV to save him from the hypocrite, while Eliza, contrary to the more familiar resolution of *My Fair Lady*, prefers to be loved by and married to Freddy, not Higgins, who has objectified her in his way as fully as Lady Bellaston did Tom. (Juxtaposing scenes from the 1938 film of *Pygmalion* and the 1964 film of *My Fair Lady* will highlight the alternate endings for this plot.) Late in *Tom Jones*, as Fielding begins the penultimate book, the narrator confronts the problem of endings head on:

> When a Comic Writer hath made his principal Characters as happy as he can; or when a Tragic Writer hath brought them to the highest Pitch of human Misery, they both conclude their Business to be done, and that their Work is come to a Period.
>
> Had we been of the Tragic Complexion, the Reader must now allow we were very nearly arrived at this Period, since it would be difficult for the Devil, or any of his Representatives on Earth, to have contrived much greater Torments for poor *Jones*, than those in which we left him in the last Chapter. . . . (875 [bk. 17, ch. 1])

Declaring it probable that Tom will be hanged and Sophia married to some odious man, Fielding laments that, as "a poor circumscribed Modern," he can only depend on "natural Means" to figure out what "may be done for poor *Jones*" (876). Lacking the mythological resources Shakespeare utilized to extricate the human lovers in *A Midsummer Night's Dream* and unwilling to write a daredevil escape like Juan's from Donna Julia's bedchamber in Byron's narrative, Fielding devotes two full books to getting Tom and Sophia married.

Both *Tom Jones* and *Tartuffe* are cited by Northrop Frye as examples among "an extraordinary number of comic stories, both in drama and fiction," that "seem to approach a potentially tragic crisis near the end," a crisis that he calls "the point of ritual death" (179). Hanging and financial ruin are not the only manifestations of this death. For instance, *A Midsummer Night's Dream* includes "[t]he most lamentable comedy and most cruel death of Pyramus and Thisby" (153), a ridiculous version of a more tragic Ovidian fable, complete with young lovers, parental tyranny, secret meetings, and double suicide, perhaps a parody of *Romeo and Juliet*. Amis adds a subtitle to *Money*, *A Suicide Note* to alert readers to the destructive and self-destructive tendencies of his Rabelaisian protagonist. Subtler versions of Frye's "ritual death" occur in other texts through allusion to tragedies, such as Tom's seeing a performance of *Hamlet* or references in *Lysistrata* to Euripides, whose plays evoke the masculine values that Athenian women turn upside down through their outrageous stratagem.

Endings that call attention to artifice and plots in which tragedy is averted should direct students to another recurrent aspect of comedy: its self-consciousness. For example, in *A Midsummer Night's Dream* Shakespeare twice includes characters watching other characters perform: Oberon and Titania observing the two pairs of lovers in the Athenian woods and Theseus and his court watching the play enacted by the rude mechanicals. Puck serves as a spokesman for such a perspective in act 3 when he asks and answers, "Shall we their fond pageant see? / Lord, what fools these mortals be!" He quickly adds, "those things do best please me / That befall prepost'rously" (162). Employing another method, the printed text of *Pygmalion* includes Shaw's extensive observations on Eliza's character and the ending the reader just completed.

Students will encounter another kind of comic self-consciousness when Pseudolus addresses the audience about his plots to trick practically everyone and when John Self in *Money* speaks to readers about their likely hatred of his crude hobbies or their own need for human reassurance and touch. Students should delight as Pseudolus compares his actions to a playwright's process and when Self befriends a writer named Martin Amis, with whom he discusses fiction. Like Fielding's self-conscious narrator, whose reader is first a guest at an ordinary and last a fellow passenger in a stagecoach, a narrator who throughout concerns himself with establishing parameters for his "new Province of Writing" (77 [bk. 2, ch. 1]), Byron's narrator establishes a familiar relationship with his reader. He foregrounds his recollections of first love, his hopes for a large readership, his use of rhyme, and his departures from epic conventions.

Several authors explicitly part ways with their readers. Byron concludes the first canto of *Don Juan* with a farewell that should register with students who have just read *Tom Jones*.

> But for the present, gentle reader, and
> Still gentler purchaser, the bard—that's I—
> Must, with permission shake you by the hand,
> And so your humble servant, and good-bye! (101)

On the page before *Money* begins, M. A. attaches a statement, supposedly written after the fact, to his suicide note: "To whom is the note addressed? To Martina, to Fielding, to Vera, to Alec, to Selina, to Barry [various characters]—to John Self? No. It is meant for you out there, the dear, the gentle" (5).

When Fielding says farewell to the reader as "my Friend," he avails himself of "this Opportunity . . . of heartily wishing thee well" and hopes he has been "an entertaining Companion" (913–14 [bk. 18, ch. 1]). These self-conscious voices, genial and mocking, friendly and skeptical, are a persistent feature of comic narratives as well as of comic drama. Speaking in character, for example, Pseudolus and Puck bid farewell even as they ask the audience to applaud.

Such self-consciousness may be one reason Horace Walpole, Fielding's contemporary, wrote this to a friend: "I have often said, and oftener think, that *this world is a comedy to those that think, a tragedy to those that feel*—a solution of why Democritus laughed and Heraclitus wept" (7: 166). Though Walpole did not like *Tom Jones*, his statement offers an appropriate binary for students to consider as they study these texts: thought and laughter. Writing about laughter, Martin C. Battestin describes Fielding's talent, as remarked by his friends, "for generating mirth that was irrepressible"; he also cites Fielding's *Craftsman* essay, which uses the persona of Democritus to vindicate laughter "as the defining faculty of humanity" ("Fielding's Anatomy" 2, 15). Since my course emphasizes laughter, it will pay more attention to the festive and carnivalesque than to the satirical and didactic.

Having taught *Tom Jones* for several decades, I cannot imagine asking students to approach this novel, especially in combination with these precursors and successors, without making comic exuberance central. Aristophanes, the first author in Fielding's invocation to Genius and his truest guide in this matter, concludes *Lysistrata* with a dance and a song that calls on Dionysus and Aphrodite. In Fielding's final chapter, Squire Western performs a similar role, singing "a merry Song, which bore some Relation to Matrimony, and the Loss of a Maidenhead" and urging Sophia to "Drink another Glass of Wine, sha't drink another Glass?" (978 [bk. 18, ch. 13]). This rustic lord of misrule continues drinking "long after that happy Hour which had surrendered the charming *Sophia* to the eager Arms of her enraptured *Jones*" (979). Despite more decorous notes in the chapter, Fielding's laughter will not be repressed. Nor, I hope, will students' joy in experiencing it.

Fielding's Critique of Governance in *Tom Jones*

Elizabeth Kraft

For much of my career, I have regularly taught *Tom Jones* as the centerpiece of The Eighteenth-Century Novel, an upper-division English literature course in our curriculum at the University of Georgia. I organize the syllabus as a chronological survey of the field, beginning invariably with Aphra Behn's *Oroonoko*. The virtue of starting with Behn rather than with, say, Daniel Defoe, is that *Oroonoko* provides (indeed demands) occasion to review the historical background of the long eighteenth century, from the civil conflicts of the 1640s through the Commonwealth, the Restoration, and the Glorious Revolution. I want the students thinking, from the beginning of the course, of the long shadow that civil war casts over a nation—because when we come to *Tom Jones*, it will be important to remember the past, envision the future, and imagine the uncertainty of living in a present that seems, by virtue of hindsight, sealed in the certainty of history. As I teach in the American South, I find it quite easy to convince my students that the wounds of civil conflict can fester unhealed for a century or more and the conflict can seem unresolved for decades upon decades after it was resolved, particularly if painful reminders of its causes and effects linger in the nightmares and dreams of the nation.

It is a fact that Charles Edward Stuart (aka Bonnie Prince Charlie) read *Tom Jones* (McLynn 520), and I share it with my students when we begin our three-week discussion of the novel. They wonder, as others have wondered before them, what Fielding's novel meant to the erstwhile heir across the water. And I encourage them to ask themselves what *Tom Jones*, which so blatantly invokes the 1745 uprising, meant to readers who longed for Charlie's return—as well as to readers who feared it. What, after all, was at stake in 1749, the year of *Tom Jones*'s publication, for the likely readership of this novel? Weren't fears calmed (and hopes dashed) at Culloden? Besides, did monarchy still matter after over twenty years of ministerial control? In the context of the times, was there consensus on the locus of leadership?

Eric Rothstein's brilliant essay "Virtues of Authority in *Tom Jones*" long ago provided me a hint on how to initiate discussion of *Tom Jones* as a novel that is, significantly, a meditation on governance. Rothstein begins his argument with a provocative reference to Richard Sennett's *Authority*:

> The narrator's control and unshakable confidence let him partake of two modes of authority, paternalism and autonomy. Richard Sennett's analysis of these two modes . . . describes the first of them, paternalism, as an offer of intimacy and protection to those who are deferent. . . . As to the second mode of authority, autonomy, Sennett discusses it partly in terms of self-possession and self-sufficiency, and of the disciplinary tool of shame. (99–100)

Rothstein proceeds through an analysis of narrative authority in Fielding's novel, demonstrating the way the narrator alternates between paternalistic authority and autonomous authority, governing the reader through a combination of nurturance and shaming.

Early in our reading of *Tom Jones*, as my students get to know both Allworthy and the narrator, I have found Rothstein's argument helpful. But because I wish to move to the question of Tom's development as an authority figure, I also want to understand what the students expect from a leader. In either the first or second class, therefore, I ask them to define *authority figure* or *leader*. Is such a person an expert? One who inspires trust? One who is in a position of power? One who can persuade? One who can punish? One who can control himself or herself as well as others? One who instills fear? (I don't articulate these options before raising the question. Here I am rhetorically reconstructing what seem, in retrospect, to be the students' thought processes.)

After we establish some general notions of leadership and governance, I turn to Sennett's *Authority* for additional organizing principles. I find particularly helpful his review of authority as an idea canvassed by thinkers from the eighteenth to the twentieth century. Sennett emphasizes Max Weber's categories of leadership—traditional authority, legal-rational authority, and charismatic authority—as well as Sigmund Freud's notion of our psychological "passion to return, to surrender" to "infantile images of strength" instead of accepting our own mature participation in the behaviors and discourses of authority (21, 23–24). It is easy to think of government leaders who have successfully defined their leadership by each of Weber's categories. The English Civil War was the beginning of a long historical process that adjudicated the advantages of Weber's first two types of national authority—to be interrupted at points by the other two. The '45 was arguably such an interruption. Bonnie Prince Charlie was charismatic, and, though he did have a purchase on tradition, by the time he invaded, that purchase had become devalued (most would say that it had been rendered invalid) by the clear establishment of another tradition. His charisma, therefore, was countered in the press by the specter of autocracy and tyranny.

It is significant that *Tom Jones* invokes these examples of authority: the traditional, which in Allworthy has stultified into neglect; the legal-rational, which too often, as in laws against poaching and highway robbery or in discourses of parliamentary power, privileges justice over mercy or focuses unproductively on partisan politics; the charismatic, which has spawned a rebellion fueled by infantile longings such as those exhibited by Partridge and Western but which also speaks to a valid desire for legitimacy. In the *Jacobite Journal,* Fielding did what he could during the actual crisis of the '45 to combat the threat to the Hanoverian succession—a succession that he, and most others of his time, supported. As John Allen Stevenson has argued, however, in *Tom Jones* Fielding is more nuanced, recognizing the "appeal" of Charles's charisma ("*Tom Jones*" 577). Perhaps this appeal partakes of a national longing of the sort Freud describes as a deep-seated hunger for return and surrender. Perhaps, as well,

Fielding's novel, unlike his journalism, eschews the specific question of who should lead the nation in its more general concern with the qualities needed to lead the nation.

I leave that possibility hanging as we turn to Tom Jones the character. At the end of the first week of discussion (which covers books 1–6), I ask my students to think of Tom as a potential leader of men who in the course of the narrative will or will not develop the skills necessary to properly govern. Since I feel that Tom in fact grows into a proper leader, I do what I can to build a case for him (always allowing—and usually receiving—student opposition, interrogation, revision). I highlight his general good character, revealed in his self-sacrifice for Black George, his behavior toward Sophia's bird, his compassion for Molly, his demeanor during Allworthy's near-fatal illness, and his joy at his adoptive father's recovery. It is true that all Tom's behavior is open to more than one interpretation, but the narrator guides us sufficiently with comments on his instinctive good nature: "for though he did not always act rightly, yet he never did otherwise without feeling and suffering for it" (173 [bk. 4, ch. 6]). Fielding's dedication announces that the didactic purpose of the novel is the inculcation of awareness that men of "Virtue and Innocence" must be wary of "Indiscretion . . . which often betrays them into the Snares that Deceit and Villainy spread for them" (7). Certainly, the novel is replete with Tom's increasing difficulty on that score. Still, as an exemplary case study of the dangers and snares that await the too trusting, too openhearted individual, his story could serve as a conduct book for leaders even today.

At this point, I reintroduce the matter of princely reception of the novel. I suggest that it might have been as conduct book that Charles Edward Stuart consulted the text. After all, Charles and Tom share a good many characteristics—love of women and drink among them. Perhaps Fielding even wrote the novel with such an audience in mind. A more likely intended regal audience would have been Frederick, prince of Wales, whose lusty Tom Jones–like youth had by 1749 given way to steady domesticity. Frederick, estranged from his father, who preferred his second son, was a favorite of the opposition party, among whom a sense of governmental change had been gratified by the fall of Walpole in 1742. Even before that year, there seems to have been a perceived need for guiding the future leader of Great Britain. In 1738, Henry St. John, Lord Bolingbroke, had penned and circulated privately *The Idea of a Patriot King*, a work that David Armitage has identified as "the last major example in the English-speaking world of that venerable humanistic genre, the mirror for a prince" (401). Many of Bolingbroke's notions are reflected in *The History of Tom Jones*.

Bolingbroke's premise is set forth early in a syllogism: "God has made us to desire happiness; he has made our happiness dependent on society; and the happiness of society dependent on good or bad government. His intention therefore was, that government should be *good*" (87). The patriot king's duty is to preserve the liberty, and therefore the happiness, of his people. To do so, however, he must cultivate virtue in himself. Of course, there are dangers: "A man of sense and virtue both will not fall into any great impropriety of character, or indecency of conduct. But he may slide or be surprized into small ones. . . . Against these, therefore, even men, who are incapable of falling into the others, must be still on their guard, and no men so much as princes" (200). In other words, to lead his people, the prince, like Tom, must learn prudence.

While I think it important to tie Fielding to discourses about governance and authority in his own time (and Bolingbroke's discussion of the patriot king is a good way of doing that), I also think that the novel's greatness, like that of any novel, lies in its ability to transcend its time by invoking categories of experience still familiar to us. Tom's journey from Paradise Hall to London can be usefully read as an examination of the crisis of authority in the modern age. Sennett invokes Hegel in asserting that "authority is renewed by periodic crises" with regard to "[c]onsciousness of lordship and bondage" between ourselves and others as well as within our individual psyches—crises that ideally lead to an "interpretation of power" based on "sympathy, sensitivity, modesty about oneself" (129).

The Hegelian model is based on a four-stage development. For Hegel, the subject in an authoritative relationship moves from stoicism to skepticism to an unhappy consciousness before emerging into the rational consciousness that represents "the final stage of freedom" necessary for proper social relationship and healthy constructs of power (Sennett 129). It would be overly schematic to suggest that Tom systematically passes through these stages, but I have found it helpful to invoke them in the discussion of his development. The Man of the Hill, for example, is the epitome of the autonomous self whose misanthropy represents a kind of stoicism rejected by Tom even before he hears the screams of a woman in distress: "I believe . . . the Abhorrence which you express for Mankind, . . . is much too general. Indeed you here fall into an Error, which, in my little Experience, I have observed to be a very common one, by taking the Character of Mankind from the worst and basest among them" (485 [bk. 8, ch. 15]).

The King of the Gypsies is more attractive to Tom, and that monarch's wisdom in adjudicating the guilt and innocence of Partridge and the Gypsy husband is exemplary, causing Tom to "sing forth the Happiness of those Subjects who live under such a Magistrate" (671 [bk. 12, ch. 12]) and causing the narrator to interrupt the narrative with a skeptical digression against the Gypsies' form of governance: "I know but of one solid Objection to absolute Monarchy. The only Defect in which excellent Constitution seems to be the Difficulty of finding any Man adequate to the Office of an absolute Monarch" (672).

The Gypsies, for whom "Shame [is] . . . the most grievous Punishment in the World" and who, in this case, find themselves ruled by a man who is adequate to the office, do not provide Tom a model of authority to embrace (673). As Martin Battestin has pointed out, the entire episode is "tinged with overtones of unreality" that mark it as an alluring but unattainable fantasy and one that it would be a mistake, given the realities of human nature, to pursue ("Tom Jones" 76). Yet it is significant that the episode includes a brief discussion about prejudice and stereotypes. When Tom applauds the king's justice, the king remarks, "Me believe you be surprize: For me suppose you have ver bad Opinion of my People; me suppose you tink us all de Tieves." Tom admits that the king is correct about the prejudice he assumes but says that experience has changed Tom's impression: "I must confess . . . I have not heard so favourable an Account of them as they seem to deserve" (671). In addition to providing a critique of absolute power (a kind of cautionary tale for Jacobite dreamers), the episode serves to highlight the sympathy, sensitivity, and modesty of Tom in his dealings with this people who are so different from him.

The road provides moments of growth and self-recognition for Tom (as well as moments of lapsed judgment and unguarded behavior). In London, however, he suffers episodes of what Sennett, after Hegel, describes as crises of "unhappy consciousness." The third week of my class on *Tom Jones* is devoted to these episodes and their resolution in the development of Tom's "rational consciousness" (Sennett 128).

I guide my students through the leadership decisions Tom makes once he enters the urban landscape. Initially he responds with physical courage, as he has been wont to do from the beginning (Sophia's bird, Molly's church degradation, the attempted rape of Mrs. Waters, etc.): he comes to Nightingale's aid in an altercation with an angry footman (702 [bk. 13, ch. 5]). He soon finds himself, however, in a morally complex situation in which his newfound wealth enables him to help Mr. Enderson, Mrs. Miller's cousin, by providing solace in the form of a fifty-pound note—an act of largesse made possible only by his submission to Lady Bellaston. On this count and others, he begins to experience excruciating episodes of internal conflict.

We glimpse moments of Tom's unhappy consciousness at many points between his entry into London and the resolution of the novel, but two paragraphs in book 13, chapter 9, crystallize the moral dilemmas with which Tom struggles in language that clearly demonstrates the conflict in his mind between lord and bondsman. Frustrated by "the Difficulties he met with in discovering *Sophia*," worried that "he had . . . disobliged her" and that she had "purposely concealed herself from him" (as Lady Bellaston reported), he is more seriously bothered by "a Difficulty . . . which it was not in the Power of his Mistress to remove, however kind her Inclination might have been." What truly troubles Tom is that "the almost inevitable Consequence" of marrying Sophia without Western's consent ("which he had no Hopes of ever obtaining") is "the exposing of her to be disinherited of all her Father's Estate" (723). The internalizing of all the strictures that define his times and his situation cause him to feel powerless in the pursuit of his desire—a worthy and honorable love.

It is not difficult to see that his state of conflicted values—a state central to so many texts of the eighteenth century that we cannot but recognize a cultural crisis—leaves Tom vulnerable to the machinations of Lady Bellaston. My students, of course, blame him for his affair with this very unsympathetic and not even particularly attractive woman. Tom "[feels] his Obligations," however. He knows that if he does not reciprocate her passion, she will "think him ungrateful; and, what is worse, he would have thought himself so" (724). This reasoning, typical of Tom, never fails to elicit a collective groan from my students. But we see here again the internalizing of standards that serve as intractable lord to the bondsman of the self's desires.

Although Tom seems trapped at times in his internal conflicts, he proves himself to be one who can bring resolution to such conflicts experienced by others, those of the young lovers Nightingale and Nancy Miller most notably. My class and I discuss that episode: Tom's eliciting Nightingale's confession of love for Nancy, his offer to mediate the situation with Nightingale's father, his strategy during that conversation (one of indirection, in which he congratulates the elder Nightingale on his son's upcoming marriage, revealing late in the conversation that he means Nancy Miller, not Miss Harris), and his good luck in finding an ally in Nightingale's uncle. Tom is a kind of diplomat in this episode. He does not please everyone (Nightingale's father is not happy with the result), but, exhibiting sympathy, sensitivity, and modesty, he manages to broker a just resolution based on both the feelings and the obligations of the parties concerned. In this episode, he earns his right to lead by virtue of his character. Later, he will discover his right to lead by virtue of his birth. To my mind, Fielding clearly indicates which is the more important. And, of course, my students, being American, tend to agree!

The end of the novel famously celebrates the marriage of Tom and Sophia, which, as Elaine McGirr has said, "models the Georgian state's domestic values" (208). The union, we are told, brings happiness to all the couple's "Relations and Friends" as well as to those who live on or near Paradise Hall: "[T]here is not a Neighbour, a Tenant, or a Servant, who doth not most gratefully bless the Day when Mr. *Jones* was married to his *Sophia*" (981–82 [bk. 18, ch. 13]). It's an interesting detail that on pledging his faith to Sophia, Tom takes her to a mirror and declares her image to be "Security . . . for my Constancy" (973 [ch. 12]). He in turn might be said to be the image in the mirror that provides security for readers, princely or otherwise, then or now, readers who seek to develop principles of leadership that will preserve the liberty and therefore ensure the happiness of those they govern.

SHAMELA, JONATHAN WILD, AND *AMELIA*

The Sham Spirit of the Age

Earla Wilputte

An Apology for the Life of Mrs. Shamela Andrews is often taught as a response to Richardson's *Pamela* or as a precursor to *Joseph Andrews*. Taught on its own, however, it lends itself well to discussions about the problems of textual interpretation, satire, and the eighteenth-century cultural propensity for sham. Hoaxes such as George Psalmanazar's posing as a native of Formosa, Mary Toft's giving birth to seventeen rabbits, and Isaac Bickerstaff's (actually Swift's) prediction of the death of John Partridge point to the audacity as well as the gullibility of the age. Shamela herself is the embodiment of the energy of the period: she is prostitute, actress, and politician combined, a con artist who manipulates her master and her mother. Students find her eminently likable even though—or perhaps because—she is not virtuous. Sham, or imposture, and society's hypocritical obsession with virtue are not vices she aims to correct but vices from which she intends to profit. A close reading of *Shamela* helps students explore Fielding's satire of the frauds and prostitutions perpetrated in three specific cultural realms—literature, politics, and religion—even as Fielding uses sham himself.

The techniques I use in the classroom to teach *Shamela* are easily applied to other eighteenth-century works, especially those that seem to require an extensive knowledge of the culture of the time. By focusing students on close reading so that they are attuned to diction and by using the authors' own prefatory-textual apparatus as signposts (either serious or ironic) for how to read their books, we can encourage students to discover the interactive element of these works. Daniel Defoe's preface to *Moll Flanders*, the textual machinery to Alexander Pope's *Dunciad*, and Eliza Haywood's *Eovaai*, not to mention Fielding's

Tragedy of Tragedies and the eclectic and bawdy Tristram in Laurence Sterne's *Tristram Shandy*, all try to control their readers' responses through precise notes and direction, and all mock bad readers. Encouraging students to slow down and notice irony, puns, wordplay, and typography helps them become aware of how they are being manipulated by the author and are complicit in the author's satire of uncareful readers.

Students enjoy the bawdiness of *Shamela* but are often confused by the material that starts the book, in which Fielding parodies the business of authorship even as he engages in that business. I invite them to pick out phrases, words, and tones from *Shamela*'s title page that indicate that the author is leading them in a particular direction. They are amused by the need to offer an "Apology" for Shamela's life and are quick to hear the vitriolic tone (emphasized by all capital letters) in the phrase "many notorious FALSHOODS and MISREPRESENTATIONS of a Book called PAMELA." I provide the barest plot summary of *Pamela; or, Virtue Rewarded*: Mr. B's attempts on the virginity of his maid, Pamela; her defense of her virtue, about which she writes home to her parents; how Mr. B., reformed by Pamela's letters, marries her, rewarding her virtue with an elevated social status. *Shamela* provides a corrected version: Pamela is not the virgin she pretends to be, but is in fact a prostitute scheming to entrap her booby master in marriage.

On the title page of *Shamela*, the phrase "Necessary to be had in all FAMILIES" leads us to a discussion of this kind of tagline affixed to books and pamphlets of religious or moral instruction, how it suggests that moral lessons can be learned from the text. *Pamela* was heralded as such a work: allegedly Pope said that it "will do more good than many volumes of sermons" (Battestin, Introduction [to *Apology*] 134). Or, as Tickletext writes to Oliver, "Happy would it be for Mankind, if all other Books were burnt . . . [*Pamela*] alone art sufficient to teach us as much Morality as we want" (*Shamela* [Journal] 155). Students find the tag comparable with modern-day advertisements for vitamin-enriched breakfast cereal and energy drinks. If *Shamela* is advertising its own moral goodness and the consumer's need to own it, shouldn't we question it as we do commercials? Fielding proposes that we question everything, because what promotes itself as true can be false, and *Shamela* is no exception. We must be active, critical readers.

The title page credits "Mr. Conny Keyber" as the author of *Shamela*, his name a combination of Colley Cibber and Conyers Middleton, real-life authors whose most recent works Fielding regarded as gambits for political favor. Cibber was a playwright, actor, and, for his politics rather than for his talent, poet laureate in Walpole's government. His autobiography, *An Apology for the Life of Colley Cibber*—his title echoed in *Shamela*'s—hides none of his vices; critics complained it was "vain, pert, and neither lucid nor elegantly written" (Fone ix). The memoir led Fielding to put Cibber on trial "for the Murder of the *English* Language" in *The Champion* (*Contributions* 319). Cibber is emblematic, then, of bad morals and bad writing both.

Middleton, a clergyman, published the *Life of Cicero*, dedicating it to Walpole's favorite, John, Lord Hervey. Fielding only slightly misquotes some of Middleton's dedication to render it the obsequious and sexually evocative "To Miss *Fanny*, &c." Hervey was named "Lord Fanny" by Pope, who was mocking him for his pretensions to poetry as well as for his effeminacy. Though students are usually hesitant to admit that they find sexual puns in the dedication, when they hear that *Fanny* and *et cetera* are slang for the female pudenda, as is *Conny* or *cunny*, they know that they are reading correctly. They point to lines like, "Madam, I must tell the World, that you have tickled up and brightned many Strokes in this Work by your Pencil," and, "I have constantly found you reading in good Books; and if ever I have drawn you upon me, I have always felt you very heavy" (150), as funny, sexual clues that Keyber's relationship with Fanny is physically intimate. His language functions as a series of Freudian slips. Students can then make the thematic connection between this suggestive language and Cibber's and Middleton's prostitution of art to curry social advancement. I don't spend any more class time on the many names and allusions in the prefatory material; however, students are given the essay option to research Cibber, Middleton, Hervey, and Walpole in more depth to ascertain the extent to which Fielding's satire of them is deserved.

Moving to the letters between Parsons Tickletext and Oliver, I ask students about the name "Tickletext." They have already encountered the verb *to tickle* in Keyber's dedication and so are aware of its sexual connotations. But how does one have a sexual relationship with a text? They soon discover sentences in which his appreciation of the novel is conflated with lustful desire for the girl. The parson mentions that in *Pamela* "the Thought is every where exactly cloathed by the Expression; and becomes its Dress as *roundly* and as close as *Pamela* her Country Habit; or *as she doth her no Habit*, when modest Beauty seeks to hide itself, by casting off the Pride of Ornament, and displays itself without any Covering" (155). He gets carried away imagining how Pamela looks naked. When he exclaims, "Oh! I feel an Emotion even while I am relating this: Methinks I see *Pamela* at this Instant, with all the Pride of Ornament cast off" (155), discussion reveals that Tickletext's "Emotion" is orgasmic, that his "tickling"meanings out of the book tickles him physically. *Pamela* performs a pornographic, not a moral, function for him. Tickletext notes that the author's imagination "has stretched out this diminutive mere Grain of Mustard-seed (a poor Girl's little, *&c.*) into a Resemblance of that Heaven, which the best of good Books has compared it to" (156). The parson's language is biblical (referencing the parable in Mark 4.30–32), but students are now familiar with *et cetera*. When they replace that term with the explicit word *vagina*, they see that stretching Pamela's "*&c.*" to resemble "Heaven" is not moral-minded at all.

I tell students that satire can be regarded as "erotic because it exposes what lies hidden, metaphorically stripping away clothes and veils," producing "a blend of pleasure and pain that satirists have often compared to tickling" (Griffin 173, 175). John Dryden in his *Discourse on Satire* states, "A witty man is tickled while he is hurt" by raillery (137). Readers of *Shamela*, then, are like Tickletext: amused by a book even as it reveals their moral shortcomings.

Parson Oliver is determined to disabuse his friend of his gullible reading and to cure him and the town of their fascination with *Pamela*, which he calls "an epidemical Phrenzy" (157). Oliver offers copies of the original letters as "an Antidote to this Poison" (194); he also voices, without satire, Fielding's theme:

> [W]orldly Honours . . . are often the Purchase of Force and Fraud, we sometimes see them in an eminent Degree possessed by Men, who are notorious for Luxury, Pride, Cruelty, Treachery, and the most abandoned Prostitution; Wretches who are ready to invent and maintain Schemes repugnant to the Interest, the Liberty, and the Happiness of Mankind, not to supply their Necessities, or even Conveniencies, but to pamper their Avarice and Ambition. (157–58)

The tone and diction here are distinct from the sexually evocative puns of the previous sections. Oliver's language is serious in its condemnation of excessive consumption, which leads to physical and moral decay. The desire for material reward distracts men from the less tangible blessings of a good conscience, the respect of good and wise men, and pleasing God. Oliver's catalog of vices—force and fraud, luxury, pride, cruelty, treachery, prostitution, avarice and ambition—emphasizes the lengths to which men will go to satisfy their desires. These vices drive society and are exercised by writers, politicians, the clergy, and everyday people.

To make the transition from the frame material to the *Shamela* story, I give two short assignments. The first is a scavenger hunt: I ask students to compile a list of malapropisms and italicized phrases from the main text and discuss their meanings and purposes. Lists always include "*Digressions*" (162), "Poluteness" (169), "Vartue" (172), and "*Pollitricks*" (190). Students notice that most of these words are mispronunciations of terms of morality or manners, indicating characters' misunderstanding of those concepts: transgressions are downplayed into digressions, politeness is polluted behavior, and politics merge with turning tricks. "Vartue," with its comical pronunciation, appears ten times in *Shamela* but is treated as an invented word, not a moral virtue. "*O what a charming Word that is, rest his Soul who first invented it*," writes Shamela (175). The fourteen italicized phrases in the text convey the perverted proverbs by which these characters live. These axiomatic sayings reflect not Christian messages of charity and virtue but selfishness. For example, "*How sweet is Revenge: Sure the Sermon Book is in the Right, in calling it the sweetest Morsel the Devil ever dropped into the Mouth of a Sinner*" (176) and "*O how foolish it is in a Woman, who hath once got the Reins into her own Hand, ever to quit them again*" (189) indicate that these "Wretches" mean only to exercise power and get even with those who cross them. There is no Christian virtue here, but the way the ideas are presented—visually, typographically, aphoristically—lends them the credibility and weight of philosophies and the appearance of good rules of behavior. Virtue, contorted into "Vartue," becomes an invented concept that one talks about over hot buttered pies until bedtime.

The second assignment is to make character sketches of Shamela, Williams, and Booby. Shamela is likable for her energy, language, and directness (with us). She loves Williams, enjoys sex, but refuses to sleep with Booby for free: "[N]othing under a regular taking into Keeping, a settled Settlement, for me, and all my Heirs, all my whole Life-time, shall do the Business—or else cross-legged, is the Word, faith, with *Sham*; and then I snapt my Fingers" (165). She knows that her "Vartue" is valuable, and she is canny enough to sell it—or at least the semblance of it. She knows how to use the system to her advantage. No sympathy is lost on Booby: he begins as a bully and turns out to be a fool. Students argue that he deserves to be deceived, because in a culture of shams and tricksters he can't detect fraud. Coveting the virginity Shamela pretends to have, he marries her. At this point students realize they have embraced the sham spirit: they applaud Shamela and mock Booby for being a dupe. They have fallen into the trap of enjoying power—they are not shammed but not shamed either. Fielding complicates matters with the character of Parson Williams.

Students do not like Williams. He is a corrupt clergyman, and he is not appreciative enough of Shamela: he loves his pipe, drink, and poaching more. He contorts meanings; he equivocates, rationalizes, and invents syllogisms to serve himself. Williams

> shewed us that the Bible doth not require too much Goodness of us, and that People very often call things Goodness that are not so. That to go to Church, and to pray, and to sing Psalms, and to honour the Clergy, and to repent, is true Religion; and 'tis not doing good to one another, for that is one of the greatest Sins we can commit, when we don't do it for the sake of Religion. . . . '[T]is not what we have to do, but what we believe, that must save us. (172)

For Fielding, Williams's insistence on faith over good works is the most reprehensible of shams because it destroys the social purpose of religion. Williams deliberately misreads the word of God so that he can live comfortably, and this misreading influences Shamela: we find that her library contains *The Whole Duty of Man* (Allestree) "with only the Duty to one's Neighbour, torn out" (181). Williams has fathered Shamela's baby but does nothing to support it. He says that if Shamela says her "Prayers as often as another, and . . . read[s] in good Books, as often as [she has] Leisure . . . that will make amends" (163). He admits that "in some Respects" he considers her his wife, "[f]or tho' the Omission of the Service was a Sin; yet, as I have told you, it was a Venial One, of which I have truly repented, as I hope you have" (171). For him, words, not actions, matter: he can be a good Christian without actually having to do anything. This is the reason that Oliver advises, "Be the reverse of *Williams*" (193).

After Shamela's marriage, Williams manipulates language to prove she needs two husbands: Booby, for the flesh, because he keeps her housed and clothed; Williams, for her spirit, because "all immaterial Substances . . . such as Love, Desire, and so forth, were guided by the Spirit" (188). His ability to recast his sexual affair with Sham as a spiritual relationship and her marriage as a tawdry "Necessity, . . . to furnish [her] with those other Conveniencies" (189) demonstrates his selfishness and corruption. His manipulation of her to get him what he wants—sex, a "Canister of Tobacco (the Saffron Cut)" (170), to prevail on Booby ("not scrupling any thing for Righteousness sake" [182]) to release him from jail—renders him criminal in students' eyes. Students do not sympathize with Booby but feel sorry for Shamela because of her inability to read Williams correctly. She is not so much outwitted as tricked by her own heart.

In her last letter, Shamela writes that Booby "is resolved to have a Book made about him and me" and that the author "can make my Husband, and me, and Parson *Williams*, to be all great People; for he *can make black white*" (192). She is reluctant to reveal her secrets but is assured: "[Y]ou mistake, Child, . . . if you apprehend any Truths are to be delivered," because "the Gentleman *who writes Lives*, never asked more than a few Names of his Customers, and that he made all the rest out of his own Head" (192). And so *Pamela* is written, "a nonsensical ridiculous Book" that imposes upon a booby society that invites delusion (193). But we are left with the question of interpretation and how to read this satire. Do we simply invert what is presented? Read white as black? "Be the reverse of *Williams*"? Understand that *Pamela* is the lie and *Shamela* is the truth—regardless of what the heroine's name warns? In *Shamela* Fielding joyfully takes advantage of the ambiguities and deceptions of eighteenth-century culture, revealing his attraction, an attraction that sometimes merges with repulsion, to language and people who are not what they seem. Like Oliver, he does not condone cruel impostures or that lethal combination of force and fraud, and yet he can delight in playful shams, tricks, puns, and disguises.

A good sham, like a good satire, should invite us to question our assumptions. Tickletext, having read "those authentick [sham] Copies" sent by Oliver, is so impatient to publish *Shamela* that he "shall not wait for the Originals" (195). He completely accepts the latest book he has read. We, on the other hand, know that *Shamela* is a sham: a counterfeit used to expose an imposture, a joke that points to the seriousness of being tricked by more calculating tricksters, and a genuine invitation to read critically.

Jonathan Wild, a Novel for all Classrooms

Manushag N. Powell

Henry Fielding's arch, sometimes atonal *Life of Mr. Jonathan Wild, the Great* (1743) is a generic puzzle, but given half a chance it is also a puzzle piece that can fit in a broad variety of teaching projects: on the novel itself, on Henry Fielding, on satire, on empire, on criminality, on economy and culture. I have also used *Wild* in units on theater and pirate tales. Fielding's is a fragmentary, heavily fictionalized account of the rise and fall of Jonathan Wild, a notorious thieftaker and mastermind of London's criminal underworld who was executed in 1725. For all its topicality, I find students can still read *Jonathan Wild* more or less without the footnotes—Fielding is only sporadically interested in the historical Wild anyway.[1] Indeed, neither generic nor cultural knowledge on its own solves the problems of *Jonathan Wild,* whose beauty is that it expands virtually every received narrative about eighteenth-century literary practices that it touches.

When I teach *Jonathan Wild*, my desire is less to have my students seek out definitive answers to the same old questions than to celebrate Fielding's achievement in writing a text with such sustained ability to upset and unsettle. In the spirit of raucous division, then, rather than offer a single approach to working this novel into the classroom, I quickly sketch out here two possibilities that pivot on different halves of the virtuous couple who receive the happy ending Jonathan Wild himself is denied, the Heartfrees: one, a performance-oriented pairing with *The Beggar's Opera*, the play Fielding invokes to contextualize Heartfree's escape from the misery that drags down most of the novel's other characters; two, a novelcentric approach that leans heavily on Mrs. Heartfree's quizzical narrative.

As this divided approach hints, *Jonathan Wild* is a text most likely to be enjoyed by a reader who can embrace multiple, even conflicting themes. Despite the rich critical activity that has grown up around the novel, some fairly fundamental questions still provoke disagreement: Is the narrative essentially comic or nihilistic? To what degree can we understand it as about Robert Walpole, who was often connected satirically to Jonathan Wild by other authors? Does the blandness of Mr. Heartfree, Wild's schoolmate and simultaneously his antithesis and quondam victim, represent the failure of sentiment or the triumph of the title character's dark powers? Is Mrs. Heartfree an insipid pre-Amelia or a self-aggrandizing liar? Such questions persist because *Jonathan Wild* is at once cohesive and fractured, its rise-and-fall arc related in a patchwork of allusions, parodies, and generic bait and switch. As Paula McDowell notes, Fielding rarely shows actual crime in *Jonathan Wild.* Instead, as in Greek drama, words dominate ("Narrative Authority" 214). Words also fail: near its conclusion, the text dissolves into fragments. The dialogue between Wild and the ordinary of Newgate descends into such extended blasphemy that both sides become long blocks of asterisks and bits of obscene words from which not even full sentences can be reconstructed (179–81). And yet, since the reader understands the main point all the same, Fielding demonstrates in his fragments that virtually no one rule of composition, probability, character, continuity, or even spelling is indispensable to the business of fiction writing.[2]

One of the rules *Jonathan Wild* briskly unsettles is the division between prose and drama. Fielding clearly has John Gay's *Beggar's Opera* (1728) on his mind, and it is enormously helpful in the classroom to preface the novel by reading the libretto of Gay's musical masterwork, which sides with the famous thief Jack Sheppard (Macheath) against thieftaker Wild (Peachum). Through Gay, students encounter the London underworld, the theatrical marketplace in which Fielding also worked, and the disreputable legends of Wild, Sheppard, and Walpole; they emerge old hands at a Newgate scene, primed to process Wild's antics and Fielding's notorious lowness. Reading Gay, they may also develop a helpful appreciation for angry satire. But shifting from Macheath to Fielding's great man is not merely telling the same story over. Instead, our attention is redirected to the Peachum figure, and the tale changes with this new emphasis: the worst source of corruption is no longer a charming rogue (Wild can persuade readily, and he is often hilarious, but he is never, even in Laetitia's eyes, charming). Wild has no Macheath-like interest in honor among thieves; his powers of subversion go instead to remaking the rules of ownership and property. Yet, like Macheath, he is a highly performative creature.

Beginning with Gay gives students the structure to appreciate the profound attachment of Fielding's *Jonathan Wild* to drama. Born as Wild was to an orange wench, this version of him has the theater, and the darkness of its profit-minded side, in his very blood. Indeed, many readers have weighed in on his thespian streak (Rawson, *Order* 261–310; Lockwood, "Fielding," esp. 27–28, 34–37; Pettit). While at points the narrator insists that Wild behaves like a prompter or puppet master (124 [bk. 3, ch. 11]), there's something showy and oratorical about his character, too; he has a gift that might well be the envy of David Garrick, "that perfect Mastery of his Temper, or rather of his Muscles, which is as necessary to form a GREAT Character as to personate it on the Stage" (59 [bk. 2, ch. 3]). Wild's story is packed with little set pieces that require few props or stunts, making them easy to exhibit casually in the classroom. Try, for example, staging his proposal to Laetitia, in which "Wild then fell on his Knees, and taking hold of her Hand, repeated a Speech which, as the Reader may easily suggest it to himself, I shall not here minutely set down": the actors need memorize no lines, for almost any set of clichés will do, if delivered with the right posture and energy (60).

Sincerity, as this exercise suggests, is utterly beside the point, for Wild wins over enemies and detractors thanks to his ability to control his emotions and sell a speech.[3] (Whether one uses Walpole or not, it is easy to transition discussion, with this point, from Wild as actor to Wild as politician, if the class is so inclined.) Wild makes thieving and thieftaking into well-managed, corporate pursuits and even seems to feel professional obligations in his guise as an actor. In Newgate Prison, he struts about in an ill-fitting costume and refuses to break character even for his own comfort after he has dethroned Roger Johnson (sometimes thought to be a stand-in for Walpole). A naturally gifted performer, the Great Man is also thoroughly committed to his craft. Wild is an evil actor run amuck in fiction; the other characters, bound by different rules of comportment, have little defense against him.

But what manner of play, we may ask ourselves, does *Jonathan Wild* stage with this hero? Alexander Pettit points to the generic ambiguity of the dramatic allusions in the novel: not only is the form of the novel conflicted by its "proximity to the drama" but also it is unclear whether the play is a comedy or tragedy (156–57). *The Beggar's Opera,* whose bitterness clearly informs Wild's ironic leveling of high and low and uses the London underworld to criticize the Walpole ministry (which was out of power in 1743 but hardly forgotten), is ambiguous in the same way. The narrator of *Jonathan Wild* denounces the ambivalent ending of *The Beggar's Opera,* in effect endorsing the conclusion of Gay's darker sequel, *Polly*. He exclaims, of Heartfree's last-minute salvation, "[L]est our Reprieve should seem to resemble that in the *Beggar's Opera*, I shall endeavour to shew . . . that this Incident, which is undoubtedly true, is at least as natural as delightful; for . . . we would rather have suffered half Mankind to be hang'd, than have saved one contrary to the strictest Rules of Writing and Probability" (152 [bk. 4, ch. 6]). My students find this moment funny but also unsettling, for while they are loath to take Fielding's denunciation of Gay seriously, they balk at what they perceive as a Marty Stu, the incredibly good magistrate who saves Heartfree and in so doing staves off Gay's open pessimism.[4]

My own suggestion is that the narrator's declared preference to murder half of humanity rather than violate the unities is Fielding's hint that setting the probable—what we might call realistic—over morality or pleasure may have undesirable consequences. *Wild*'s characters receive their sudden reversals with less aplomb than the cheerful dancers at the close of Gay's ballad opera. Heartfree's last-minute reprieve is so unexpected that a surgeon is called to bleed all the principal characters, and the narrator worries that his reader "may almost want the Surgeon's Assistance also" to cope with this shocking turn (152 [bk. 4, ch. 8]). The dual forces speeding the narrative to a happy conclusion, the inexhaustible goodness of the magistrate and the return of the ultrachaste Mrs. Heartfree, barely stay within the bounds of the possible. It is by uniting the fantastic potentialities from different generic lines that *Jonathan Wild* builds its momentum to a satisfying ending.

Just as the return of Mrs. Heartfree triggers a rejection of *The Beggar's Opera* and, with it, of the dramatic forms of the Jonathan Wild legend, her adventures open up a second set of generic traditions for scrutiny.[5] *Jonathan Wild* troubles the link from epic to modern prose when it locates Wild's initial corruption in his schoolboy's interest in Caesar and Alexander, a corruption that denies neoclassicism's utility as a sure basis for order. Yet *Wild* makes ample room for representation of the romance, a genre built with the same heroic ideals as the epic, though arguably through a lower, more populist form. Mrs. Heartfree's narrative is often configured as Fielding's acerbic send-up of the credulous readers of travelogues, but it is better understood as a modern romance, a feminocentric travel tale of kidnapping and voyages, similar to the fare created by Jane Barker, Penelope Aubin, or Eliza Haywood. In a novel studies syllabus, *Wild* works better if it is not opposed to *Pamela* but set instead alongside titles such as Barker's *Exilius* (1714), Aubin's *The Noble Slaves* (1722), or Haywood's *Philidore and Placentia* (1727) (all of which also teach surprisingly well).[6]

Some readers may feel uncomfortable even with the classification of *Jonathan Wild* as a novel. Fielding prestidigitates, neither copying a pattern nor making something new out of whole cloth but filching from other genres for his patchwork. Jesse Molesworth takes the entire text to be an elaborate confidence game, noting that the narrator cheerfully admits to practicing literary theft (156), and Jenny Davidson calls Fielding's approach in *Jonathan Wild* a "tactical pillaging" of almost every popular genre available: "history, epic, biography, the novel, and the picaresque" (66). We ought to recognize *Jonathan Wild* as an iconic example of the dynamism of a time before novelists felt compelled to "reclothe their baggy monsters in uniforms" (Hunter, "Serious Reflections" 279). To demonstrate that dynamism, I suggest including a heroine in an adventure tale with Wild: this pairing unlocks the patterns that undergird the narrative of Mrs. Heartfree, who is the element that most often keeps readers from embracing Fielding's generic pastiche.

Like many romances, *Jonathan Wild* delights in men's unsuccessful attempts to rape powerful women. Wild's passion for the chaste Laetitia is "extremely violent": during their courtship, we are told, the lady is "more indebted to her own Strength for the Preservation of her Virtue" than to Wild's respect (33 [bk. 1, ch. 9]).[7] When Wild turns his attention to the fair Mrs. Heartfree, taking advantage of her husband's imprisonment to trick her, they are caught in a tempest at sea, but Wild resolves to risk everything rather than abandon his plans for ravishment. Less Amazonian than Laetitia, Mrs. Heartfree calls for help, and the captain comes to her assistance, asking if Wild has "no more Christianity in him than to ravish a Woman in a Storm!" (79 [bk. 2, ch. 10]).[8] Soon their ship is taken by a French privateer, and fortunately Mrs. Heartfree understands French "perfectly well" (80 [bk. 2, ch. 10]), showing a linguistic power that even Wild (whose verbal skills do not exceed English) lacks, and at this point the third-person narrative breaks off. When it resumes, Mrs. Heartfree is in command.

As both narrators and genres shift through *Jonathan Wild*, it becomes clear that as much as society may be desperate for order, the novel, the form that represents society, thrives on chaos. Mrs. Heartfree, a romance heroine, meets no man who can long resist her, yet back in England she suffers interruptions from various male parties who do not give her the awestruck respect due such a heroine. Students may dismiss Mrs. Heartfree as conceited or worse, because her extensive catalog of violent suitors drives most of her narrative's action. I point out to them, however, that rejecting Mrs. Heartfree's adventures as mere lies means siding with Wild and therefore choosing Newgate over romance instead of seeing how both are presided over by the too benevolent magistrate.

Readers are understandably made uneasy by the long series of sexual assaults she suffers, and both Susan Staves and Simon Dickie ("Fielding's Rape Jokes") rightly take Fielding to task for his weakness for rape humor in her tale. But calling this trope the realism of misogyny may blind us to what Fielding is getting at, because in romance, ravishment is both ubiquitous in the attempt and inevitably fruitless. My contention is not that the impotence of the rapist must lessen our suspense for Mrs. Heartfree or that rape was not then, as it continues to be, a terrible crime but rather that the rhetorical conventions Mrs. Heartfree invokes make her trials obligatory. I do not question the feminist problem with rape humor but note that a specific literary tradition is complicit here: Mrs. Heartfree is not Sophia or Amelia; her narrative is not presented as realistic in either the psychological or formal sense. Fielding is wrong to use attempted rape as a totem for attractiveness and virtue, but it is hardly strange for him to do so when writing an inset romance.

Foregrounding Mrs. Heartfree's narrative in class leads to an appreciation of the value of convention, and even clichés, for a strong, original author. The French privateer captain develops a violent passion but uses "softer Methods" to persuade Mrs. Heartfree (155 [bk. 4, ch. 7]). When an English man-of-war takes the privateer, though, the next captain is a lout, "much rougher and less gallant than the *Frenchman* had been" (156). It requires little nudging for students to see the national satire here. What they may not know is that the plot in which a virtuous woman is rescued from respectful pirates only to be threatened by a lawful sea captain is common (satirical pirating, I like to call it, because the prime function of the pirate here is to be the lesser of two evils).

The plot is common, but Mrs. Heartfree's response makes the episode special: a Richardsonian heroine avoids rape by fainting and Aubin's romance heroines start stabbing and setting fires, but Mrs. Heartfree outthinks her assailant. She asks for a drink and goes bumper for bumper with the captain, "as fast as possible," until he is totally incapacitated. She remarks that at any other time she would have been soused, "but at the present [the drinking] did not affect me" (158). (My students find her miraculous tolerance of alcohol unbelievable.) Mrs. Heartfree brilliantly uses language to deceive and delay Count La Ruse, protecting the figurative jewel of her chastity while also recovering her actual family jewels. Eventually the ship is blown by storm to the coast of Africa, where she encounters monsters, further rudeness, and a naked hairy hermit.[9] Her ingenuity in defending herself is a sign of her canny merchant-class resourcefulness and of her maturity—she is older than the rest of Fielding's heroines. Like a female Crusoe, she begins to interpret her successive, and successful, adventures as marks of God's special favor and desire for her prosperity. Her spirits are assisted by, as she says, "the Repossession of our Jewels by an Accident, so strongly savouring of the Disposition of Providence in my Favour" (168 [bk. 4, ch. 10]). From this point, her struggle to preserve her chastity falls less into doubt than her ability to dictate the terms of her narration.

The fair Mrs. Heartfree's repetition of the hermit's "many . . . Compliments" is cut off by a "horrid Uproar," for Wild has just "caught *Fireblood* in the Arms of his lovely *Laetitia*" (169–70), a deliberate juxtaposition of chastity and unchastity. Mrs. Heartfree resumes, recalling that she "was beginning to repeat some of the Compliments made me," but the benevolent Justice, evidently willing to trade gallantry for the sake of expediency, insists, "Just as you had finished them" (172 [ch. 12]). Affronted, she continues. Finally she makes her way to a settlement where an African "Mayor" offers her a rich gift to make love to him, then presents her "with a very rich Jewel" when she turns him down. She finds a passage back home and is courted by the latest sea captain, but this time with great civility: he "behaved in a manner very pleasing to me, regarding my Sex only so far as to pay me a Deference, which is very agreeable to us all." This is a deference that she has not received from the audience currently around her (175).

To conclude, Mrs. Heartfree is not a liar but an author who understands that a narrative of virtue and respect for women may be easier to find by accessing genres outside satire. The moral tale going on around her, a rejoinder against false greatness and an affirmation of the goodness of people who love virtue, is all very well and worthy, but it is not compatible with the part of her that desires to write her story as a heroine. Her narrative is tonally jarring. In students it rouses suspicion but also attention: its improbability, in the end, is no more a marker of defect than her spouse's deeply improbable last-minute legal reprieve, which was used to reject but also acknowledge the dramatic ancestry of *Jonathan Wild* (just as Mrs. Heartfree's narrative rejects but also acknowledges the ambiguous place of romance).

My students tend to read in favor of narrative patterns that adhere to formal realism, often without realizing that they have been trained to do so. I return to, and try to illustrate for them, J. M. S. Tompkins's observation that "[i]t is always important to remember that the realism of detail [is] only intermittently interesting to eighteenth-century writers; they will consult it for a space and then discard it, without any scruples, in favour of other qualities" (358–59). *Jonathan Wild* is interested in "the realism of detail" mainly to demonstrate its mendacity. The ability of Wild to fend off the law depends on alibis, on how well he can persuade others to accept his performances and fictions as truth. Despite his thespian gifts and many false witnesses, Mrs. Heartfree and her jewels carry the day; the magistrate is convinced more by them than by her attacker's lies.

With its intentionally jagged mix of urban, Newgate settings, seafaring, honor, and epic, *Jonathan Wild* may, in the end, be more at home among the travel yarns and hybrid novel-romances dominant in the 1720s than among the interiorized character studies we tend to prize from the 1740s. The text makes the point that, when it comes to narrative value, facts and probability are in the province of the narrator. The novel's ultimate strength is in being about many things while committing to none: Wild's values are deeply vulgar, and although Fielding sees the usefulness of what Wild rejects (i.e., the Heartfrees and their extrageneric improbabilities), he also enjoys Wild's antics. *Jonathan Wild* is greater than the vantage point of any of its characters, none of whom quite understand the others. The reader should strive to stand above them all.

NOTES

[1] In a moment always worth a good discussion, Fielding uses the preface to the *Miscellanies* to explain defensively, "[M]y Narrative is rather of such Actions which [Wild] might have performed, or would, or should have performed, than what he really did" (9).

[2] *Jonathan Wild*, composed in 1740 or 1742, may be Fielding at his most experimental (and hence most himself). It also presents a nexus of many facets of his career that were external to the novel: his abiding interest in the law (he was called to the bar in 1740), his work as a periodicalist (there's a strong affiliation between *Jonathan Wild* and Fielding's *Champion*), and his work as a dramatist. On the *Champion*, which is essential to decoding the "Of Hats" chapter, see Goldgar. Both the novel and the journal attack Alexander the Great and connect him to the historical Wild, and there are Wildean echoes in Fielding's Court of Censorial Enquiry, a critical device that runs throughout his periodicals.

[3] This point is not undermined later when the narrator admits he's been cleaning up and elevating Wild's language (108–09 [bk. 3, ch. 6]): it's not the words that win over his hearers but Wild's performance of them.

[4] John Bender argues that the narrator is pushing for some separation, that the irony of Wild is more contained, more lamented than in Gay (*Imagining* 151–53).

[5] Critics are deeply divided on how we should read Mrs. Heartfree. Earla Wilputte favors Mrs. Heartfree's narrative by arguing that while the male characters of the text are all good or bad, Mrs. Heartfree is human: mostly good, but fallible, a "hybrid heroine" ("Autodiegetic Power" 230). In contrast, for Michael McKeon, Fielding wrestles with how to deliver truth through narrative in *Jonathan Wild*, rejecting both "old, romancing histories" that mislabel evil as heroic and newer "naive empiricism" (383). Missing or rejecting the possibility of feminocentric romance, McKeon finds Mrs. Heartfree a spectacularly unreliable narrator, more akin to Wild than her husband is; Heartfree becomes the dupe of both Wild and Mrs. Heartfree (which somewhat complicates his flatly idealized character [391]).

[6] *Romance* is a slippery term, but here I employ it in a sense following Barbara Fuchs's argument that romance, readily recognizable but hard to define, is essentially more a mode than a text, one best understood "as a literary strategy that appears in a variety of genres" and written traditions, "one of many voices within the novel" (10).

[7] In a very *Shamela*-like moment, she scratches his face liberally until he retreats, at which point "[s]he then proceeded to talk of her Virtue, which Wild bid her carry to the Devil" (34).

[8] Ian Watt's amused recollection of this moment constitutes the only mention of *Jonathan Wild* in his *Rise of the Novel* (284).

[9] Fielding's revised version of *Jonathan Wild* deleted chapter nine of book 4, which he called "a Burlesque on the extravagant Accounts of Travellers" (11 [preface]). Subsequent reprintings in the eighteenth century followed suit, although modern editions usually reinstate it. The chapter relates the shipwrecked crew's encounter with fabulous monsters. Its deletion, instead of increasing the probability of the entire (but still highly improbable) book 4 of *Jonathan Wild*, effectively strengthens the coherence of Mrs. Heartfree's romance.

Destined for Greatness: Hero Worship and *Jonathan Wild*

Carl Fisher

The traditional hero motif changed significantly in the eighteenth century, driven by dynamic social conditions, new narrative forms, and a burgeoning commercial market. The main characters of novels, from Daniel Defoe to Samuel Richardson, became more modest. There were adventures, both physical and spiritual, but not the epic exploits of warriors and rulers that would once have placed a figure in histories or romances. Fielding's *Jonathan Wild*, both the novel and the character, wrestles with the heroic concepts operative in the period. Fielding brings both levity and gravity to what, on the surface, might seem like a standard criminal biography or a historical revisionist romp.

Throughout the novel, Fielding plays with audience expectation in ways that allow the narrative to be read as a paean to greatness, an attack on popular subculture, a serious satire on a specific political moment, or a broader critique of human morality. The multiplicity of potential interpretations is what makes *Jonathan Wild* so teachable. Students can be guided through traditional heroic tropes, sensitized to the instability of the narrative tone, and provided context to see how the novel is deeply embedded in eighteenth-century contexts but extremely modern in the treatment of criminality, power relations, celebrity culture, and hero worship.

The hero concept is as old as epic narrative, from Gilgamesh to the Greek and Roman figures Fielding knew well. Heroes, ideally, stand out from the crowd, are spectacular leaders, perform daring feats, and have the public good as a primary goal. Whether warrior-kings or modern rulers, they sometimes seem superhuman, almost immortal. But the world is not governed by the same rules as mythology, and Fielding uses sustained irony, an eighteenth-century staple, to reveal corruption and suggest the need for reform. He also uses it as an implicit criticism of contemporary hero characters, such as Robinson Crusoe or Pamela, whom he sees as inane or insipid. Other satiric works by Fielding, such as his plays or *Shamela*, which a student would probably not know but which an instructor could explain, provide useful background in understanding the heroic/mock-heroic axis of the novel.

This is not to say that Fielding's novel is one or the other exclusively. Fielding certainly knew the heroic archetype and believed in authority and order, but he also imagined literature as an opportunity to discipline both powerful figures and average people who were immoral or hypocritical. Drama and narrative could be used to reveal truths to audiences that might be hidden or not immediately obvious. In the classroom, then, Fielding's protagonist can be effectively situated in some of the best-known conceptions of the heroic and then complicated through specific satiric aspects. This parallax vision provides a fuller reading of the novel and the contextualization that most students need.

Jonathan Wild the Great: The Heroic Archetype and Continuum

Fielding's heroic can be traced to classical models but should also be situated in a history of ideas that foregrounds human agency, from Niccolò Machiavelli to Thomas Carlyle. Positioning the novel this way gets students to reflect on modern concepts of the individual and the hero, on our leaders and our idols.

Machiavelli reconceived the classical heroic model, which often depended on divinity and adulation. Heroic power, in Machiavelli's view, required political ruthlessness, practical intelligence, and psychological insight. Reading Wild as a Machiavellian hero makes sense because Wild's defining principle is that it is better "to be feared than to be loved" (Machiavelli, *Prince* 58). Wild rules by threats and intimidation, with "a bold Heart, a thundering Voice, and a steddy Countenance" (54 [bk. 2, ch. 2]). All leaders need followers or "Tools," as the narrator says (104 [bk. 3, ch. 5]), and by the third book, far into his progression, "Wild had now brought his Gang to great Regularity: He was obeyed and feared by them all" (107 [ch. 6]). As Wild consolidates his power and fights off rebellion, ". . . he flattered himself that Fear would keep them in Order . . ." (134 [ch. 14]). In rulership, for Machiavelli, the end justifies the means, and Wild will use any means to achieve his desires. His willingness to sacrifice others for his own benefit follows Machiavelli's idea of how to maintain control in a contingent world. However, being brought down by one of his inner circle (Fireblood) shows that Wild has overestimated his Machiavellian skills.[1]

Equally relevant to *Jonathan Wild* is Machiavelli's satiric play *The Mandragola*, which Fielding probably knew (see Keymer, "Fielding's Machiavellian Moment" 85); it shows what can happen when manipulative people are too clever or overconfident. The main character, Callimaco, wants to sleep with Lucrezia, a young woman married to an older man. Callimaco intrigues to fool the husband, an intricate plot involving a mandrake plant, and ultimately does get his wish. Lineaments of this plot can be found in Wild's intense pursuit of Mrs. Heartfree. Wild sees sexual conquest as a primary force, although it is hard to know whether his desire for the wife or the opportunity to humiliate the husband provides greater motivation.

Another useful extratextual source for analyzing Wild is Thomas Hobbes's civil society in *Leviathan*. Hobbes argues that in the state of nature, individual desire holds sway and that everyone is at odds with everyone else, what he calls "a warre, as is of every man, against every man." To avoid constantly being a prey to others, human beings agree to a social contract that accepts behavioral limitations in return for security. Hobbes writes that without this contract we would live in "continuall feare, and danger of violent death" and that under these conditions human life would be "solitary, poore, nasty, brutish, and short" (70). Wild's world sounds rather close to Hobbes's state of nature, and the contrast between an abstracted nature and a developed civilization is stark.

Hobbes's concept of the heroic also tells us something about the mid-eighteenth-century world Fielding describes. For Hobbes, reason fights with nature, or with physical appetite, for power and control and allows for adaptation. The hero must behave well; to do so earns respect and brings honor. A hero may have gained his high social place from intrinsic causes—strength or wit—but he keeps it by deserving it. Respect is the source of true power. Wild lusts for power but accrues no respect. He learns many of his behaviors not from experience but through the exemplary heroes featured in tales of his schoolboy days, what Claude Rawson calls "tyrant thugs."[2]

Fielding presents Wild as mechanically driven. Wild cannot help behaving as he does: he learned many of his negative behaviors from the stories he read and seems to have gained none of positive qualities of the heroic, including the ability to curb his urges. But there is nuance here, which can be explored in a classroom. Wild is not simply a cardboard villain, easy to despise. Students should be asked to analyze him in different ways. Why does Fielding show how natural and cultural forces play out in Wild's character? To what extent does Wild represent the amoral or antiheroic, and to what extent does he reflect a society in which, to gain wealth or status, the end justifies the means? Viewing Wild through this lens allows an interrogation of what ends are desirable in a society, and students will recognize how the novel speaks to our present—for example, put *Jonathan Wild* in juxtaposition with Martin Scorsese's *The Wolf of Wall Street*.

Most significant is that Wild uses reason instrumentally to take advantage of others, and, immune to shame, guilt, or regret, he enjoys that game. Fielding evokes his scheming toward greatness when he describes how Wild sees his world: "Mankind are first properly to be considered under two grand Divisions, those that use their Hands, and those who employ Hands" (47 [bk. 1, ch. 14]). His logic continues on a slippery slope until he convinces himself that he alone has greatness, that he should employ the hands of others to do his bidding, and that he will "convert those Laws which are made for the Benefit and Protection of Society, to [his] single Use" (48). His thinking process is worth a close reading in the classroom and can lead to fruitful discussion of the relation between the ego and social or communal values, between selfish desire and the greatest good. These are not merely Enlightenment brain twisters but concepts that have been played out by each successive generation. Wild wants to be autocratic in a dialectical world. His self-interest is very human, but, if taken to an extreme, it is socially dangerous.

Fielding's self-serving hero imagines society as designed for his own use and pleasure. He does not care about consequences or any dishonor should his manipulations be revealed. To Wild, truth is fungible, and reality should bend to him. He cares about what other people think only insofar as it will allow him to succeed. Fielding would have known Machiavelli and Hobbes well, but it is surprising how forward-looking his sense of the hero was. A more modern view of the hero, and a productive comparison of it with Fielding's, can be found in the writing of Carlyle almost a century later. In *Sartor Resartus* (1833), Carlyle criticizes civil society as a miasma of negativity, corruption, and self-indulgence. In *On Heroes, Hero Worship, and the Heroic in History* (1840), he examines heroes through history, from the pagan to the Christian, and concludes that we willingly subordinate ourselves to "Kings" and "Commanders," because it is in our best interest, and heroes ". . . may be reckoned the most important of Great Men" (169). His philosophical system has a Hegelian bent, to which he gives a spiritual twist. He believes heroes are great when they manage the will of the people through their personal agency to maintain social order. Societies in which heroes do not exist, or do not rise to the occasion, are prone to strife. His greatest opprobrium is reserved for heroes who misuse the will of others, who will stop at nothing to achieve inappropriate goals. He highlights Napoleon as a hero whose ambition destroyed many and whose conclusion in exile is "almost tragical to consider. . . . Having once parted with Reality, he tumbles helpless in Vacuity . . . our last Great Man!" (208).

Situating Fielding's novel on the heroic continuum helps students read Jonathan Wild. How, they could be asked, does society reconcile the need for heroes with the realities of the heroes' lives? Many recent news stories about famous figures illustrate the difference between public faces and private facts, between what is on the surface and what lies beneath it. And, to extend the discussion, how does the fall of a hero, or the revelation of facts different from what we expect, keep us from falling into complete cynicism or distrust? How, in a fictional landscape, does the hero provide us with a way to test our own values?

Fielding's narrator assiduously frames Wild in the mold of Alexander and Caesar, and Wild, caught up in ideas of power and authority, sees himself in that light. Yet he has more in common with Tony Soprano or Walter White than with warriors or royalty. In modern parlance, read realistically, he would be considered a sociopath, having just enough humanity to keep him interesting but too self-interested to sustain any personal relationship.

Wild's story follows the traditional arc of the hero, a history from ancestry through birth, upbringing, development, and adulthood, and ultimately to death. In this arc are some natural qualities and some nurtured and developed. That Wild acts with passion and the absolute certainty of his greatness, much to the detriment of others and always in conflict with anything good or productive in society, guides a reader to see how greatness can function pejoratively. There might be true heroes for Fielding, but Wild is not one of them.

The Mock-Heroic: Jonathan Wild *and the Satiric Spectrum*

When Fielding announces, early in the novel, that ". . . Greatness consists in bringing all Manner of Mischief on Mankind . . ." (9 [bk. 1, ch. 1]), he destabilizes the hero concept and reduces Wild to a mock-heroic figure. Wild idealizes the heroes of history, but Fielding makes sure, using many elements of the satiric toolbox, that it is impossible to read him as a role model. In fact, the satiric intensity can seem heavy-handed and repetitive to the point that it threatens the fabric of the work. The novel's satiric density, however, is a great opportunity to teach critical thinking skills. Students recognize in *Jonathan Wild* many of the same rhetorical moves they see on *The Daily Show* or *Saturday Night Live*'s "Weekend Update." The satire is essentially the same. When Fielding uses the trope of the puppet show in describing powerful figures who pull the strings but try to hide their true intentions—performing "Pollitricks" (67 [bk. 2, ch. 5]), "Where it is the Master of the Show who dances and moves everything" (124 [bk. 3, ch. 11])—his criticism of the two-faced politician rings true for anyone who has seen a modern political scandal unfold or knows the axiom that often it is not the crime but the cover-up that snares a politician.

Students understand satiric irony, the voice that indicates that things are not what they seem on the surface. Everything human, especially behavioral norms and political structures, is subject to caricature. Caricature portrays leaders as human beings and not idols, prey to error and desire, neither infallible nor unassailable. Leaders like Wild, especially politicians, too often betray the public trust. That the correlation of power and priggery is obvious for Fielding should make his readers suspicious—and, hopefully, "sagacious."

Satirists use an arsenal of weapons to attack what they perceive to be dangerous or disruptive in society. They write satire to shine a light, so that readers can see what they might not see on their own, in part because of a public tendency to want to trust leaders, in part because it is not in the interest of the leaders to be transparent. Satire lays them bare, shows the emperor without clothes, so to speak. Satire complicates the public viewpoint and encourages critical analysis.

In *Wild*, Fielding attacks selfishness, greed, vanity, and hypocrisy in the tradition of Menippean satire, which makes the text a medley (the reason it seems at times disjointed), sprinkled with classical and modern quotations, proverbs (82–86 [bk. 2, ch. 12]), maxims (191–92 [bk. 4, ch. 16]), monologues, and theatrical dialogues (112–18 [bk. 3, ch. 80], 178–84 [bk. 4, ch. 14]). Fielding also mines the broad mock-heroic genre—a comic tradition from Lucian to Rabelais to Cervantes—as well as the mock-epic, for which he had many contemporary verse examples, from John Dryden's *Absalom and Achitophel* to Alexander Pope's *Dunciad*, works he knew well. Fielding criticizes and parodies virtually every form of heroism, including the newly rising sentimental hero.

The first chapter places the life of Wild in the context of both heroic and criminal biographies and points out the dual purpose of entertaining and instructing. Fielding's narrator straightforwardly announces that in hero narratives we have "lively Examples of whatever is amiable or detestable, worthy of Admiration or Abhorrence, and are consequently taught in a Manner infinitely more effectual than by Precept, what we are eagerly to imitate or carefully to avoid" (7). The narrator claims that judgment can be complicated because many heroes are "of the mixt Kind; neither totally good nor bad" (8). It is hard to know whether Wild has the sharpness of a Shakespearean villain or the dullness of a Hobbesian mechanistic man. Both are dangerous but not equally engaging. It is the writer's responsibility to narrate honestly, the audience's to be attentive to nuance. Fielding knows the pleasure of the text as entertainment but also, aware that writing can be manipulative and that irony makes a text open to both interpretation and misreading, understands the need to read critically. This call for insight can encourage students to read closely.

Throughout *Jonathan Wild*, students recognize satire but sometimes need guidance in its structures and contexts. Instructors should discuss how Fielding's satiric thrusts direct the reader—for example, when Fielding wonders, implicitly if not explicitly, as Horace does in his satires, why there is no middle ground, no golden mean. Or when he highlights the antithetical relation between greatness and goodness, where the great is ironically apotheosized while the good is ridiculed for small-minded sentimentality. He redefines these terms for his audience. Greatness is not heroic, not admirable, but at best a chimera for the self-inflated, at worst a misuse of public power and will. The mask of goodness is very different from real goodness, and unreflective goodness (e.g., that of Heartfree) is not only easily victimized but also insipid, almost as inhuman and lacking in character as greatness. The thinking process for a hero, in Wild's world, must differ from "that pitiful Order of Mortals, who are in Contempt called 'Good-natured' " (50 [bk. 2, ch. 1]).

Fielding's theatrical background, mostly in comedies, influences the novel's characterization, but it is important to note that his dramatic career was closer to the satiric conventions of Restoration comedy than to the emergent world of sentimental comedy. One of the most popular contemporary playwrights until the Licensing Act of 1737, Fielding had translated Aristophanes, adapted Roman comedies, and was well known for both his farces (e.g., *Tom Thumb*) and his scathing political commentaries (e.g., *Pasquin*). He retained, in both storytelling and dialogue construction, the forms of drama when he focused on fiction. The soliloquies that Wild performs, for example, are critical indicators of his character. In book 2, chapter 4, after a fruitless evening of seeking the count, Wild retires to a night cellar with punch and quietly speaks of his hopes and dreams—and ultimately explains his rationale for being what he is. He starts with the rhetorical question, "How vain is human Greatness!," expresses concern about contingency and the existential solitude of thievery, and concludes that it is the "inward glory" of making others miserable that drives the great man (62). This soliloquy sounds like something out of Aristophanes, such as Kinesias's parody of a tragic monologue in *Lysistrata*, full of self-pity and despair for his inability to fulfill a nefarious scheme. It shows the ethical slippery slope that Wild travels, licking his wounds while simultaneously plotting his next move.

The contrast to Wild's soliloquy is Heartfree's when all seems lost (94–97 [bk. 3, ch. 2]). Heartfree is undoubtedly mocked as much as Wild, but a close reading of his soliloquy shows an unselfish man primarily concerned with the evils of the world and the future of his family. He too starts with a rhetorical question: "What shall I do? Shall I abandon myself to a dispirited Despair, or fly in the Face of the Almighty!" (95). He comes to a conclusion very different from that of Wild's, espousing a philosophy that sounds almost like the Horatian golden mean, that it is the middle road and the simple pleasures that lead to happiness. But instead of idealizing Heartfree, Fielding's chapter heading notes that this soliloquy is "without a Syllable of Greatness," and the narrator characterizes Heartfree's speech as "base" and "low" (94). Heartfree has not passion but enthusiasm, and this quality marks his thinking as extreme and a poor basis for reality. This soliloquy may be more reflective and generous than Wild's, but it lacks wisdom and insight.

Fielding's use of contrast for satiric effect, and to highlight extremes, was a popular rhetorical style—after all, Fielding is writing in the wake of Dryden, Pope, and Jonathan Swift, among others. One of the best eighteenth-century comparative examples for extreme irony is Voltaire's *Candide* (1759). Published less than two decades after *Jonathan Wild*, it has a good hero easily victimized by the great. Candide's misadventures demonstrate for readers the horrors of a world in which vanity, vainglory, corruption, and greed are the driving forces. Anyone who doesn't recognize these underpinnings and accepts surface reality, the satire shouts, is easily manipulated. But even when these underpinnings are recognized, victimization seems the way of the world and justice is a rare commodity.

The heroic final scene of justice, Wild's "Consummation" at the gallows (186–89 [bk. 4, ch. 15]), concentrates irony and reveals some of Fielding's preoccupations. The execution scenario is one Fielding had written about before and one that he would come back to in later journalism and as a judge, because in eighteenth-century London executions represented the axis of order and disorder, private and public, crime and punishment. (An instructor might use Hogarth's *Idleness and Industry* as a visual referent, esp. plate 11, *The Idle 'Prentice Executed at Tyburn*.) The mob scene that the narrator describes can be read in different ways, just as the eighteenth-century mob meant different things depending on the perspective of the viewer. Were the crowds applauding justice? Were they identifying with the criminals? Was an execution carnivalesque, a social safety valve? Was it a moment of potential rebellion in which the people, unleashed, could create havoc? The world, Fielding imagines, is less stable than it should be, and crime and power form an unholy alliance that the public permits unless it is taught to see otherwise.

One of the most unsettling aspects of *Jonathan Wild* is this ending. Wild's last-minute picking of a pocket is little different from what his ancestor Longfinger did, who stole from individuals and whose key ally, Hubert de Burgh, "Doth the Pocket of the Nation fang" (11 [bk. 1, ch. 2]). If nothing can truly be done to change our natures, if the apple never falls far from the tree, what is the point of setting examples?

But if reading histories and heroic narrative provides a teachable moment, "in a Manner infinitely more effectual than by Precept, what we are eagerly to imitate or carefully to avoid" (7 [bk. 1, ch. 1]), then satire can have a salutary or prophylactic effect. Satire strips away the veneer of greatness, shows the pettiness of power as well as the consequences of its misuse. It is the audience who benefits from this critical insight. Ultimately the novel works as an antidote to hero worship, in an age in which the idea of the hero was increasingly contested. It is not enough for us to avoid being Wild; it is equally important that we recognize and unveil the many Wilds who populate the world, whether they are public figures or private citizens.

Finding the Golden Mean in Wild's Extremes

Wild's final fall into justice is not a validation, underlining how justice can function only when facts and evidence are revealed. Similarly, what Hugh Amory calls Heartfree's "heroic passivity" is in no way validated by "the novel's farcically happy ending" (qtd. in Fielding, *Miscellanies: Volume Three* 213 ["Textual Introduction"]). Heroes need to be shown in a clear light and through the fullness of time to be judged properly. For Fielding, the ending is the beginning for readers to recognize the thoroughgoing irony and draw an appropriate message. As he notes about both puppet shows and romances, viewers and readers can be duped only when they "agree to be deceived" (125 [bk. 3, ch. 11]). The critique of power—whether that power is exercised by the politician pulling strings or by the author manipulating opinion—implicates the audience as well.

Fielding uses satire to reveal character, and the comic narrative drives readers to see their own world in new ways, to become aware of the realities of unchecked power. *Jonathan Wild* is a critical stopping point on a tour of Fielding. After it, he becomes identified more for the milder, moral humor of *Joseph Andrews* and *Tom Jones*, although the darker elements of *Amelia* have their seeds in *Wild*, and the satirized great man turns into a protogothic figure, where the veneer of society and hierarchy provide cover for misdeeds and perverse desires.

Wild reveals a flawed society but also holds the possibility for change. Like a Machiavellian figure, Jonathan Wild governs with fear and lies—except that he is not a prince. Like a Hobbesian madman, he automatically expresses his true nature—except that he is living not in nature but in civil society. Like Carlyle's Napoleon, he is a tyrant who sees nothing but self-interest and has no goal but manipulation. His portrayal is a humanist attack on greatness as selfish, self-aggrandizing, and socially destructive. Greatness may be his destiny, but it is also his downfall. That he doesn't seem to care is his most poignant and most distressing quality.

NOTES

[1] One caveat about seeing Fielding's hero only through the Machiavellian lens is worth noting, especially in the specific eighteenth-century context. Critical discussion of *Jona-*

than Wild often compares the main character with Robert Walpole, the prime minister to whom Fielding was often opposed. Walpole was considered a particularly Machiavellian politician by his opponents. Comparing Walpole and Wild, the prime minister and the criminal mastermind, has a certain value, as does comparing government flunkies with criminal prigs, but Thomas Keymer points out that during Walpole's period in office, Machiavelli had a topical edge and could be invoked for a number of reasons: "the nature of virtue, and the definition of greatness, in modern commercial society; the preservation of liberty in conditions of degeneracy and corruption; the means of achieving personal and collective ends in a world of contingency and fortune; the relationship between public interest and private motive; the applicability of moral restraints to political calculation and action" ("Fielding's Machiavellian Moment" 58).

[2] Rawson's concept of the "tyrant thug" situates *Jonathan Wild* first in reference to the great figures Wild admires, the Homeric heroes who manifest excessive violence or the emperors who rule by force and cunning, but Rawson also sees Wild as part of a literary line that follows the criminal hero, from Gay's *Beggar's Opera* (1728) to Brecht's *Threepenny Opera* (1928). He argues that these idealized images conflate "heroes, thugs, criminals, national leaders . . . corrupt tyrannical regimes . . . [and] the world of boys' schools, of schoolboys and their masters, epitomized by the comic but murderous tyrant Ubu Roi. . ." ("Avatars" 93).

Amelia on Trial

Regina Janes

TRIAL. 1. Test; examination . . . 2. Experience; act of examining by experience . . . 3. Experiment; experimental knowledge . . . 4. Judicial examination.
EXPERIMENT. Trial of any thing; something done in order to discover an uncertain or unknown effect.
BOOTH. A house built of boards, or boughs, to be used for a short time. "Much mischief will be done at Bartholomew fair, by the fall of a *booth*."

—*Swift's Predictions* (Johnson's *Dictionary*, 1755)

Except for his bookseller, no one was more surprised or dismayed than Henry Fielding when his last novel, *Amelia,* elicited sneers instead of applause and failed to sell like *The History of Tom Jones, a Foundling*. The admirers of *Amelia* seemed to be only those who, like Samuel Johnson, had detested Fielding's earlier work. To love Fielding was not to like *Amelia,* and to love *Amelia* was not to like (the rest of) Fielding. There were, of course, those, like Samuel Richardson, who hated all Fielding and made no exception for any text ("Letters, 1752"). Little has changed: admirers of *Tom Jones* racing for the next installment relish the prison scene but stumble over the monologues; miss the confident, prefacing, child-watching narrator; and fail to respond to the charms of Billy Booth and his noseless wife. As Thomas Lockwood protests, "Why wasn't *Amelia* funny?" ("Why"). Alerting students that a text has excited hostility since it first appeared and that they too may hate it liberates everyone. Students invited to participate in the controversy often spring to Fielding's defense when *Amelia* is presented as an ambitious, flawed experiment, the first attempt to write a total novel when the model for such a work was still the epic. One way to shape entry into this critical dispute is to follow Dianne Osland's suggestion and propose that the class reenact Fielding's own trial of *Amelia* in the *Covent-Garden Journal,* numbers 6–8. In this judicial process, students can slide back and forth between Fielding's contemporaries and modern critics, while engaging more deeply with their own assumptions about the craft of fiction.

Fielding had already contributed to the rising novel current political and religious discourse and aesthetic autonomy, videlicet the "comic Epic-Poem in Prose" (*Joseph Andrews* 4) perfected in the trajectory from *Shamela* and *Joseph Andrews* to *Tom Jones*.[1] In *Amelia*, he was once again on to something new: the novel of social and psychological reform. Going beyond the marriage plot into the novel of marriage, he sent a married, and even less prudent, Tom Jones (i.e., Booth) and Sophia (i.e., Amelia) into a world where, unprotected by her property or his commission, they must negotiate public and private corruption. She succeeds, he fails, and her face providentially saves them both (Potkay, "Liberty" 357). Martin Battestin describes *Amelia* as an "experiment" and the first novel of social protest and reform before Charles Dickens (Introduction [to *Amelia*] xv). Like modern experimental novelists, Fielding recast generic conventions, challenged the comfort of his readers, provided them with fragments rather than an exquisitely orchestrated whole, and remade their conceptions of reality by remaking the forms of art. As an experiment *Amelia* blew up in his face, but writers have been poking around in the ashes ever since. Unlike the perfect *Tom Jones*, the flawed *Amelia* left room for improvement, becoming, as J. Paul Hunter observes, Fielding's most influential novel (*Occasional Form* 193) and paralleling his contributions as magistrate. When Émile Zola's lovely Nana rots away, hideous in her dying, it is well to remember Fielding's Bleareyed Moll and the noble peer so rotten that he stunk aboveground.

If *Amelia* did not amuse, Fielding's account of her failure does. Calling *Amelia* "a Romance," Fielding issued process to bring the book before "*The* Court *of* Censorial Enquiry" in the *Covent-Garden Journal*, number 6 ("*Covent-Garden Journal*" 51). *Amelia* was arraigned in number 7 by Counsellor Town, and evidence was heard from Lady Dilly Dally. In number 8, while a great crowd of "Beaus, Rakes, fine Ladies, and several formal Persons" pushed forward to offer themselves as witnesses, "a grave Man" begged to be heard. Offering no defense, he identified himself as the parent of "this poor Girl the Prisoner at the Bar," declared her his "favourite Child," claimed to have taken great pains in her education, insisted she "will be found to deviate very little from the strictest Observation of all those Rules . . . of those who are acknowledged to have writ best on the Subject." He had followed the rules as closely as Homer and especially Vergil, "the noble model, which I made use of on this Occasion" (65), and finally he volunteered to "trouble the World no more with any Children of mine by the same Muse." That declaration was received with "a loud Huzza"; the girl was restored to her parent; an end was put to the cause, but "several very grave and well looking Men, who knew the whole Merits, asserted, that the Lady ought to have been honourably acquitted" (66). In the case of *Amelia*, then, the charges still stand.

The classroom project may be informal, a student-led discussion, or formal, a jury, prosecution, and defense, with witnesses on each side. To imitate the eighteenth-century courtrooms Fielding often represented, a prejudiced judge, one whose mind is already made up or who has been paid off, may volunteer to instruct the jury.[2] Students will need to choose their briefs before they start reading, so as to prepare their cases as they go. Some will seize on the charges Counsellor Town brought; others will be more interested in charges that Fielding omitted but his contemporaries raised (readily available in Paulson and Lockwood's *Critical Heritage* volume). Still others will want to focus on current problems related to the art of fiction. The verdict remains in suspense: Should *Amelia* hang—that is, should the book be taken off the syllabus? Or does *Amelia* have, as Linda Bree suggests (Introduction 29), strengths that warrant keeping it alive?

Counsellor Town's arraignment engages both Fielding's intentions and contemporary responses to his work: dullness; the humor of the age (and what opposition to it means); the characters of Amelia, Bath, Harrison; and the jail scene (the low). From Fielding's defense come the role of Vergil and the gendering of Fielding's attackers and defenders (Fielding supposes more male readers than female, and only male readers defend his book). Charges brought by his contemporaries that Fielding did not address include women's learning and Mrs. Bennet-Atkinson, Booth's character and "botch[ed]" conversion (Chapone 1: 46), and the too providential catastrophe. Among the issues raised by neither Fielding nor his contemporaries but that should now be addressed are the intrusiveness of his narrator (or is the narrator not intrusive enough?), his social and legal criticism (praised by Lady Orrery, however), the too lengthy personal histories, the irrelevant episodes (Harrison and the political peer, Harrison and the father-son clerics, Amelia's shattered idyll at Vauxhall, Booth's literary criticism in the sponging house), and Fielding's technical limitations.

Indicting *Amelia* on the statute of dullness, Counsellor Town seeks "a dreadful Example to all future Books, how they dare stand up in Opposition to the Humour of the Age" (*"Covent-Garden Journal"* 59). Through this charge, Fielding situates his text as oppositional, setting the counselor against the fiction's innovations, embodied in three characters and the opening in Newgate. The counselor arraigns the once idealized, now vexed character of Amelia as wife and mother; Colonel Bath, Fielding's cross-dressing, sister-doting, walking attack on dueling; and Dr. Harrison, an idiosyncratic cleric, prickly, dogmatic, pedantic, following Jonathan Swift and preceding Laurence Sterne.

In Harrison, Fielding revisits his other novels' absurd (Adams), brutal, dissolute, and venal parsons. Bath and Harrison provide an opportunity for students to consider what makes comedy work and how comedy fails. The jail scene Town condemns as *"low and unmeaning,* and brought in by Head and Shoulders, without any Reason, or Design" (59). Through this scene, Booth's unjust imprisonment and his unjustifiable amour with Miss Matthews, Fielding links his public and private purposes. Systemic, institutional corruption, to which Town is oblivious, is evident in the jailing of Booth for an attempted rescue and private corruptibility in adultery's easy undermining of marriage, facilitated by Miss Matthews's (and others') cash in hand.

Counsellor Town's characters continue to be controversial. Bath tends to be overlooked in discussions of Fielding on dueling. More nuanced than Allworthy in *Tom Jones*, Harrison is regarded by Gary Gautier (114) and Hester Mulso Chapone (1: 46–47, 50–51) as a paragon and by Adam Potkay as a butt ("Liberty" 355).[3] For Robert Alter, Harrison is merely charmless (*Fielding* 162). As for Amelia, students are likely to be surprised—and delighted—that women reading in the eighteenth century were as infuriated by her and Mrs. Bennet-Atkinson as they are. Lady Orrery thought Amelia good but silly. Anne Donnellan was sharper: "[P]oor Amelia, she is so great a fool we pity her, but cannot be humble enough to desire to imitate her," adding of Mrs. Atkinson, "Must we suppose that if a woman knows a little Greek and Latin she must be a drunkard, and virago?"

Counsellor Town finds Amelia low, a fool, a milksop; she faints and drinks water, taps a bottle of wine and drinks two glasses; she is too kind to her children, too forgiving of her husband's faults, reproving neither his infidelity nor his losing their money at play. She forgives the loss of money because his heart was almost broken by it (as if his remorse offset the harm caused by his folly). She prepares her husband's supper, dresses her children, submits to every servile office, and she has no nose. Fielding indeed dreams of domesticity like a man who married his maid.

Fielding's tender domestic scenes elicited broad parodies (Thornton 321–24; Kenrick 333). Even John Cleland found the low characters too frequently repeated; they "disgust even those, who, from their distance in rank or circumstances from these subjects, may be curious to have some idea of them, and can only come at it in such description" (306). The "humour of the age" moved not against sentiment but against insufficiently comic low characters in low situations. The detail of a newly realistic domesticity, sunk beneath the comfortable standards assumed for the gentry, did not please.

Creating a new and complex role, the positive alternative to the mother of *Tom Jones*'s Sophia, abused, silent, dead, and unloved (Wilputte, "Women" 328–29), Fielding attempted to affix cultural prestige to the effaced role of selfless wife and mother (Cleland 304). Amelia embodies bourgeois values, the sanctification of the private sphere. Feminist objections notwithstanding, Amelia is the first heroine ever to cook or open a bottle of wine, Booth the first husband present at the birth of his child, and some students might like to investigate where Amelia does her marketing. Gautier's "Marriage and Family in Fielding's Fiction" can help students describe the revaluation of women's traditional occupations that elevated their roles' status to equality in separate spheres but also forestalled demands for their access to learning and public life, demands represented in Mrs. Bennet-Atkinson.

A new cultural type is being created, and the novel is not unaware of the problems associated with Amelia as ideal. Fielding shows Booth's husbandly contempt for his wife's thinking on religious and moral questions, his disastrous disregard of her dislike of card playing (Molesworth 178), and the inability of her virtues or his love to effect any change in his behavior. Even her legal status under couverture is recognized, in Harrison's letter on adultery. The mocked Mrs. Bennet-Atkinson, by contrast, secures for her husband the commission Booth fails to get for himself. In the novel's last lines, Fielding's "ART OF LIFE" celebrates a reciprocal love that remains a cultural ideal and invites a contrast with the life of the town lady, a life attacked by authors from Alexander Pope to Mary Wollstonecraft, by way of Mrs. James and Lady Dilly Dally.

Having no nose suggests that Amelia has had too much of what Tristram Shandy will lack (Fielding gives Booth his own "Proboscis" [448 (bk. 11, ch. 1)]). Lost noses code venereal disease and sexual excess, while the Shandys have never had enough nose to keep their women satisfied. The battered nose, anticipating the plainness of Jane Eyre, recalls Fielding's first wife, as his contemporaries observed without sympathy. The scandal crosses over from an eighteenth-century bawdy joke to modern concerns with class. Although Fielding argues that sympathy should not be bounded by status, he reveals his own inability to register continuities across class barriers. Choosing to damage Amelia's nose, he failed to recognize the venereal connotations of a missing nose even though he had already drawn Blear-eyed Moll.

Booth explains his author's error: "Compassion . . . will, I believe, appear to be the Fellow-feeling only of Men of the same Rank and Degree of Life for one another, on account of the Evils to which they themselves are liable. Our Sensations are . . . very cold towards those who are at a great Distance from us, and whose Calamities can consequently never reach us" (443 [bk. 10, ch. 9]). Amelia corrects Booth's aperçu to widen the reach of sympathy, but their author remains caught in his particular subject position. Why, after all, should Booth deserve a commission more than Colonel James's two footmen? Is Atkinson the equal of Booth at the novel's end, when his family pays a visit of three months to Booth and Amelia? Is the maid Betty's violation of trust more or less blameworthy than Booth's gambling losses, which immediately precede it? Is Amelia's damaged nose an oversight caused by Fielding's class prejudices or a purposeful ambiguity? The question is not easy. The reader is on trial, too.

Fielding's intentions are clearer elsewhere. Through Counsellor Town's attack on his jail scene as without design, Fielding lays claim to his artistic lineage. This exchange in the trial enables wide-ranging discussion of what the rules did for Augustans and what Fielding contributed to the development of the genre of the novel. Pleading the rules followed (not invented) by Homer and especially Vergil, Fielding redefines the novel as an epic poem in prose, but this time not comic, that combines public and private worlds in an integrated, unified design. Grounding his fable in his jail scene, he moves from corruption, deception, and fallacious appearances at society's lowest level (the prison) to its highest (various peers) and holiest (parsons). Imbricating individual and institutional corruption (the justice, Booth, Amelia's sister), he parallels private and public, sexual and monetary, all the way up the social scale. Vergil dignifies Fielding's project, ballasts his satiric, social, psychological, and philosophical purposes, and enables Fielding to augur epic's displacement by his new form of romance.

The critical debate on Vergil usually centers on structural parallels: twelve books commence in medias res at the nadir and include an underworld scene, a story told to a dangerously amorous lady, and a home reestablished in another country. Bree suggests that Fielding drops Vergil after the opening chapters, though Mrs. Atkinson and Dr. Harrison keep quarreling through Vergil (Introduction 12). Thereafter, Fielding trusts his fable to ramify and carry its own developing weight. The exegeses of Lyall Powers, Maurice Johnson, and the comical intervention of Michael Irwin (who calls Powers's analogues far-fetched but then adds a far-fetched analogue of his own [115]) allow students to assess intertextuality's limits. How far is too far, what constitutes a meaningful allusion and what is critical wiredrawing, a pleasure in its own right? Was Samuel Richardson correct that *Amelia* is "Virgil Travestied" ("Letters" 336)? Perhaps Fielding predicts *Ulysses,* trading Vergil's establishment of an empire for domesticity and panic over adultery (Tanner 15, 369–71), as the triumph of bourgeois values? (Richardson, nota bene, would have thought no better of James Joyce.)

Vergil, fable, and design also inform the controversies over Booth's character, "botch[ed]" conversion, and the providential catastrophe, teased since Chapone's superb attack on Booth (1: 45–47, 48–52).[4] Fielding's epic queries the relation between pervasive social corruption, where his characters are victims, and individual responsibility, where they do and do not victimize themselves. The Augustan sense of fable informs Booth's fecklessness: the agonizing trajectory of his losses follows Fielding's design, from (private) gambling with Trent to (public) donation to the patron-pike. Redemption comes—designedly—from below, through Robinson, the fleecing, fatalist gamester encountered at the opening in Newgate, at the pawnshop, and above the sponging house.

Ultimately, as Potkay observes, moving along a debate to which many commentators have contributed (Sherburn, "Fielding's *Amelia*"; Battestin, "Problem"; Hunter, *Occasional Form*; Mulford), Booth converts from a philosophical view that because actions proceed from whatever passion is uppermost, they can have neither merit nor demerit ("Liberty"). Harrison cites as meritorious Christianity's appeal to the passions. In Newgate, as the novel opens, Robinson assures Booth fatalistically that what is cannot be otherwise. When Robinson sees Amelia in distress, he ought to shrug. Instead he acts on his emotions and saves Amelia's family. Reformed for a time, he later relapses to be hanged. What Booth realizes and Harrison endorses, Robinson does. He acts from a prevailing passion *and* accrues merit or demerit in doing so.

Students interested in the developing art of fiction might want to address such technical questions as how the personal histories of Miss Matthews, Booth, and Mrs. Bennet are given. Much longer than Fielding's other interpolated narratives (that of the Man of the Hill or Mrs. Fitzgerald in *Tom Jones*), they take up about a quarter of the novel. Matthews and Booth echo Dido and Aeneas, but Fielding invites readers to contrast Mrs. Bennet's story with that of Miss Matthews (282 [bk. 7, ch. 1]). Readers might also compare his technique with Jane Austen's way of presenting Mrs. Smith in *Persuasion.* Episodes that appear irrelevant give Fielding's sociopolitical commentary a wider range. Inquiry might also be made into the particular legal reforms Fielding proposes, some already enacted, others not (Wolff 44–45).

Fielding's narrator has been attacked for abandoning the "art of the novel" (Hassall, "Fielding's *Amelia*" 228) for the "ART OF LIFE" (58 [bk. 1, ch. 1]), for slipping from satire to didacticism and sentiment. Anthony Hassall's attack on Fielding's narrator can be challenged by the argument that Fielding makes increased demands on the reader, who must negotiate uncertain ground (Osland; Wanko). Contributing to the irresolution of moral and social dilemmas are

Fielding's old narrative tricks, such as deceptive signposting. When Atkinson joins Mrs. Ellison, Mrs. Bennet, and Amelia at supper, Fielding both marks and conceals a contrast between the widowed Mrs. Bennet and the widowed Mrs. Ellison in their approach to the eligible bachelor Atkinson. Mrs. Ellison was so pleased

> with what she had heard of him, and what she saw of him, that when a little warmed with Wine, for she was no Flincher at the Bottle, she began to indulge some Freedoms in her Discourse towards him, that a little offended *Amelia*'s Delicacy, nay, they did not seem to be highly relished by the other Lady. Tho' I am far from insinuating that these exceeded the Bounds of Decorum, or were indeed greater Liberties than Ladies of the middle Age, and especially Widows, do frequently allow to themselves.
> (221 [bk. 5, ch. 3])

Pointing to Mrs. Ellison conceals the other widow, Mrs. Bennet, and sets up the later confusion over who has proposed to Atkinson. It also differentiates Ellison's broad coquetry from Bennet's marital mindedness and defends behavior later correlated with the profession of procuress. Judgment is supplied not by the narrator but, in the scene, by the responses of Amelia and Mrs. Bennet.

The narrator sometimes obtrudes but more often leaves his readers to work through a complex layering of narrative silence and characters' actions and speech. He affirms that a servant's claim "was really the Truth" (61 [bk. 1, ch. 2]) but remains silent on Mrs. Bennet's claim that her disease did not kill her husband (314 [bk. 7, ch. 9]). Cleland admired the multifaceted representation of Mrs. James (307), whose character shifts as she is viewed through the narrator or by Amelia or in her own actions. She reconciles with Amelia; desires Billy, Amelia's husband; and quarrels with her own spouse. Fielding leaves her complexities to his reader to plumb.

Certain technical means Fielding did not have available. Unlike Dickens, he had not learned from the gothic novel, still to be invented, to make stones, roads, buildings, and things speak. Admiring William Hogarth, Fielding saw the people, not the architecture and objects, so his fiction remained a play of voices. Still, his favorite child, imbricating individuals with institutions, using the rules to create new forms, mingling autobiography and art, may gain new respect and affection as an experiment meant to trouble the present and touch the future.

NOTES

[1] Ian Watt had difficulty fitting the Augustan, satirical Fielding into formal realism; Michael McKeon solved the problem. For a discussion of the issues, see Richetti, "Legacy" 106.

[2] The judge might argue, "This book is two hundred and sixty years old and six hundred pages too long; besides, who reads anymore?"

[3] Harrison, unlike Allworthy but like Tom Jones, worsens his circumstances to do others good (488–89 [bk. 12, ch. 3]).

[4] Chapone's attack is reprinted in *Henry Fielding: The Critical Heritage*, where it is attributed, incorrectly, to Sarah Chapone (Paulson and Lockwood 318–19, 351–52).

Friendship and Marriage in *Amelia*

George E. Haggerty

Henry Fielding's last novel, *Amelia* (1752), is a deeply personal and reflective, if not to say valedictory, work. Written when Fielding was wracked with ill health and pressured by the demands of his position as local magistrate, it has neither the delight of discovery that is to be found in *Joseph Andrews* nor the comic majesty of *Tom Jones*. For some, it is badly written and overly sentimental (Sabor 105). What it offers in place of Fielding's earlier achievement, however, is a deeply felt account of the complexities of contemporary life and of the burdens to be borne by a young married couple of limited means. While in his earlier novels, topics like friendship or marriage might have been discussed or even represented, in *Amelia* the terms of representation are more serious and the concepts themselves are subjected to the exigencies of the lived experience of the author. In the classroom, therefore, *Amelia* offers a new way of understanding Fielding and a useful perspective from which to view his earlier work.

Friendship in the novel is often celebrated, but it is also shown to be less than ideal. For one thing, it is almost always measured in mercenary terms: a friend is considered more or less stalwart according to how much money he can lend. This observation is made so often in the novel as to seem like a solid tenet. For another, male friendship almost always founders because of rivalry over a woman. In her description of "homosocial" relationships in English literature, Eve Kosofsky Sedgwick talks about how male bonds are charged with emotion, even if that emotion emerges from such negative forces as jealousy or hatred (20–21). *Amelia* gives us several examples of friendship that involves erotic rivalry, which often creates its own kind of emotional bond. Booth and James recognize the bitter rivalry between them yet remain friends.

Marriage too, although central to Fielding's plan in *Amelia*, never shows itself to be the flawless and consoling structure Fielding sometimes describes. Marriage offers a spectacle of debility for his hero: Captain Booth rarely has enough money to support his wife and growing family; he squanders what little money he has through silly investments or loses it in gambling; he has sex outside marriage and puts his wife, Amelia, in one untenable situation after another; and he is jealous to a fault. Despite all these pressures and tensions, however, marriage emerges intact in *Amelia*, and that success is due primarily to the strong personality of the title character. Fielding is trying to show that friendship and marriage are flawed and self-defeating in various ways but also finds a method of taking strength from the very structures he deconstructs.

Critics have often noted that it is the figure of the masquerade that represents metonymically everything that Fielding thinks is wrong about contemporary culture, which includes friendship and marriage. Linda Bree writes, for instance:

> The centerpiece of *Tom Jones* had been at the inn at Upton, a location embodying temporariness and transition, arrivals and departures, where most of the main characters came together, misunderstood each other, and separated again. It is hugely significant that the equivalent scene in *Amelia* takes place at the much less neutral, much more duplicitous, location of a masquerade.

The masquerade, revealing what Bree calls the heart of "deception" in the novel, offers an opportunity for "genteel men and women to throw off the ceremonies and formalities of their society and act in transgressive ways" (Introduction 15). For the novelist, moreover, it offers the chance to show how friendship and marriage function under extraordinary duress. From the long tale that Mrs. Bennet tells Amelia, the masquerade can be seen as a snare for young women, married or unmarried, and it becomes almost immediately clear that Amelia is the intended victim of just such a scheme. Even before the Noble Peer attempts to seduce an unsuspecting Amelia at the climactic masquerade of the novel, she has been made aware of the ways in which the traps inherent in the masquerade can destroy a woman and ruin her marriage (see Castle, *Masquerade* 219–22). Of course, that does not happen, because Amelia and Mrs. Bennet devise a way to avoid the danger.

If Amelia can prove herself in one situation, however, her integrity is continuously under attack from other quarters. The Noble Peer befriends her and offers trinkets to her children, warming her heart but placing her in more danger than she realizes; meanwhile, Colonel James, her husband's dear friend, offers her tickets to the masquerade and tries everything in his power to persuade her to attend. Later James tries to get Booth a posting abroad so that James can bring Amelia and her children to reside with him and his increasingly dishonest wife. Because Amelia has already caught on to James's ploys and because she fears to tell her husband about his attempts at seduction (lest a duel result), she takes matters into her own hands. Readers are not told that she switches places with Mrs. Atkinson, who attends the masquerade in her place. Afterward Amelia reassures her husband, who thought he saw her in her mask conversing with the Noble Peer, and Mr. Atkinson admits that in her disguise as Amelia she procured some advancement for Mrs. Atkinson. In this way, both women defeat the power that the masquerade held over them.

What is even more remarkable about the masquerade is the public reading of a pointed sermon on adultery that entertains a gang of young bucks there. The sermon, meant, it seems, for the ears of Colonel James, has been penned by none other than Dr. Harrison, who is the dear friend of Booth and Amelia and hovers as a force of beneficence over most of the novel.

The adultery sermon addresses topics of friendship and marriage from another perspective: it points out the deficiencies of friendship and the ways in which it undermines the very meaning of marriage. Dr. Harrison begins by reminding his listeners of the punishments for adultery promised in Scripture, but then he gives a detailed outline of the sin itself:

> And for what will you submit yourself to this Punishment? Or for what Reward will you inflict all this Misery on another? I will add on your Friend? For the Possession of a Woman; for the Pleasure of a Moment? But if neither Virtue nor Religion can restrain your inordinate Appetites, are there not many Women as handsome as your Friend's Wife, whom, though not with Innocence, you may possess with much less Degree of Guilt? What Motive can thus hurry you on to the Destruction of yourself and your Friend? (411–12 [bk. 10, ch. 2])

By posing the question in this way, Dr. Harrison articulates one of the main ideas of the novel: friendship fails whenever sexual desire for a woman intervenes. He seems to feel that the threat of adultery to friendship is of greater concern than the threat of adultery to a woman and her reputation. The rivalry of friends is central to this idea.

This tension between friends happens twice in the novel, first when it turns out that Miss Mathews, the woman with whom Booth had a brief affair while in prison, much to his later chagrin, is also the object of Colonel James's long-standing desire. When Booth confides in James that he would like to rid himself of the responsibility he feels toward Miss Mathews, James is only too happy to take this woman off his hands. The generosity that James shows to Booth is therefore already tempered by sexual jealousy and a sense of libertine rivalry.

Booth might seem above such rivalry in certain ways, but Amelia knows that he would fight a duel with James if Booth discovered that James was pursuing her. Later in the novel, James actually sends Booth a challenge, but Amelia intercepts it to protect her husband. She understands the power of their masculine rivalry and that it can destroy her marriage if she does not take care.

Booth thinks of James as a friend who will support him in any adversity. The language of celebration of this friendship is excessive. When James visits Booth in the sponging house, for instance, we are given this poetic account:

> The unexpected Visit of a beloved Friend to a Man in Affliction, especially in Mr. *Booth's* Situation, is a Comfort which can scarce be equalled; not barely from the Hopes of Relief, or Redress, by his Assistance; but, as it is an Evidence of sincere Friendship, which scarce admits of any Doubt or Suspicion. Such an Instance doth, indeed, make a Man amends for all ordinary Troubles and Distresses; and we ought to think ourselves Gainers, by having had such an Opportunity of discovering, that we are possessed of one of the most valuable of all human Possessions.

The passage, when the reader is already suspecting James's hypocrisy, points to how short of the ideal their friendship falls. Even as the narrator articulates these values, moreover, he is unable to resist exposing James, to the reader if not to Booth:

> In Truth, the Colonel, tho' a very generous Man, had not the least Grain of Tenderness in his Disposition. His Mind was formed of those firm Materials, of which Nature formerly hammered out the Stoic, and upon which the Sorrows of no Man living could make an Impression. A Man of this Temper, who doth not much value Danger, will fight for the Person he calls his Friend; and the man that hath but little Value for his Money will give it him; but such Friendship is never to be absolutely depended on: For whenever the favourite Passion interposes with it, it is sure to subside and vanish into Air. (339 [bk. 8, ch. 5])

If what the narrator calls "the favourite Passion," in this case sexual intrigue, can cause all the value of friendship "to subside and vanish into Air," then a mind like James's is not really suitable for the kind of friendship that Fielding has articulated. The closest thing to a friend, as classically defined, in the novel, James turns out to be instead a perverse and double-dealing enemy.

In her wonderful book about Fielding, Jill Campbell notes the tension between two sets of values in the novel. Booth is often "paralyzed or isolated by a conflict between, on the one hand, Christian ideals and the Cavalier or military code" and, on the other, more modern and forward-looking versions of masculinity (*Natural Masques* 215). By devoting himself to the friend who turns out to be false, Booth is trying to uphold values that are utterly outmoded.

We can see how outmoded they are by attending briefly to another friend: Colonel Bath. Bath is rendered ridiculous by readiness to rush into a duel for the sake of his honor. No friend is safe from the occasional ire of this fire-breather, who is at other times as sweet and charming as can be. "A Man of Honour wears his Law by his Side," Bath tells Dr. Harrison when the older man tries to show him the speciousness of arguments in favor of dueling (368 [bk. 9, ch. 3]). Bath is not convinced, and he leaves the novel bristling with irritation that shortly brings about his demise: "killed in a Duel," as the narrator announces (514 [bk. 12, ch. 9]). The older cavalier values that Campbell mentions are mocked in the figure of Bath, and, with James, equivalent libertine codes of sexual license are also questioned.

Male friendship is hampered by a conflict not only of libidos but also of codes. Booth and his friends are victims of competing allegiances. Given to sexual jealousy as much as any other character in the novel, he finds himself hounded by a sense of honor and what it demands of him in one situation after another. If friendship is only rivalry, as it often seems here, and male relations can lead only to conflict, what hope is there for a culture that is structured around them?

Fielding offers two clear models of friendship. Dr. Harrison stands out as a friend: the honorable older man supports Booth and Amelia and does his best to make their path easy. He challenges Booth when he sees that Booth is going astray, and he helps the couple discover the deceit, a discovery that leads to the happy ending.

Sergeant Atkinson can also function as a friend, devoted as he is and as ready with his purse: when he can least afford to spare any cash, he hands considerable amounts over to Booth. But Booth treats him as little more than a servant, as Campbell reminds us. "Assumptions about class and assumptions about the relative importance of homosocial and heterosexual bonds," she writes, "both influence Booth's understanding of Atkinson, whose actions and motivations he consistently either overlooks or mistakes" (*Natural Masques* 221). Although Atkinson distinguishes himself as a stalwart friend, he remains a minor character.

The friendship that stands out as the best and most forward-looking relationship in the novel is the one between Booth and Amelia. Fielding does not offer an idealized version of his first marriage, as is often suggested (e.g., Battestin, Introduction [*Amelia*] xvi–xxi), but uses this novel to examine the state of marriage itself; and, far from sugarcoating marriage, he shows the stress it is under and the various ways in which it could easily fail. Booth's relationship with Amelia, unlike his relationship with James, which seems rooted in an idealized past, is not only rooted in the present but also constantly redefined as the novel proceeds. Campbell reminds us that with

> no more means than Booth to sustain her little family economically, but from quite early in their story, [Amelia] is given a sphere of honorable activity and self-definition in the labor of caring for their home and children. . . . [Her] function as housekeeper and mother . . . provides the present economic as well as moral anchor of the Booth household.
> (*Natural Masques* 206–07)

If Bree feels that Amelia "never converts [her] rhetoric [of devotion] into any practical action to improve the family's position" (Introduction 20); she nevertheless asserts, "[T]he scenes between Booth and Amelia offer a convincing representation of a husband and wife, who know each other well and are still in love with each other despite the pressures of a hostile world, whether they are exchanging informal intimacies, gossipy jokes, delicate half-truths, or uncomfortable lies" (17–18).

This "convincing representation" is the whole point of the novel.[1] A mutual relationship based on respect that nourishes both members of it and enables them to function together in a way that neither could function alone—this is the definition of marriage that Fielding offers, and it would be hard to find a better or more progressive definition of friendship. The degree that marriage is modeled on friendship in the later eighteenth century has only begun to be told (Bray 307–23). Betty Rizzo reminds us that even so-called "companionate marriage" makes it clear that relations were askew to the point that wives felt subservient (22–24). But what Fielding is offering is something else—something based on a model of friendship that celebrates mutual love and trust. What Booth and Amelia have together rarely appears in earlier English fiction.

Some critics point out that deception creeps even into this relationship, but deception to protect is quite different from the other kinds of deception that circulate in the novel (Bree, Introduction 15). When Amelia tricks Booth into thinking that she has gone to the masquerade, she avoids having to admit her fears about James and involve Booth in them directly; moreover, she shows her faith in Booth in her knowledge that he will forgive and even celebrate her absence from the masquerade, as he does. Booth transgresses with Miss Mathews while in prison, but Amelia both understands and forgives that transgression. Also, it is her inheritance that provides for them at the novel's conclusion. Booth's love might seem feckless at times, but her faith in him, that he is the husband and friend who will sustain her in the world of multiplied dangers, is solid.

"Domestic Happiness is the End of almost all our Pursuits," Dr. Harrison says in his sermon on adultery (411 [bk. 10, ch. 2]), and that statement does seem to be the one lesson that this novel argues convincingly. Many critics have said that *Amelia* was ahead of its time in dealing with social life realistically (see Battestin, Introduction [to *Amelia*] xxxix; Battestin and Battestin 535). In this articulation of marriage as a kind of friendship, Fielding is an unlikely source for such an important advance in gender relations but, because he is one of the greatest novelists in the English literary tradition, it is a fitting source.

NOTE

[1] I develop this argument in "Amelia's Nose."

Amelia and the "Choice of Life" Novel

Jennifer Preston Wilson

At Appalachian State University, I teach *Amelia* (1752) as the beginning text in an undergraduate honors class focused on eighteenth- and nineteenth-century British novels. The course structure arose from my interest in situating *Amelia* not as Fielding's last (and least accomplished) novel or his last (and most capitulatory) response to Samuel Richardson—although those views have some truth to them—but as a forward-looking, experimental work. I connect *Amelia* instead with Amelia Opie's *Adeline Mowbray* (1804) and Charles Dickens's *Bleak House* (1853), novels selected for their close study of a suffering domestic heroine, an unyielding social environment, and the unreliable bulwarks of marriage and friendship.[1] The rest of the syllabus consists of supplementary background readings to help undergraduates place these works in formal, historical, and ideological contexts.

As I begin any class, I find it worthwhile to check students' prior reading experience, but for this honors course such checking proves necessary, since undergraduate knowledge of the pre-1900 novel varies widely. Most students know Charlotte Brontë's *Jane Eyre*, Nathaniel Hawthorne's *The Scarlet Letter*, and Jane Austen's *Pride and Prejudice* from high school English courses and film adaptations. We use these familiar texts to discuss some common plot configurations, noting how narratives of courtship made the novel popular in England. As a part of this conversation, we consider Ian Watt's claim that the rise of the novel was "connected with the much greater freedom of women in modern society, a freedom which, especially as regards marriage, was achieved earlier and more completely in England than elsewhere" (138). Watt's argument that a surge in individual liberties and economic independence created conditions that were favorable for and reflected in the courtshipcentric plots of the early novel is an appealing story in itself because it foregrounds dynamic agency and growth.

Yet what of the works that subverted the marriage-plot paradigm of this time period? What occurs when courtship is blocked either by marriage itself or a host of other reasons—principled objection to the institution of matrimony, class conflict, nationalist differences, legal restrictions? I encourage students to weigh the possibilities before we go any further. We discuss the dramatic portrayal of marriage in many different media, from Shakespeare to television sitcoms, and ask, along with Christine Roulston in her *Narrating Marriage in Eighteenth-Century England and France*, why the novel tradition of eighteenth century avoids focusing on day-to-day married life (1–2). We also take notice of Kelly Hager's claim that the "failed-marriage plot" is more prevalent than we acknowledge but has been ignored in favor of the closure offered by the courtship model (12–13).

Once these questions have been aired, we begin *Amelia*. We read through the initial Newgate scenes and into direct observation of the Booths' marriage and compare our reading experience against that of a conventional courtship novel. Particularly useful to provoke discussion is D. A. Miller's unequivocal pronouncement that marriage is "nonnarratable" (3–4). Likewise, Peter Brooks's claim that the end of the narrative is always already present in the beginning (22–23) does not mesh with the "ongoing middle" of married life (Roulston 11). If, as Brooks, Tony Tanner, and René Girard all suggest, the courtship plot is adept at enabling other forms of desire, how is the reader engaged when courtship does not drive the plot? My students are quick to respond with alternative models of readerly interest. In *Amelia* and the ensuing novels in our class, we relate to a tenacious character who, in a state of privation, tries to achieve the basic conditions of human happiness. Sometimes this protagonist has done nothing wrong yet suffers nonetheless.[2] At other times, he or she knowingly or unknowingly blocks his or her own advancement. The narrative focus is on this character's choices, not on the choice of marriage, which is either blocked or was already made.

The protagonist in such a "choice of life" novel typically begins his or her story at a disadvantage.[3] Language of lack or of indebtedness describes his or her insufficiency and sets a tone of anxiety from the very start. *Amelia* initiates this theme of compromised identity that will continue in the semester's subsequent novels. In discussion, we note how the love story between Will Booth and Amelia Harris originates from a carriage accident: her noble behavior in response to her damaged nose and social status draws Booth's admiration for her "Firmness of Soul" even when "deprived" of her "exquisite Beauty" (98–99 [bk. 2, ch. 1]). In *Adeline Mowbray*, we attend to the heroine's imbalanced education at the whim of an overly confident, theory-addled mother: "like an animal in an exhausted receiver, [Adeline] had during her short existence been tormented by the experimental philosophy of her mother" (5). Parental intercession causes harm, functioning like a vacuum pump that extracts vitality from the child. Our third heroine, Esther Summerson of *Bleak House*, suffers a blight from birth, when her guardian condemns her illegitimate origin while refusing at the same time to ever speak of it. Esther feels guilt for having offended without knowing how, acknowledging, "Imperfect as my understanding of my sorrow was, I knew that I had brought no joy, at any time, to anybody's heart" (27). Like her counterparts, Amelia and Adeline, Esther sets her life course in response to her perceived inadequacy.

Beginning with *Amelia* (and later continuing with *Adeline Mowbray* and *Bleak House*), we examine supporting materials to contextualize the heroine's loss in her particular social setting. Amelia's disfigurement had specific implications for an eighteenth-century woman. We read Samuel Johnson's "The Vanity of Human Wishes," especially tuning in to the stanza on daughters blessed with "the fortune of a face" (2850 [line 320]) and on other holders of transitory power, such as the rich man, the general, and the king—all cited by Booth as analogies for his wife. We also give a close reading of Amelia's appearance against that of Blear-eyed Moll to analyze how we are to regard Amelia's nose "beat all to pieces," incorporating William Hogarth's *A Harlot's Progress* for its depiction of syphilitic decay. Does Amelia's flawed nose suggest flawed virtue? Note that Booth says he never would have turned his thoughts to her before her accident (98 [bk. 2, ch. 1]). Or could her nose be an emblem of her humility and mindfulness of her imperfect nature? Why, for example, does she sit for a miniature portrait after enduring the accident, surgery, and mockery of her peers (136 [bk. 3, ch.3])?

We examine the liabilities of the other protagonists in the same way. The cultural significance of Adeline Mowbray's imbalanced education becomes clearer with excerpts from Mary Wollstonecraft's *A Vindication of the Rights of Woman* and Hannah More's *Essays on Various Subjects, Principally Designed for Young Ladies*; we also analyze the didactic 1785 print *Keep within Compass* for its portrayal of a woman's prescribed sphere. In the Victorian era, the ambiguous class identity of Esther makes her an outcast; only a philanthropist like John Jarndyce would adopt her into his social circle. To better understand her plight, we read the imprecatory biblical verses hurled at her by her evangelical godmother and discuss the solace the young girl seeks in the nonjudgmental company of her doll. Sharon Marcus's analysis of nineteenth-century doll tales and play (158–62) and images of Victorian dolls at the *Victoria and Albert Museum* (http://collections.vam.ac.uk) help us further analyze Esther's stunted childhood.

With these and other materials, my students counter the allure of the courtship plot with interest in an outsider protagonist who suffers early trauma. The stakes grow higher and the choices become more limited even as our heroines move forward to experience public life in grand, urban settings. In this ironic progress all three of our novels expand to encompass complex social systems: masquerade balls, spa towns, country estates, St. James Park, the Court of Chancery, the House of Commons, and the streets of London. For both the heroine and readers, these settings pose intense problems of navigation and interpretation of social codes, a process of sharing that creates what Eric Rothstein calls "epistemological empathy" in the reader (*Systems* 154–55). My students discuss this concept as they analyze the excitement and danger created by the portrayal of social circulation. The panoramic effect of these scenes lets the reader mill through the crowd along with the characters, but such spectacles also serve to stress the isolation of the protagonist. The teeming environment of the masquerade in Fielding (bk. 10, ch. 2), Adeline's frenzied dashing through Fleet Street and the Strand in Opie (206–08), and the nightlong search for Lady Dedlock in Dickens (801–19, 833–47), offer extended examples of this panorama and isolation.

Lost in the multitudinous city, our heroines are also alone in their closest domestic relationships. Amelia waits up late for Booth on a number of occasions, and we see her hope dwindling as the reheated dinner congeals. Adeline is separated from her partner by his illness and eventual death; when she later succumbs to custom and consents to a legitimate marriage, she still experiences many nights alone since her spouse is too embarrassed by her past history to introduce her into company. Esther keeps busy to ignore her isolation in Jarndyce's Bleak House, but it is revealed at night when she returns to her room and cries, feeling "as if an old chord had been more coarsely touched that it ever had been since the days of the dear old doll, long buried in the garden" (142). These ironic moments of being solitary in relationship build psychological pressure as the range of possible action increasingly narrows.

My students notice that friendship offers no relief to our heroines; rather, it proves intense and complicated, if not outright threatening. These liaisons develop, as Terry Castle has noted, from a structural doubling of roles that points the reader to larger societal patterns (*Masquerade* 110). When Amelia listens to Mrs. Bennet's history,[4] her epiphany that it is also her own story evokes an eerie awareness that the forces endangering her have perpetrated serial crimes. Mrs. Bennet tells of her experience at the Oratorio:

> At these Words, Amelia cried, "O gracious Heavens!" and fell back in her Chair, Mrs. Bennet, with proper Applications, brought her back to Life; and then Amelia acquainted her, that she herself had first seen the same Person in the same Place, and in the same Disguise. "O! Mrs. Bennet," cried she, "how am I indebted to you!" (309 [bk. 7, ch. 7])

Amelia faints on recognizing that, as a victim in a series of victims of the noble lord, she would lose agency and become a discardable object of his desire. Her outcry of indebtedness to her friend signals the interchange of narrative obligation: hearing Mrs. Bennet's story has delivered her from a terrible fate.

J. Paul Hunter observes that the central trait of Amelia is not virtue but caution (*Occasional Form* 195). She withstands temptation because of her avoidance of risk. It is her friendship with Mrs. Bennet that enables her to make these safe moves time and again (thanks to Bennet's life history, her warning about Colonel James's intentions, and her frankness about Mr. Atkinson's affection for Amelia). But Amelia's relationship with this friend is by no means perfect. The malleability of Bennet's morals—the result of suffering (or possibly causing?)[5] early family loss, further bereavement, and a tarnished reputation—grates against Amelia's nicety. Yet in Amelia carefulness does not lead to ingratitude, and she remains attached to the woman who sacrificed her own privacy to protect a friend at a crucial moment.

Once we complete *Amelia*, my students find that a similar awareness of self in others occurs in *Adeline Mowbray* and *Bleak House*. When Adeline sees that Savannah, a mulatto woman, is being carted off to jail with her dying, impoverished husband and hears the language of abuse heaped by the creditor on the faithful wife, she acts against injustice by paying off the debt, although she notes the cost to her own fate. Thus the friendship of the two women begins in recognition, emotion, and debt: "Adeline thought on Glenmurray's danger, and shuddered as she beheld the scene [of Savannah and William's illness and imminent imprisonment]; she felt it but a too probable anticipation of the one in which she might soon be an actor" (138). In Opie's portrayal of this pivotal moment, life is a script in which characters might find ourselves acting the same part that others have been assigned to play. Shared sympathy draws Adeline and Savannah together, yet their mutual support is interrupted by William's final relapse.

Dickens also explores the eerie connectedness in the child Jo's mistaken yet correct feeling that Esther is Esther's mother, Lady Dedlock. On being assured that Esther is her own person, he hesitates: "'Is it?' returned the boy doubtfully, and surveying me with his arm held out above his burning eyes. 'She looks to me the t'other one. It ain't the bonnet, nor yet it ain't the gownd, but she looks to me the t'other one'" (451). Although Esther has no way of knowing who "t'other one" is in Jo's feverish talk, she has felt a similar uncertainty when observing Lady Dedlock. This realization is evoked through Jo, though Esther will soon catch the disease he carries and lose the looks that might allow others to connect her to her mother. Her face will no longer link her to her parent, but she will unconsciously proceed along a similar life course. Like her mother before her, she recoils from unattainable romantic love and instead consents to marry an older guardian figure. The channeling of history into repeated patterns leads us, here as throughout the semester, to inspect the societal conditions that limit human choice.

As it turns out, Esther winds up with a fate very different from that of her mother. The endings of these choice of life fictions tend to be either histrionically tragic or, calling attention to their own artifice, providentially comic. But if the protagonist's conflict resolves, the social backdrop is understood to continue when the book is closed. The system persists. The plot of these three novels—the protagonist's early debility, circumscribed choices, ironic isolation in a cosmopolitan environment, recognition of self in others, and a nonrealistic ending—is admittedly more complicated than the resounding movement toward union in the courtship novel. All the same, these selections work well in the classroom with a "teach the problem" approach that foregrounds their difference from the mainstream tradition. While Adam Potkay has recently illumined the influence of David Hume's *Philosophical Essays* on Will Booth's final conversion, arguing that Booth more accurately might be said to realize that "[c]haracter is determined and that we are nonetheless responsible for it" ("Liberty" 348), *Amelia* also asks how individuals who assume that responsibility might withstand an onslaught of external adversity. Given a choice of how to respond to her accident, Amelia is sent whirling through a long series of consequences, and the depiction of her endurance aligns her with later protagonists under duress in the nineteenth-century novel.

NOTES

[1] The theme of my course might be pursued with other novels as well: Frances Burney's *Cecilia* (1782), Maria Edgeworth's *Belinda* (1801), William Makepeace Thackeray's *Vanity Fair* (1848), Anthony Trollope's *Phineas Finn* (1868), George Eliot's *Daniel Deronda*

(1876), and Henry James's *The Portrait of a Lady* (1881) also might complement *Amelia* because of their shared focus on marriage, money, risk, and tenacity.

[2] Although Booth is most often named the protagonist of *Amelia*, an association supported by the initial comparison of him with Aeneas, I would argue that in Fielding's text two characters function as a protagonist: by the end of the book, the reader has spent as much if not more time considering Amelia's reality as Booth's.

[3] Samuel Johnson's *Rasselas* is self-conscious of the endless time and money that might be devoted to the paradoxical pursuit of the "*choice of life*" (35). *Amelia* and its like are similarly ironic in depicting choices limited by contingency and want.

[4] I use the name "Mrs. Bennet" in this essay because I dwell on this character's early history and relation of it; she remarries and becomes "Mrs. Atkinson" later in the novel.

[5] Peter Sabor suggests that Mrs. Bennet might be hiding her culpability, retelling her history to further her own interests (101).

NOTES ON CONTRIBUTORS

Stephen C. Behrendt is university professor and George Holmes Distinguished Professor of English at the University of Nebraska. He is author of *Royal Mourning and Regency Culture: Elegies and Memorials of Princess Charlotte* (1997) and *British Women Poets and the Romantic Writing Community* (2009) and editor of *Romanticism, Radicalism, and the Press* (1997) and, with Harriet Kramer Linkin, *Romanticism and Women Poets: Opening the Doors of Reception* (1999).

Scott Black, associate professor of English at the University of Utah, has contributed essays to *Henry Fielding in Our Time* (2008), *The Cambridge History of the English Novel* (2012), and *The Oxford Handbook of the Eighteenth-Century Novel* (2014). He is the author of *Of Essays and Reading in Early Modern Britain* (2006) and has published articles on Hume, Ortega, and Heliodorus.

Pamela S. Bromberg is professor and director of the Graduate Program in English at Simmons College. Her teaching and scholarly work engages a broad variety of writers, including contemporary women and postcolonial novelists. She has published articles on William Blake's visual art and on the work of Margaret Drabble, Margaret Atwood, Lillian Hellman, and Buchi Emecheta. She has contributed to Approaches to Teaching World Literature volumes on Jane Austen's *Emma*, *Pride and Prejudice*, and *Mansfield Park*.

Jill Campbell, professor of English at Yale University, is the author of *Natural Masques: Gender and Identity in Fielding's Plays and Novels* (1995) and essays on Lady Mary Worthy Montagu, Alexander Pope, Horace Walpole, Maria Edgeworth, and women novelists of the Romantic period. Her edition of Fielding's *The Author's Farce* appears in *The Broadview Anthology of Restoration and Eighteenth-Century Drama*.

Leigh G. Dillard is assistant professor of English at the University of North Georgia, where she teaches composition, British literature, and technical writing. Among her recent publications are "Illustrating *Tom Jones*: The Visual Culture of Fielding's Realism" (2008) and "Drawing outside the Book: Parallel Illustration and Building of a Visual Culture" (2011). She is currently working on a book-length study of British illustration in the long eighteenth century.

J. A. Downie is professor of English in the Department of English and Comparative Literature at Goldsmiths, University of London. Among his books are *Robert Harley and the Press: Propaganda and Public Opinion in the Age of Swift and Defoe* (1979), *Jonathan Swift, Political Writer* (1984), *To Settle the Succession of the State: Literature and Politics, 1678–1750* (1994), and *A Political Biography of Henry Fielding* (2009). He is editor of the forthcoming *Oxford Handbook of the Eighteenth-Century Novel*.

James Evans, professor of English at the University of North Carolina, Greensboro, is the author of "Writing London in *Tom Jones*" (2008), *Comedy: An Annotated Bibliography of Theory and Criticism* (1987), "'The Dullissimo Maccaroni': Masculinities in *She Stoops to Conquer*" (2011), and "*Evelina*, the Rustic Girls of Congreve and Abington, and Surrogation in the 1770s" (2011). He won the ASECS Teaching Competition in 2000.

Carl Fisher, professor of comparative literature and chair of the Departments of Comparative World Literature and Classics and of Human Development at California State University, Long Beach, is the coeditor, with Maximillian E. Novak, of *Approaches to Teaching Defoe's Robinson Crusoe* (2005) and, with Robert Maniquis, of *Defoe's Footprints: Essays in Honour of Maximilliam Novak* (2009). He is author of "Pleasing the Public: Fielding's Afterpieces as Satyr Plays" (2007).

Joshua Grasso, associate professor of English at East Central University, is the author of "'An Enemy of his Country's Prosperity and Safety': Mapping the English Traveler in Defoe's *Robinson Crusoe*" (2008), "The Providence of Pirates: Defoe and the 'True-Bred Merchant'" (2010), and essays for Scribner's British Writers Supplement Series. He is currently writing a book about eighteenth-century musical travelogues.

George E. Haggerty is distinguished professor of English at University of California, Riverside. Among his books are *Gothic Fiction / Gothic Form* (1989), *Unnatural Affections: Women and Fiction in the Later Eighteenth Century* (1998), *Men in Love: Masculinity and Sexuality in the Eighteenth Century* (1999), *Queer Gothic* (2006), and *Horace Walpole's Letters: Masculinity and Friendship in the Eighteenth Century* (2011).

Anthony J. Hassall is professor emeritus of English literature at James Cook University and honorary professor at the University of Queensland. He has published extensively on eighteenth-century English literature, including Henry Fielding's *Tom Jones* (1979), and on Australian literature, including *Strange Country: A Study of Randolph Stow* (1986) and *Dancing on Hot Macadam: Peter Carey's Fiction* (1994).

Nicholas Hudson, professor of English at the University of British Columbia, is author of *Samuel Johnson and Eighteenth-Century Thought* (1988), *Writing and European Thought* (1994), *Samuel Johnson and the Making of Modern English* (2003), and *A Political Biography of Samuel Johnson* (2013) and coeditor, with Aaron Santesso, of *Swift's Travels: Eighteenth-Century British Satire and Its Legacy*.

Regina Janes, professor of English at Skidmore College, is author of *Gabriel García Márquez: Revolutions in Wonderland* (1981), One Hundred Years of Solitude*: Modes of Reading* (1991), *Edmund Burke and Irish Affairs* (2002), *Losing Our Heads: Beheadings in Literature and Culture* (2005), "Fielding and the Case of the Misguided Reader" (2008), "Henry Fielding Reinvents the Afterlife" (2011), and "Henry Fielding Straddles a Moving Theme" (2012).

Christopher D. Johnson is professor and chair of English, modern languages, and philosophy at Francis Marion University. He is the editor of *The Lives of Cleopatra and Octavia*, by Sarah Fielding (1994), and *New Perspectives on Eighteenth-Century British Fiction, "Hearts Resolved and Hands Prepared": New Essays in Honor of Jerry C. Beasley* (2011). He is presently working on a critical edition of Sarah Fielding's *The History of the Countess of Dellwyn* and on *Sarah Fielding: A Political Biography*.

Elizabeth Kraft is professor of English at the University of Georgia. She is author of *Character and Consciousness in Eighteenth-Century Comic Fiction* (1992), *Laurence Sterne Revisited* (1996), and *Women Novelists and the Ethics of Desire, 1684–1814* (2008). She has edited and coedited works by Charlotte Smith, Anna Letitia Barbauld, and Samuel Richardson. She is currently completing a critical work on Restoration courtship comedies and Hollywood comedies of remarriage.

Eric Leuschner is associate professor of English at Fort Hays State University. Among his essays are "'Utterly, Insurmountably, Unsaleable': Collected Editions, Prefaces, and the 'Failure' of Henry James's New York Edition" (2001), "Body Damage: Dis-figuring the Academic in Academic Fiction" (2006), and "Beginning with the Ephemeral: Reading the Eighteenth-Century Preface" (2012). He is working on a book project on campus novels.

Nancy A. Mace, professor of English at the U.S. Naval Academy, is author of *Henry Fielding's Novels and the Classical Tradition* (1996), "Fielding, Theobald, and *The Tragedy of Tragedies*" (1987), "Henry Fielding's Classical Learning" (1991), and numerous articles on late-eighteenth-century music printing and publishing.

Lisa Maruca is associate professor, associate chair, and director of Undergraduate Studies in English at Wayne State University. She is the author of *The Work of Print: Authorship and the English Text Trades, 1660–1760* (2007); has written articles on copyright, plagiarism, and bookselling; and is presently engaged in a book project, "Writing Readers: Educational Technologies of the English Enlightenment."

Brian McCrea is professor emeritus of English at the University of Florida and visiting lecturer in English at Flagler College. Among his books are *Impotent Fathers: Patriarchy and Demographic Crisis in the Eighteenth-Century Novel* (1998) and *Frances Burney and Narrative Prior to Ideology* (2013). He has contributed essays to The Spectator*: Emerging Discourses*, *Hermeneutics at the Crossroads*, *A Celebration of Frances Burney*, and *Henry Fielding in Our Time*.

Adam Potkay, professor of English and William R. Kenan Professor of Humanities at the College of William and Mary, is the author of *The Fate of Eloquence in the Age of Hume* (1994), *The Passion for Happiness: Samuel Johnson and David Hume* (2000), *The Story of Joy from the Bible to Late Romanticism* (2007), and *Wordsworth's Ethics* (2012). He is the editor of the Longman Cultural Edition of *Joseph Andrews* (2008).

Manushag N. Powell, associate professor of English at Purdue University, is the author of *Performing Authorship in Eighteenth-Century English Periodicals* (2012); the coauthor, with Frederick Burwick, of *British Pirates in Print and Performance* (2015); and the coeditor, with Rivka Swenson, of *Sensational Subjects*, a special issue of *The Eighteenth Century: Theory and Interpretation* (2013).

Chloe Wigston Smith, associate professor of English at the University of Georgia, is the author of *Women, Work, and Clothes in the Eighteenth-Century Novel* (2013). She has published also on costume books, trade cards, object narratives, and theatrical portraiture.

Rivka Swenson is assistant professor of English at Virginia Commonwealth University. Her book *Essential Scots and the Idea of Unionism in Anglo-Scottish Literature, 1603–1832* is forthcoming. She recently coedited, with Manushag N. Powell, *Sensational Subjects*, a special issue of *The Eighteenth Century: Theory and Interpretation* (2013), and is coediting, with John Richetti, Defoe's *The Farther Adventures of Robinson Crusoe*.

Earla Wilputte is professor of English at St. Francis Xavier University. She is the author of *Passion and Language in Eighteenth-Century Literature: The Aesthetic Sublime in the Work of Eliza Haywood, Aaron Hill, and Martha Fowke* (2014) and the editor of Eliza

Haywood's *Three Novellas* (1995) and *Adventures of Eovaai* (1999). Among her published essays are "Haywood's Tabloid Journalism: *Dalinda: or, The Double Marriage* and the Cresswell Bigamy Case" and "'Paper Cannot Blush': Martha Fowke, an Eighteenth-Century Abandoned Woman."

Jennifer Preston Wilson, associate professor at Appalachian State University, is the author of "*Clarissa*: The Nation Misrul'd" (2003), "'One Has Got All the Goodness, and the Other All the Appearance of It': The Development of Darcy in *Pride and Prejudice*" (2004), and "On Honor and Consequences: The Duel in *The Small House at Allington*" (2012). Her current project analyzes the influence of Samuel Richardson's novels on the works of Shirley Jackson.

SURVEY PARTICIPANTS

Stephen C. Behrendt, *University of Nebraska*
John Bender, *Stanford University*
Lisa Berglund, *Buffalo State College, State University of New York*
Melissa Bissonette, *St. John Fisher College*
Scott Black, *University of Utah*
Erik Bond, *University of Michigan, Dearborn*
Pamela S. Bromberg, *Simmons College*
Jill Campbell, *Yale University*
Terra A. Caputo, *Allegheny College*
Keith Clavin, *Auburn University*
Leigh G. Dillard, *University of North Georgia*
J. A. Downie, *Goldsmiths, University of London*
James Evans, *University of North Carolina, Greensboro*
Carl Fisher, *California State University, Long Beach*
Mark K. Fulk, *Buffalo State College, State University of New York*
Joshua Grasso, *East Central University*
George E. Haggerty, *University of California, Riverside*
Anthony J. Hassall, *James Cook University and University of Queensland*
Melanie Holm, *Rutgers University*
Nicole Horejsi, *Columbia University*
Nicholas Hudson, *University of British Columbia, Vancouver*
Regina Janes, *Skidmore College*
Christopher D. Johnson, *Francis Marion University*
Katherine Kickel, *Miami University of Ohio*
Elizabeth Kraft, *University of Georgia*
Marta Kvande, *Texas Tech University*
Anthony W. Lee, *Arkansas Tech University*
Eric Leuschner, *Fort Hays State University*
Nancy A. Mace, *U.S. Naval Academy*
Lisa Maruca, *Wayne State University*
Brian McCrea, *University of Florida and Flagler College*
Will McMorran, *Queen Mary, University of London*
Jason H. Pearl, *Florida International University*
Adam Potkay, *College of William and Mary*
Manushag N. Powell, *Purdue University*
Dale J. Pratt, *Brigham Young University*
Raymond J. Ricketts, *Bryn Mawr College*
Daniel Robinson, *Widener University*
Richard Rosengarten, *University of Chicago*
Robin Runia, *Angelo State University*
Carole Sargent, *Georgetown University*
Carrie Shanafelt, *Grinnell College*
Chloe Wigston Smith, *University of Georgia*

Anne Stevens, *University of Nevada, Las Vegas*
Rivka Swenson, *Virginia Commonwealth University*
Connie Capers Thorson, *University of New Mexico, Albuquerque*
David L. Vander Meulen, *University of Virginia*
Elizabeth Way, *Wake Forest University*
Anne Widmayer, *University of Wisconsin, Washington County*
Earla Wilputte, *St. Francis Xavier University*
Jennifer Preston Wilson, *Appalachian State University*
James Woolley, *Lafayette College*
Linda Zionkowski, *Ohio University*

WORKS CITED

[Allestree, Richard]. *The Whole Duty of Man Laid Down in a Plain and Familiar Way for the Use of All*. London, 1714. Print.

Allott, Miriam. "A Note on Fielding's Mr. Square." *Modern Language Review* 56 (1961): 69–72. Print.

Alter, Robert. *Fielding and the Nature of the Novel*. Cambridge: Harvard UP, 1968. Print.

———. "Fielding's Legacy in Fiction." Rawson, *Henry Fielding, 1707–1754* 314–24.

———. *Partial Magic: The Novel as a Self-Conscious Genre*. Berkeley: U of California P, 1975. Print.

Amis, Martin. *Money: A Suicide Note*. New York: Penguin, 1985. Print.

Amory, Hugh. "Fielding's Lisbon Letters." *Huntington Library Quarterly* 35.1 (1971): 65–83. Print.

Anderson, Howard. "Answers to the Author of *Clarissa*: Theme and Narrative Technique in *Tom Jones* and *Tristram Shandy*." *Philological Quarterly* 51 (1972): 859–73. Print.

Arabian Nights' Entertainments. Ed. Robert L. Mack. Oxford: Oxford UP, 2009. Print.

Aravamudan, Srinivas. *Enlightenment Orientalism: Resisting the Rise of the Novel*. Chicago: U of Chicago P, 2012. Print.

Arbuthnot, Archibald. *Memoirs of the Remarkable Life and Surprising Adventures of Miss Jenny Cameron*. London: R. Walker, 1746. Print.

Ardila, J. A. G. "Henry Fielding, from Quixotic Satire to the Cervantean Novel." *The Cervantean Heritage: Reception and Influence of Cervantes in Britain*. Ed. Ardila. London: Modern Humanities Research Assn., 2009. 124–41. Print.

Aristophanes. *Lysistrata*. Trans. Douglass Parker. New York: Signet, 2009. Print.

Armitage, David. "A Patriot for Whom? The Afterlife of Bolingbroke's Patriot King." *Journal of British Studies* 36 (1997): 397–418. Print.

Armstrong, Nancy. *Desire and Domestic Fiction: A Political History of the Novel*. Oxford: Oxford UP, 1987. Print.

Backscheider, Paula R., and John J. Richetti, eds. *Popular Fiction by Women, 1660–1730*. Oxford: Clarendon, 1996. Print.

Baines, Paul. "*Joseph Andrews*." Rawson, *Cambridge Companion* 50–64.

Baker, Sheridan. "Bridget Allworthy: The Creative Pressures of Fielding's Plot." *Papers of the Michigan Academy of Science, Arts, and Letters* 52 (1967): 345–56. Print.

———. "Bridget Allworthy: The Creative Pressures of Fielding's Plot." Fielding, *Tom Jones* [ed. Baker] 906–16.

———. "Fielding: The Comic Reality of Fiction." *Tennessee Studies in Literature* 25 (1985): 102–42. Print.

———. "Fielding's Comic Epic-in-Prose Romances Again." *Philological Quarterly* 58 (1979): 63–81. Print.

———. "The Idea of Romance in the Eighteenth-Century Novel." *Papers of the Michigan Academy of Science, Arts, and Letters* 49 (1964): 507–22. Print.

Bakhtin, M. M. "Discourse in the Novel." *The Dialogic Imagination*. Trans. Caryl Emerson and Michael Holquist. Austin: U of Texas P, 1981. 259–422. Print.

———. *Rabelais and His World*. Trans. Hélène Iswolsky. Bloomington: Indiana UP, 1984. Print.

———. "Response to a Question from the *Novy Mir* Editorial Staff." *"Speech Genres" and Other Late Essays*. Trans. Vern W. McGhee. Austin: U Texas P, 1986. 1–9. Print.

Bal, Mieke. *Narratology: Introduction to the Theory of Narrative*. 1985. Toronto: U of Toronto P, 2009. Print.

Ballaster, Rosalind. *Fabulous Orients: Fictions of the East in England, 1662–1785*. Oxford: Oxford UP, 2005. Print.

———. *Seductive Forms: Women's Amatory Fiction, 1684–1740*. Oxford: Oxford UP, 1998. Print.

Banerjee, Jacqueline. "Coram and the Foundling Hospital." *The Victorian Web*. Ed. Philip V. Allingham and Banerjee. Victorian Web, n.d. Web. 13 Mar. 2014.

Bannet, Eve Tavor. *Empire of Letters: Letter Manuals and Transatlantic Correspondence, 1680–1820*. Cambridge: Cambridge UP, 2005. Print.

———. *Transatlantic Stories and the History of Reading, 1720–1810: Migrant Fictions*. Cambridge: Cambridge UP, 2011. Print.

Barker, Jane. *Love Intrigues*. Backscheider and Richetti 81–112.

Barthes, Roland. "The Death of the Author." *Image-Music-Text*. Trans. Stephen Heath. New York: Hill, 1977. 143–47. Print.

———. *S/Z*. Trans. Richard Miller. New York: Hill, 1974. Print.

Battestin, Martin C. "Adapting Fielding for Film and Television." *Eighteenth-Century Fiction on Screen*. Ed. Robert Mayer. Cambridge: Cambridge UP, 2002. 88–105. Print.

———. "Fielding's Anatomy of Laughter." Downie, *Henry Fielding* 1–26.

———. "Fielding's Definition of Wisdom: Some Functions of Ambiguity and Emblem in *Tom Jones*." *ELH* 35 (1968): 188–217. Print.

———. *A Henry Fielding Companion*. Westport: Greenwood, 2000. Print.

———. Introduction. Fielding, *Amelia* [Battestin] xv–lxi.

———. Introduction to *An Apology for the Life of Mrs. Shamela Andrews (1741)*. Fielding, Journal 133–45.

———. *The Moral Basis of Fielding's Art: A Study of* Joseph Andrews. Middletown: Wesleyan UP, 1959. Print.

———. "The Problem of *Amelia*: Hume, Barrow, and the Conversion of Captain Booth." *ELH* 41.4 (1974): 613–48. Print.

———. "Tom Jones and 'His *Egyptian* Majesty': Fielding's Parable of Government." *PMLA* 82.1 (1967): 68–77. Print.

Battestin, Martin C., and Ruthe R. Battestin. *Henry Fielding: A Life*. London: Routledge, 1989. Print.

Battigelli, Anna. "ASECS Summary of 'Some Noisy Feedback.'" *Early Modern Online Bibliography*. Battigelli, 27 Mar. 2010. Web. 15 May 2013.

Bean, Richard. *One Man, Two Guvnors*. London: Oberon, 2011. Print.

Behn, Aphra. *Oroonoko*. Ed. Catherine Gallagher. Boston: Bedford, 2000. Print.

Behrens, Laurence. "The Argument of *Tom Jones*." *Film/Literature Quarterly* 8.1 (1980): 22–34. Print.

Bell, Ian A. *Henry Fielding: Authorship and Authority*. London: Longman, 1994. Print.

Bender, John. *Imagining the Penitentiary: Fiction and the Architecture of Mind in Eighteenth-Century England.* Chicago: U of Chicago P, 1987. Print.

———. Introduction. Fielding, *Tom Jones* [ed. Bender and Stern] ix–xxxiv.

Benedict, Barbara M. *Making the Modern Reader: Cultural Mediation in Early Modern Literary Anthologies*. Princeton: Princeton UP, 1996. Print.

Bertelsen, Lance. *Henry Fielding at Work: Magistrate, Businessman, Writer*. Basingstoke: Palgrave, 2000. Print.

Bindman, David, Frédéric Ogée, and Peter Wagner, eds. *Hogarth: Representing Nature's Machines*. Manchester: Manchester UP, 2001. Print.

Black, Scott. "The Adventures of Love in *Tom Jones*." Downie, *Henry Fielding* 27–50.

———. "Anachronism and the Uses of Form in *Joseph Andrews*." *Novel* 38 (2005): 147–64. Print.

———. *Of Essays and Reading in Early Modern Britain*. New York: Palgrave, 2006. Print.

Blewett, David, ed. *Reconsidering the Rise of the Novel*. Spec. issue of *Eighteenth-Century Fiction* 12 (2000): 141–49. Web. 12 Mar. 2014.

Bohls, Elizabeth, and Ian Duncan, eds. *Travel Writing, 1700–1830: An Anthology*. Oxford: Oxford UP, 2005. Print.

Bolingbroke, Henry St. John. *Letters on the Spirit of Patriotism, on the Idea of a Patriot King, and on the State of Parties, at the Accession of King George the First*. London: A. Millar, 1749. Print.

Bonnell, Thomas F. *The Most Disreputable Trade: Publishing the Classics of English Poetry, 1765–1810*. Oxford: Oxford UP, 2008. Print.

"Bonnie Jeanie Cameron." *Ancient Scots Ballads with Their Traditional Airs*. Glasgow: Bayley and Ferguson, 1894. Print.

Booth, Wayne C. "Fielding in *Tom Jones*." Booth, *Rhetoric* 215–18.

———. "Fielding in *Tom Jones*." Fielding, *Tom Jones* [ed. Baker] 893–95.

———. The *Rhetoric of Fiction*. Chicago: U of Chicago P, 1971. Print.

Boswell, James. *Life of Johnson*. Ed. R. W. Chapman. Oxford: Oxford UP, 1980. Print.

Braudy, Leo. *Narrative Form in History and Fiction: Hume, Fielding, and Gibbon*. Princeton: Princeton UP, 1970. Print.

Bray, Alan. *The Friend.* Chicago: U of Chicago P, 2003. Print.

Bree, Linda. "Henry and Sarah Fielding: A Literary Relationship." Rawson, *Henry Fielding, 1707–1754* 145–72.

———. "Henry Fielding's Life." Rawson, *Cambridge Companion* 3–16.

———. Introduction. Fielding, *Amelia* [ed. Bree] 9–30.

Brewer, John. *The Pleasures of the Imagination: English Culture in the Eighteenth Century*. London: Harper, 1997. Print.

———. *Sense and Sensation: English Culture in the Eighteenth Century.* Dir. Ian Leese. Illuminations, 2002. DVD.

Broadside Band. The Beggar's Opera*: Original Songs and Airs.* Perf. Patrizia Kwella and Paul Elliot. Harmonia Mundi, 2003. CD.

The Broadview Anthology of British Literature: The Restoration and Eighteenth Century. Ed. Joseph Black et al. Peterborough: Broadview, 2012. Print.

Brooks, Peter. *Reading for the Plot: Design and Intention in Narrative.* New York: Knopf, 1984. Print.

Brown, Homer O. *Institutions of the English Novel: From Defoe to Scott*. Philadelphia: U of Pennsylvania P, 1997. Print.

Bunyan, John. The Pilgrim's Progress*: An Authoritative Text, Contexts, Criticism*. Ed. Cynthia Wall. New York: Norton, 2009. Print.

Burke, John J. "Fielding's Epic Combat with Milton in *Tom Jones*." Downie, *Henry Fielding* 51–64.

Burnet, Gilbert. *History of His Own Time.* Vol. 1. London, 1724. Print.

Burney, Frances. *Evelina*. Ed. Stewart J. Cooke. New York: Norton, 1998. Print.

———. *The Wanderer; or, Female Difficulties*. *Internet Archive*. Internet Archive, 30 June 2010. Web. 22 Sept. 2014.

Butler, Gerald J. "Fielding's Disruptive Heterosexuality." Downie, *Henry Fielding* 65–80.

———. "Making Fielding's Novels Speak for Law and Order." Richter, *Ideology* 75–88.

Byron, George Gordon. *Don Juan*. Ed. T. G. Steffan et al. New Haven: Yale UP, 1982. Print.

Campbell, Jill. "Fielding and the Novel at Mid-Century." Richetti, *Columbia History* 102–26.

———. "Fielding's Style." *ELH* 72 (2005): 407–28. Print.

———. *Natural Masques: Gender and Identity in Fielding's Plays and Novels.* Stanford: Stanford UP, 1995. Print.

Canfield, J. Douglas, ed. *The Broadview Anthology of Restoration and Early-Eighteenth-Century Drama*. Peterborough: Broadview, 2001. Print.

Carlton, Peter J. "The Mitigated Truth: Tom Jones's Double Heroism." *Studies in the Novel* 19.4 (1987): 397–409. Print.

———. "*Tom Jones* and the '45 Once Again." *Studies in the Novel* 20.4 (1988): 361–73. Print.

Carlyle, Thomas. *On Heroes, Hero Worship, and the Heroic in History*. 1840. Berkeley: U of California P, 1993. Print.

———. *Sartor Resartus*. 1833. Oxford: Oxford UP, 2008. Print.

Carter, Elizabeth. Letter. Paulson and Lockwood 123.

Cascardi, Anthony J. "*Don Quixote* and the Invention of the Novel." *Cambridge Companion to Cervantes*. Ed. Cascardi. Cambridge: Cambridge UP, 2002. 58–79. Print.

Caserio, Robert L., and Clement Hawes, eds. *The Cambridge History of the English Novel*. Cambridge: Cambridge UP, 2012. Print.

Castle, Terry. *The Female Thermometer: Eighteenth-Century Culture and the Invention of the Uncanny*. Oxford: Oxford UP, 1995. Print.

———. *Masquerade and Civilization: The Carnivalesque in Eighteenth-Century English Culture and Fiction*. Stanford: Stanford UP, 1986. Print.

Cavendish, Margaret. *Paper Bodies: A Margaret Cavendish Reader*. Ed. Sylvia Bowerbank and Sara Mendelson. Peterborough: Broadview, 2000. Print.

Cervantes, Miguel de. *Don Quixote*. Trans. Peter Motteux and John Ozell. 4 vols. London, 1743. Print.

———. *Don Quixote*. Trans. Tobias Smollett. New York: Modern Lib., 2001. Print.

Chapone, Hester Mulso. *The Posthumous Works of Mrs. Chapone: Containing Her Correspondence with Mr. Richardson: A Series of Letters to Mrs. Elizabeth Carter, and Some Fugitive Pieces Never before Published.* 2 vols. London, 1807. Print.

Chibka, Robert L. "Henry Fielding, Mentalist: Ins and Outs of Narration in *Tom Jones*." Downie, *Henry Fielding* 81–112.

Cibber, Colley. *An Apology for the Life of Mr. Colley Cibber*. Mineola: Dover, 1968. Print.

Cleland, John. Rev. *Monthly Review* Dec. 1751. Paulson and Lockwood 304–09.

Cody, David. "Methodism." *The Victorian Web*. Ed. Philip V. Allingham and Jacqueline Banerjee. Victorian Web, n.d. Web. 13 Mar. 2014.

Compton, Neil, ed. *Henry Fielding:* Tom Jones*: A Casebook*. London: Macmillan, 1970. Print.

Conway, Alison. *The Protestant Whore: Courtesan Narrative and Religious Controversy in England, 1680–1750*. Toronto: U of Toronto P, 2010. Print.

Cooke, Charles. *Plan and Catalogue of Cooke's Uniform, Cheap, and Elegant Pocket Library*. London, [1795?]. Print.

Coolidge, John S. "Fielding and 'Conservation of Character.'" *Modern Philology* 57 (1960): 245–59. Print.

Craig, Maggie. *Damn' Rebel Bitches: The Women of the '45*. Edinburgh: Mainstream, 1997. Print.

Crane, R. S. "The Concept of Plot and the Plot of *Tom Jones*." *Journal of General Education* 4 (1950): 112–30. Print.

———. "The Concept of Plot and the Plot of *Tom Jones*." Fielding, *Tom Jones* [ed. Baker] 844–69.

Cross, Wilbur L. *The History of Henry Fielding*. 3 vols. New Haven: Yale UP, 1918. Print.

Cruise, James. "Fielding, Authority, and the New Commercialism in *Joseph Andrews*." *ELH* 54.2 (1987): 253–76. Print.

"Curate." *Dictionary of the English Language*. 2 vols. London, 1755. Print.

Davenport, G., S. Agamanolis, B. Barry, B. Bradley, and K. Brooks. "Synergistic Storyscapes and Constructionist Cinematic Sharing." *IBM Systems Journal* 39.3–4 (2000): 456–69. Print.

Davidson, Jenny. "*Jonathan Wild.*" Rawson, *Cambridge Companion* 65–79.

Davis, Leith A. *Acts of Union: Scotland and the Literary Negotiation of the British Nation, 1707–1830*. Stanford: Stanford UP, 1998. Print.

Davis, Lennard. *Bending Over Backwards: Disability, Dismodernism, and Other Difficult Positions*. New York: New York UP, 2002. Print.

———. *Factual Fictions: The Origins of the English Novel*. Philadelphia: U of Pennsylvania P, 1983. Print.

Defoe, Daniel. *Robinson Crusoe*. Ed. John Richetti. New York: Penguin, 2001. Print.

De Voogd, Peter Jan. *Henry Fielding and William Hogarth: The Correspondences of the Arts*. Amsterdam: Rodopi, 1981. Print.

Dickens, Charles. *Bleak House*. Ed. Stephen Gill. Oxford: Oxford UP, 2008. Print.

Dickie, Simon. "*Amelia*, Sex, and Fielding's Woman Question." Rawson, *Henry Fielding, 1707–1754* 115–42.

———. *Cruelty and Laughter: Forgotten Comic Literature and the Unsentimental Eighteenth Century*. Chicago: U of Chicago P, 2011. Print.

———. "Fielding's Rape Jokes." *Review of English Studies* 61.251 (2010): 572–88. Print.

Diderot, Denis. *De la poésie dramatique*. 1758. *Œuvres esthétiques*. Ed. Paul Venière. Paris: Garnier, 1994. 189–287. Print. Classiques Garnier.

Dillard, Leigh G. "Illustrating *Tom Jones*: The Visual Culture of Fielding's Realism." *Word and Image in the Eighteenth Century: An Interdisciplinary Dialogue*. Ed. Christina Ionescu and Renata Schellenberg. Newcastle upon Tyne: Cambridge Scholars, 2008. 134–53. Print.

Doody, Margaret. *The True Story of the Novel*. New Brunswick: Rutgers UP, 1996. Print.

Downie, J. A. "Biographical Form in the Novel." Caserio and Hawes 30–45.

———, ed. *Henry Fielding in Our Time: Papers Presented at the Tercentenary Conference*. Newcastle upon Tyne: Cambridge Scholars, 2008. Print.

———. "Henry Fielding, Magistrate." Downie, *Henry Fielding* 113–31.

———. *A Political Biography of Henry Fielding*. London: Pickering, 2009. Print.

Drake, George A. "Ritual in *Joseph Andrews*." Downie, *Henry Fielding* 133–46.

Dryden, John. "A Discourse concerning the Original and Progress of Satire." 1693. *"Of Dramatic Poesy" and Other Critical Essays*. Vol. 2. Ed. George Watson. Dent: London, 1962. 71–155. Print.

Dudden, F. Homes. *Henry Fielding: His Life, Works, and Times*. 2 vols. Oxford: Clarendon, 1952. Print.

Dunton, John. *The Life and Errors of John Dunton, Citizen of London*. 1705. London: J. Nichols, Son, and Bentley, 1818. *Google Books*. Web. 1 May 2013.

Earle, William. *Obi; or, The History of Three-Fingered Jack*. Ed. Srinivas Aravamudan. Peterborough: Broadview, 2005. Print.

Empson, William. "*Tom Jones.*" Paulson, *Fielding* 123–45.

Erskine-Hill, Howard. "The 'New World' of Pope's *Dunciad*." *Essential Articles for the Study of Alexander Pope*. Hamden: Archon, 1964. 739–60. Print.

An Essay on the New Species of Writing Founded by Mr. Fielding. 1751. Ed. Alan D. McKillop. Los Angeles: William Andrews Clark Memorial Lib., 1962. Print. Augustan Rpt. Soc. 95.

Evans, James. "Writing London in *Tom Jones*." Downie, *Henry Fielding* 147–64.

"Extract of a Letter from a Lady at Preston, to Her Friend in Town, Dated December 14: Concerning the Young Pretender and His Retinue." *Gentleman's Magazine* 15 (Dec. 1745): 644. Print.

Ezell, Margaret J. M. "Making a Classic: The Advent of the Literary Series." *South Central Review* 11.2 (1994): 2–16. Print.

The Female American; or, The Adventures of Unca Eliza Winkfield. Ed. Michelle Burnham. Peterborough: Broadview, 2001. Print.

Festa, Lynn. *Sentimental Figures of Empire: Eighteenth-Century Britain and France.* Baltimore: Johns Hopkins UP, 2006. Print.

Fielding, Henry. *Amelia.* Ed. Martin Battestin. Oxford: Clarendon, 1983. Print. Wesleyan Ed. of the Works of Henry Fielding.

———. *Amelia.* Ed. Linda Bree. Peterborough: Broadview, 2010. Print.

———. *The Author's Farce. Plays: Volume One, 1728–1731.* Ed. Thomas Lockwood. Oxford: Clarendon, 2004. 221–90. Print. Wesleyan Ed. of the Works of Henry Fielding.

———. *A Clear State of the Case of Elizabeth Canning.* London: A. Millar, 1753. Print.

———. *Contributions to* The Champion *and Related Writings.* Ed. W. B. Coley. Oxford: Clarendon, 2003. Print. Wesleyan Ed. of the Works of Henry Fielding.

———. *"The Covent-Garden Journal" and "A Plan of the Universal Register-Office."* Ed. Bertrand A. Goldgar. Oxford: Clarendon, 1988. Print. Wesleyan Ed. of the Works of Henry Fielding.

———. An Enquiry into the Causes of the Late Increase of Robbers, *and Related Writings.* Ed. Malvin R. Zirker. Oxford: Clarendon, 1988. Print. Wesleyan Ed. of the Works of Henry Fielding.

———. *An Essay on the Knowledge of the Characters of Men. Miscellanies by Henry Fielding, Esq.* Vol. 1. London: A. Millar, 1743. 181–227. Print.

———. *The Grub-Street Opera.* Ed. Edgar V. Roberts. Lincoln: U of Nebraska P, 1968. Print.

———. *The History of the Adventures of Joseph Andrews.* Ed. Adam Potkay. New York: Pearson, 2007. Print.

———. *The History of the Adventures of Joseph Andrews, and His Friend Mr. Abraham Adams: Written in Imitation of the Manner of Cervantes, Author of* Don Quixote. 2 vols. London: A. Millar, 1742. Print.

———. *The History of Tom Jones, A Foundling.* Ed. Fredson Bowers. Introd. and commentary by Martin C. Battestin. 2 vols. Oxford: Clarendon, 1974. Print. Wesleyan Ed. of the Works of Henry Fielding.

———. *The History of Tom Jones, A Foundling.* Ed. Thomas Keymer and Alice Wakely. London: Penguin, 2005. Print.

———. *Jonathan Wild.* Ed. Hugh Amory. Oxford: Oxford UP, 2008. Print.

———. *Jonathan Wild. Miscellanies: Volume Three*. Ed. Hugh Amory. Introd. and commentary by Bertrand A. Goldgar. Oxford: Clarendon, 1997. Print. Wesleyan Ed. of the Works of Henry Fielding.

———. *Joseph Andrews*. Ed. Martin C. Battestin. Oxford: Clarendon, 1967. Print. Wesleyan Ed. of the Works of Henry Fielding.

———. *Joseph Andrews*. Ed. Paul A. Scanlon. Peterborough: Broadview, 2001. Print.

———. Joseph Andrews *and* Shamela. Ed. Douglas Brooks-Davies. Rev. Thomas Keymer. Oxford: Oxford UP, 1999. Print.

———. Joseph Andrews *and* Shamela. Ed. Judith Hawley. London: Penguin, 1999. Print.

———. Joseph Andrews *with* Shamela *and Related Writings*. Ed. Homer Goldberg. New York: Norton, 1987. Print.

———. The Journal of a Voyage to Lisbon, Shamela, *and Occasional Writings*. Ed. Martin C. Battestin, Sheridan W. Baker, Jr., and Hugh Amory. Oxford: Clarendon, 2008. Print. Wesleyan Ed. of the Works of Henry Fielding.

———. *Miscellanies*. Vol. 1. Ed. Henry Knight Miller. Oxford: Clarendon, 1972. Print. Wesleyan Ed. of the Works of Henry Fielding.

———. *Miscellanies*. Vol. 3. Ed. Hugh Amory. Oxford: Clarendon, 1997. Print. Wesleyan Ed. of the Works of Henry Fielding.

———. *Shamela*. Fielding, Journal 133–95.

———. *Shamela*. Anti-Pamela *and* Shamela. Ed. Catherine Ingrassia. Peterborough: Broadview, 2004. 229–76. Print.

———. *Tom Jones*. Ed. Sheridan Baker. 2nd ed. New York: Norton, 1995. Print.

———. *Tom Jones*. Ed. John Bender and Simon Stern. Oxford: Oxford UP, 1996. Print.

———. *The Wesleyan Edition of the Works of Henry Fielding*. 15 vols. in 16. Executive ed. W. B. Coley. Oxford: Clarendon, 1967–2011. Print.

Fielding, Henry, and Sarah Fielding. *The Correspondence of Henry and Sarah Fielding*. Ed. Martin C. Battestin and Clive T. Probyn. Oxford: Clarendon, 1993. Print.

Flynn, Carol Houlihan. "Closing Down the Theater and Other Critical Abuses." Richter, *Ideology* 89–103.

Fone, B. R. S. Introduction. Cibber, *Apology* [1968] ix–xxvii.

Forcione, Alban K. *Cervantes, Aristotle, and the* Persiles. Princeton: Princeton UP, 1970. Print.

Forster, E. M. "Jane Austen." *Abinger Harvest*. 1936. New York: Meridian, 1955. 140–56. Print.

Foucault, Michel. "What Is an Author?" *The Foucault Reader*. Ed. Paul Rabinow. New York: Pantheon, 1969. 101–20. Print.

Fowler, Alastair. "The Two Histories." *Theoretical Issues in Literary History*. Ed. David Perkins. Cambridge: Harvard UP, 1991. 114–30. Print.

Fox, Christopher. "Swift and the Rabble Reformation: *A Tale of a Tub* and the State of the Church in the 1690s." *Swift as Priest and Satirist*. Ed. Todd C. Parker. Newark: U of Delaware P, 2009. 102–22. Print.

Francus, Marilyn. "The Monstrous Mother: Reproductive Anxiety in Swift and Pope." *ELH* 61.4 (1994): 829–51. Print.

Freeman, Lisa A. *Character's Theater: Genre and Identity on the Eighteenth-Century English Stage.* Philadelphia: U of Pennsylvania P, 2001. Print.

Frye, Northrop. *Anatomy of Criticism: Four Essays*. Princeton: Princeton UP, 1957. Print.

Fuchs, Barbara. *Romance*. New York: Routledge, 2004. Print. New Critical Idiom.

A Funny Thing Happened on the Way to the Forum. Dir. Richard Lester. Perf. Zero Mostel, Phil Silvers, and Buster Keaton. United Artists, 1966. DVD.

Fussell, Paul. *The Rhetorical World of Augustan Humanism: Ethics and Imagery from Swift to Burke*. Oxford: Clarendon, 1965. Print.

Gautier, Gary. "Marriage and Family in Fielding's Fiction." *Studies in the Novel* 27.2 (1995): 111–28. Print.

Gay, John. *The Beggar's Opera.* Canfield 1332–73.

———. *Polly.* Canfield 1545–93.

Gee, Sophie. *Making Waste: Leftovers and the Eighteenth-Century Imagination*. Princeton: Princeton UP, 2010. Print.

Genette, Gérard. *Narrative Discourse: An Essay in Method*. Trans. Jane E. Lewen. Ithaca: Cornell UP, 1980. Print.

———. *Paratexts: Thresholds of Interpretation*. Cambridge: Cambridge UP, 1997. Print.

Gilbert, Sandra M., and Susan Gubar. *The Madwoman in the Attic: The Woman Writer and the Nineteenth-Century Literary Imagination.* 2nd ed. New Haven: Yale UP, 2000. Print.

Girard, René. *Deceit, Desire, and the Novel: Self and Other in Literary Structure*. Trans. Yvonne Freccero. Baltimore: Johns Hopkins UP, 1965. Print.

Girouard, Mark. *Life in the English Country House: A Social and Architectural History*. New York: Penguin, 1980. Print.

Gladfelder, Hal. *Criminality and Narrative in Eighteenth-Century England: Beyond the Law*. Baltimore: Johns Hopkins UP, 2001. Print.

Goldberg, Homer. "Comic Prose Epic or Comic Romance: The Argument of the Preface to *Joseph Andrews*." *Philological Quarterly* 43 (1964): 193–215. Print.

Goldgar, Bertrand A. "The *Champion* and the Chapter on Hats in *Jonathan Wild*." *Philological Quarterly* 72.4 (1993): 443–50. *Gale Biography in Context*. Web. 16 Oct. 2012.

Gottfried, Leon. "The Odyssean Form." *Essays on European Literature in Honour of Liselotte Dieckmann*. Ed. Peter Uwe Hohendahl, Herbert Samuel Lindenberger, and Egon Schwarz. Saint Louis: Washington UP, 1972. 19–43. Print.

Greene, Donald. *The Age of Exuberance: Backgrounds to Eighteenth-Century Literature*. New York: Random, 1970. Print.

Greene, Jody. *The Trouble with Ownership: Literary Property and Authorial Liability in England, 1660–1730.* Philadelphia: U of Pennsylvania P, 2005. Print.

Greenfield, Sayre N. "Undergraduate Use of Search Engines in *EEBO* and *ECCO*." *Eighteenth-Century Intelligencer* 23.3 (2009): 13–16. Print.

Griffin, Dustin. *Satire: A Critical Reintroduction*. Lexington: UP of Kentucky, 1994. Print.

Gubar, Susan. "The Female Monster in Augustan Satire." *Signs: A Journal of Women in Culture and Society* 3 (1977): 380–94. Print.

Guerinot, J. V., and Rodney D. Jilg. *Contexts 1:* The Beggar's Opera. Hamden: Archon, 1976. Print.

Habermas, Jürgen. *The Structural Transformation of the Public Sphere: An Inquiry into a Category of Bourgeois Society*. Trans. Thomas Burger. Cambridge: MIT, 1989. Print.

Haefner, Joel. "'In Tangled Mazes Wrought': Hypertext and Teaching Romantic Women Poets." *Approaches to Teaching British Women Poets of the Romantic Period*. Ed. Stephen C. Behrendt and Harriet Kramer Linkin. New York: MLA, 1997. 45–50. Print.

Hager, Kelly. *Dickens and the Rise of Divorce: The Failed-Marriage Plot and the Novel Tradition*. Burlington: Ashgate, 2010. Print.

Haggerty, George E. "Amelia's Nose; or, Sensibility and Its Symptoms." *The Eighteenth Century: Theory and Interpretation* 36 (1995): 139–56. Print.

Hahn, H. George. *Henry Fielding: An Annotated Bibliography.* Metuchen: Scarecrow, 1979. Print.

Hamilton, Elizabeth. *Translation of the Letters of a Hindoo Rajah*. Ed. Pamela Perkins and Shannon Russell. Peterborough: Broadview, 1999. Print.

Harrison, Bernard. *Henry Fielding's* Tom Jones*: The Novelist as Moral Philosopher*. Sussex: Sussex UP, 1975. Print.

Hassall, Anthony J. "The Authorial Dimension in the Plays of Henry Fielding." *Komos* 1 (1967): 4–18. Print.

———. "Fielding's *Amelia*: Dramatic and Authorial Narration." *Novel* 5.3 (1972): 225–33. Print.

———. "Women in Richardson and Fielding." *Novel: A Forum on Fiction* 19 (1981): 168–74. Print.

Hatfield, Glenn W. *Henry Fielding and the Language of Irony*. Chicago: U of Chicago P, 1968. Print.

Hawes, Clement. "Novelistic History." Caserio and Hawes 63–79.

Hay, Douglas. "Property, Authority, and the Criminal Law." *Albion's Fatal Tree: Crime and Society in Eighteenth-Century England*. Ed. Hay, Peter Linebaugh, John G. Rule, E. P. Thompson, and Cal Winslow. London: Lane, 1975. 17–66. Print.

Haywood, Eliza. *Fantomina*. Backscheider and Richetti 226–48.

———. *The History of Miss Betsy Thoughtless*. *Project Gutenburg*. Project Gutenburg, 21 July 2014. Web. 22 Sept. 2014.

Haywood, Eliza, and Henry Fielding. *Anti-Pamela; or, Feign'd Innocence Detected* and *An Apology for the Life of Mrs. Shamela Andrews.* Ed. Catherine Ingrassia. Peterborough: Broadview, 2004. Print.

Hees, Amy, Ismat Mangla, Steve Porentas, and Libby Reece. *The World Upside Down: Eighteenth Century Masquerades*. Dept. of English, U of Michigan, 8 Dec. 2000. Web. 13 Mar. 2014.

Heliodorus. *The Adventures of Theagenes and Chariclia: A Romance*. 2 vols. London, 1717. Print.

Hilles, Frederick W. "Art and Artifice in *Tom Jones*." *Imagined Worlds: Essays on Some English Novels and Novelists in Honour of John Butt*. Ed. Maynard Mack and Ian Gregor. London: Methuen, 1968. Print.

———. "Art and Artifice in *Tom Jones*." Fielding, *Tom Jones* [ed. Baker] 786–800.

Hirsch, E. D., Jr. *Validity in Interpretation*. New Haven: Yale UP, 1967. Print.

"History." Def. 1. *Oxford English Dictionary*. 2nd ed. 1989. Print.

The History of Tom Jones, A Foundling. Dir. Metin Hüseyin. BBC; A&E, 1997. DVD.

Hoadly, Benjamin. *A Plain Account of the Nature and End of the Sacrament of the Lord's Supper*. 3rd ed. London, 1735. Print.

Hobbes, Thomas. *Leviathan*. Ed. Richard E. Flathman and David Johnston. New York: Norton, 1997. Print.

Hodnett, Edward. *Image and Text: Studies in the Illustration of English Literature*. London: Scolar, 1982. Print.

Hogarth, William. *Characters and Caricaturas*. 1743. British Lib., London. Engraving.

———. *A Harlot's Progress*. Plate 4. 1732. British Museum, London. Engraving.

———. *The Idle 'Prentice Executed at Tyburn*. *Idleness and Industry*. Plate 11. 1747. British Museum, London. Engraving.

Holmes, Geoffrey. *Augustan England: Professions, State and Society, 1680–1730*. London: Allen, 1982. Print.

Homer. *Iliad, Books XIII–XXIV*. 4th ed., rev. Ed. D. B. Monro. Oxford: Oxford UP, 1968. Print.

Horace. *The Art of Poetry: An Epistle to the Pisos*. Trans. George Colman. London, 1783. *Internet Archive*. Web. 6 May 2015.

———. *De arte poetica liber*. Ed. C. Smart. *Perseus*. Web. 4 May 2015.

Hudson, Nicholas. "Fielding at Three Hundred: Elusive, Confusing, Misappropriated, or (Perhaps) Obvious?" *Modern Philology* 108 (2010): 224–62. Print.

———. "Fielding's *Plays* and the Completion of the Wesleyan Edition." *Huntington Library Quarterly* 75.3 (2012): 447–63. Print.

———. "*Tom Jones*." Rawson, *Cambridge Companion* 80–93.

Hume, Robert D. *Henry Fielding and the London Theatre, 1728–1737*. Oxford: Clarendon, 1988. Print.

———. *The London Theatre World, 1600–1800*. Carbondale: Southern Illinois UP, 1980. Print.

Hunter, J. Paul. *Before Novels: The Cultural Contexts of Eighteenth-Century English Fiction*. New York: Norton, 1990. Print.

———. "Manliness and Poetry, and Pope: Gender, Language, Nation." *Imagining Selves: Essays in Honor of Patricia Meyer Spacks*. Ed. Rivka Swenson and Elise Lauterbach. Newark: U of Delaware P, 2008. 170–90. Print.

———. *Occasional Form: Henry Fielding and the Chains of Circumstance*. Baltimore: Johns Hopkins UP, 1975. Print.

———. "Rethinking Form in *Tom Jones*." *The Eighteenth-Century Novel* 6–7 (2009): 309–34. Print.

———. "Serious Reflections on Farther Adventures: Resistance to Closure in Eighteenth-Century Novels." *Augustan Subjects: Essays in Honor of Martin C. Battestin*. Ed. Albert J. Rivero. Newark: U of Delaware P, 1997. 276–94. Print.

———. "The World as Stage and Closet." *British Theatre and the Other Arts, 1660–1800.* Ed. Shirley Strum Kenney. Washington: Folger Shakespeare Lib., 1984. 271–87. Print.

Hunter, Lynette, and Peter Lichtenfels, eds. *Shakespeare, Language, and the Stage: The Fifth Wall: Approaches to Shakespeare from Criticism, Performance and Theatre Studies*. London: Arden Shakespeare, 2005. Print.

Hutchens, Eleanor. *Irony in* Tom Jones. University: U of Alabama P, 1965. Print.

Hutcheon, Linda. *Narcissistic Narrative: The Metafictional Paradox.* Waterloo: Wilfrid Laurier UP, 1980. Print.

Ingrassia, Catherine. *Authorship, Commerce, and Gender in Early-Eighteenth-Century England: A Culture of Paper Credit.* Cambridge: Cambridge UP, 1998. Print.

Ionescu, Christina, ed. *Book Illustration in the Long Eighteenth Century: Reconfiguring the Visual Periphery of the Text*. Newcastle upon Tyne: Cambridge Scholars, 2011. Print.

Irwin, Michael. *Henry Fielding: The Tentative Realist.* Oxford: Clarendon, 1968. Print.

Iser, Wolfgang. *The Implied Reader*. Baltimore: Johns Hopkins UP, 1974. Print.

Israel, Jonathan. *Radical Enlightenment: Philosophy and the Making of Modernity, 1650–1750*. Oxford: Oxford UP, 2001. Print.

———. *A Revolution of the Mind: Radical Enlightenment and the Intellectual Origins of Modern Democracy*. Princeton: Princeton UP, 2011. Print.

James, Henry. Preface to "The Princess Casamassima." *The Art of the Novel: Critical Prefaces*. 1934. New York: Scribner's, 1962. 59–78. Print.

Janes, Regina. "Fielding and the Case of the Misguided Reader." Downie, *Henry Fielding* 165–86.

Jenkins, Henry. "Transmedia Storytelling 101." *Confessions of an Aca-Fan*. Jenkins, 22 Mar. 2007. Web. 15 Mar. 2013.

Johns, Adrian. *The Nature of the Book: Print and Knowledge in the Making*. Chicago: U of Chicago P, 1998. Print.

———. *Piracy: The Intellectual Property Wars from Gutenberg to Gates*. Chicago: U of Chicago P, 2009. Print.

Johnson, Christopher D. "Well Bless His Heart: Teaching Fielding in the American South." Downie, *Henry Fielding* 187–200.

Johnson, Maurice. *Fielding's Art of Fiction: Eleven Essays on* Shamela, Joseph Andrews, Tom Jones, *and* Amelia. Philadelphia: U of Pennsylvania P, 1961. Print.

Johnson, Samuel. *A Dictionary of the English Language*. 2 vols. London: W. Strahan, 1755. Print.

———. *The History of Rasselas, Prince of Abissinia*. Ed. Thomas Keymer. Oxford: Oxford UP, 2009. Print.

———. "Letter to Chesterfield." *Samuel Johnson: The Major Works*. Ed. Donald Greene. Oxford: Oxford UP, 2009. 782–83. Print.

———. *The Plan of an English Dictionary*. 1747. Ed. Jack Lynch. *Eighteenth-Century E-texts*. Rutgers U, n.d. Web. 1 May 2010.

———. *Preface to the* Dictionary. 1755. Ed. Jack Lynch. *Eighteenth-Century E-texts*. Rutgers U, n.d. Web. 1 May 2010.

———. *Rambler* 4. 31 Mar. 1750. Ed. Michael Gamer. U of Pennsylvania, n.d. Web. 24 Apr. 2014.

———. "The Vanity of Human Wishes." *Norton Anthology* 2843–51.

Joseph Andrews. Dir. Tony Richardson. Perf. Ann-Margaret, Peter Firth, Michael Hordern, Beryl Reid, and Jim Dale. United Artists, 1977. DVD.

Kaul, Suvir. *Eighteenth-Century British Literature and Postcolonial Studies*. Edinburgh: U of Edinburgh P, 2009. Print.

Kearney, Anthony. "Tom Jones and the Forty-Five." *ARIEL* 4.2 (1973): 68–78. Print.

Keep within Compass. [1785?]. Lewis Walpole Lib., Farmington, CT. Mezzotint with etching.

Kelleher, Paul. "'The Glorious Lust of Doing Good': *Tom Jones* and the Virtues of Sexuality." *Novel: A Forum on Fiction* 38.2–3 (2005): 165–92. Print.

Kenrick, William. Excerpt from *Fun: A Parodi-tragi-comical Satire*. Paulson and Lockwood 333.

Keymer, Thomas. "Fielding's Library: An Annotated Catalogue." *Review of English Studies* 49 (1998): 363–66. Print.

———. "Fielding's Machiavellian Moment." Rawson, *Henry Fielding, 1707–1754* 58–90.

———. "Fielding's Theatrical Career." Rawson, *Cambridge Companion* 17–37.

———. "Obscenity and the Erotics of Fiction." Caserio and Hawes 131–46.

Keymer, Thomas, and Peter Sabor. Pamela *in the Marketplace: Literary Controversy and Print Culture in Eighteenth-Century Britain and Ireland.* Cambridge: Cambridge UP, 2005. Print.

Kimber, Edward. *The History of the Life and Adventures of Mr. Anderson*. Ed. Matthew Mason and Nicholas Mason. Peterborough: Broadview, 2008. Print.

King, Kathryn. "Henry and Eliza: Feudlings or Friends?" Downie, *Henry Fielding* 215–32.

Kirkman, Francis. *The Unlucky Citizen Experimentally Described in the Various Misfortunes of an Unlucky Londoner. . . .* London, 1673. *Early English Books Online*. Web. 1 May 2013.

Knight, Charles A. "Fielding's Afterlife." Rawson, *Cambridge Companion* 175–89.

———. "*Joseph Andrews* and the Failure of Authority." *Critical Essays on Henry Fielding*. Ed. Albert J. Rivero. New York: Hall, 1998. 69–82. Print.

Koppel, Gene S. "Sexual Education and Sexual Values in *Tom Jones*: Confusion at the Core?" *Studies in the Novel* 12 (1980): 1–11. Print.

Kraft, Elizabeth. *Character and Consciousness in Eighteenth-Century Comic Fiction*. Athens: U of Georgia P, 1992. Print.

Kropf, Carl R. "A Certain Absence: *Joseph Andrews* as Affirmation of Heterosexuality." *Studies in the Novel* 20 (1988): 16–26. Print.

Kundera, Milan. *The Curtain*. Trans. Linda Asher. New York: Harper, 2006. Print.

———. *The Unbearable Lightness of Being*. Trans. Michael Henry Heim. New York: Harper, 1984. Print.

Laban, Lawrence F. "Visualizing Fielding's Point of View." *The English Novel and the Movies*. Ed. Michael Klein and Gillian Parker. New York: Unger, 1981. 28–35. Print.

Langbein, John H. "Shaping the Eighteenth-Century Criminal Trial: A View from the Ryder Sources." *University of Chicago Law Review* 50.1 (1983): 1–136. Print.

Langille, Edward. "Fielding, La Place's *Histoire de Tom Jones* and *Candide*." Downie, *Henry Fielding* 233–56.

Lawrence, D. H. *Studies in Classic American Literature*. 1923. Ed. Ezra Greenspan, Lindsey Vasey, and John Worthen. Cambridge: Cambridge UP, 2003. Print.

Le Bossu, René. *Treatise of the Epic Poem: Le Bossu and Voltaire on the Epic*. Introd. Stuart Curran. Gainesville: Scholars' Facsims. and Rpts., 1970. Print.

Lembke, Janet. *Bronze and Iron: Old Latin Poetry from Its Beginnings to 500 B.C.* Berkeley: U of California P, 1973. Print.

Levin, Harry. *Playboys and Killjoys: An Essay on the Theory and Practice of Comedy*. Oxford: Oxford UP, 1987. Print.

Lewis, C. S. *A Preface to* Paradise Lost. Oxford: Oxford UP, 1942. Print.

Locke, John. *The Educational Writings of John Locke*. Ed. James L. Axtell. Cambridge: Cambridge UP, 1968. Print.

———. *The Selected Political Writings of John Locke*. New York: Norton, 2005. Print.

Lockwood, Thomas. "Fielding from Stage to Page." Rawson, *Henry Fielding, 1707–1754* 21–39.

———. Introduction. Fielding, *Author's Farce* 285–20.

———. "*Shamela*." Rawson, *Cambridge Companion* 38–49.

———. "Why Wasn't *Amelia* Funny?" Amer. Soc. for Eighteenth-Century Studies Conf. Sheraton Vancouver Wall Centre Hotel, Vancouver. 17 Mar. 2011. Address.

Loewenstein, Joseph. *The Author's Due: Printing and the Prehistory of Copyright*. Chicago: U of Chicago P, 1992. Print.

London, April. "Controlling the Text: Women in *Tom Jones*." *Studies in the Novel* 19 (1987): 323–33. Print.

The Longman Anthology of British Literature, Vol 1C: The Restoration and Eighteenth Century. Ed. Kevin J. H. Dettmar and Stuart Sherman. 4th ed. New York: Longman, 2009. Print.

Lund, Roger. "Augustan Burlesque and the Genesis of *Joseph Andrews*." *Studies in Philology* 103 (2006): 88–119. Print.

———. "The Problem with Parsons: *Joseph Andrews* and the 'Contempt of the Clergy' Revisited." Downie, *Henry Fielding* 257–86.

Lupton, Christina. "Marriage as a Literary Problem in Fielding's *Amelia*." Downie, *Henry Fielding* 287–302.

Lynch, Deidre. *The Economy of Character: Novels, Market Culture, and the Business of Inner Meaning*. Chicago: U of Chicago P, 1998. Print.

Lynch, James L. *Henry Fielding and the Heliodoran Novel: Romance, Epic, and Fielding's New Province of Writing*. Cranbury: Assoc. UPs, 1986. Print.

Mace, Nancy A. *Henry Fielding's Novels and the Classical Tradition*. Newark: U of Delaware P, 1996. Print.

———. "Using *ECCO* in Undergraduate Survey Courses." *Eighteenth-Century Intelligencer* 23.3 (2009): 2–4. Print.

Machiavelli, Niccolò. *The Mandragola*. Trans. Mera Flaumenhaft. Prospect Heights: Waveland, 1981. Print.

———. *The Prince*. Trans. Peter Bondanella. Oxford: Oxford UP, 2008. Print.

Mack, Maynard. "*Joseph Andrews* and *Pamela*." Paulson, *Fielding: A Collection* 52–58.

MacKenzie, Scott. "'Stock the Parish with Beauties': Henry Fielding's Parochial Vision." *PMLA* 125.3 (2010): 606–21. Print.

Mackie, Erin. *The Commerce of Everyday Life: Selections from* The Tatler *and* The Spectator. Boston: Bedford–St. Martin's, 1998. Print.

Macpherson, Sandra. *Harm's Way: Tragic Responsibility and the Novel Form*. Baltimore: Johns Hopkins UP, 2010. Print.

Mander, Jenny, ed. *Remapping the Rise of the European Novel*. Oxford: Voltaire Foundation, 2007. Print.

Marcus, Sharon. *Between Women: Friendship, Desire, and Marriage in Victorian England*. Princeton: Princeton UP, 2007. Print.

Maresca, Thomas E. *Epic to Novel*. Columbus: Ohio State UP, 1974. Print.

Marshall, Ashley. *The Practice of Satire in England, 1658–1700*. Baltimore: Johns Hopkins UP, 2013. Print.

Maruca, Lisa. *The Work of Print: Authorship and the English Text Trades, 1660–1760*. Seattle: U of Washington P, 2007. Print.

McCrea, Brian. "Fielding's Omniscient Narrator: Romances, Newspapers and the Partial Magic of True History." Downie, *Henry Fielding* 303–14.

———. *Impotent Fathers: Patriarchy and Demographic Crisis in the Eighteenth-Century Novel*. Newark: U of Delaware P, 1998. Print.

McDowell, Paula. "Narrative Authority, Critical Complicity: The Case of *Jonathan Wild*." *Studies in the Novel* 30.2 (1998): 211–31. *ProQuest*. Web. 17 Oct. 2012.

———. *The Women of Grub Street: Press, Politics, and Gender in the London Literary Marketplace, 1678–1730*. Oxford: Oxford UP, 1998. Print.

McGirr, Elaine. *Heroic Mode and Political Crisis, 1660–1745*. Newark: U of Delaware P, 2009. Print.

McKeon, Michael. *The Origins of the English Novel, 1600–1740*. Baltimore: Johns Hopkins UP, 1987. Print.

McLynn, Frank. *Charles Edward Stuart: A Tragedy in Many Acts*. Oxford: Oxford UP, 1991. Print.

McMorran, Will. *The Inn and the Traveller: Digressive Topographies in the Early Modern European Novel*. Oxford: Legenda, 2002. Print.

Michie, Allen. *Richardson and Fielding: The Dynamics of a Critical Rivalry*. Lewisburg: Bucknell UP, 1999. Print.

Middleton, Conyers. *The History of the Life of Marcus Tullius Cicero*. 2 vols. London, 1741. Print.

Miller, D. A. *Narrative and Its Discontents*. Princeton: Princeton UP, 1981. Print.

Miller, Henry Knight. *Henry Fielding's* Tom Jones *and the Romance Tradition*. Victoria: U of Victoria, 1976. Print. U of Victoria English Lit. Studies 6.

Milton, John. *Areopagitica*. *John Milton: Complete Poems and Major Prose*. Ed. Merritt Y. Hughes. New York: Odyssey, 1957. 716–49. Print.

Molesworth, Jesse. *Chance and the Eighteenth-Century Novel: Realism, Probability, Magic*. Cambridge: Cambridge UP, 2010. Print.

Molière. *Tartuffe: A New Verse Translation*. Trans. Constance Congdon. Ed. Virginia Scott. New York: Norton, 2007. Print.

Montagu, Mary Wortley. *The Turkish Embassy Letters*. Ed. Teresa Heffernan and Daniel O'Quinn. Peterborough: Broadview, 2012. Print.

Moody, Ellen. "Affectionately Dedicated to Mr. Fielding: The 1997 A&E/BBC *Tom Jones*." *Ellen and Jim Have a Blog, Two*. N.p., 2 June 2010. Web. 13 Mar. 2014.

———. "Stanley Kubrick's *Barry Lyndon* and Tony Richardson's *Tom Jones* Compared." *Ellen and Jim Have a Blog, Two*. N.p., 24 Oct. 2009. Web. 13 Mar. 2014.

Moore, Robert E. *Hogarth's Literary Relationships*. Minneapolis: U of Minnesota P, 1948. Print.

Moore, Steven. *The Novel, an Alternative History: Beginnings to 1600*. New York: Continuum, 2010. Print.

More, Hannah. *Essays on Various Subjects, Principally Designed for Young Ladies*. London: J. Wilkie and T. Cadell, 1777. *Eighteenth-Century Collections Online*. Web. 7 Feb. 2015.

Moretti, Franco. *The Novel*. 2 vols. Princeton: Princeton UP, 2006. Print.

———. "The Novel: History and Theory." *New Left Review* 52 (2008): 111–24. Print.

Morissey, L. J. *Henry Fielding: A Reference Guide*. Boston: Hall, 1980. Print.

Mozart, Leopold. *Cassation in G Major for Orchestra and Toys* ["Toy Symphony"]. Royal Philharmonic Orchestra. Cond. Yan Pascal Tortielier. *YouTube*. YouTube, 11 Sept. 2011. Web. 8 May 2012.

Mulford, Carla. "Booth's Progress and the Resolution of *Amelia*." *Studies in the Novel* 16.1 (1984): 20–31. Print.

Nixon, Cheryl, ed. *Novel Definitions: An Anthology of Commentary on the Novel, 1688–1815*. Peterborough: Broadview, 2009. Print.

The Norton Anthology of English Literature, Vol. C: The Restoration and Eighteenth Century. Gen. ed. Stephen Greenblatt. 9th ed. New York: Norton, 2013. Print.

Nussbaum, Felicity A. *Torrid Zones: Maternity, Sexuality, and Empire in Eighteenth-Century English Narratives*. Baltimore: Johns Hopkins UP, 1995. Print.

O'Brien, John. *Harlequin Britain: Pantomime and Entertainment, 1690–1760*. Baltimore: Johns Hopkins UP, 2004. Print.

O'Brien, Timothy. "The Hungry Author and Narrative Performance in *Tom Jones*." *Studies in English Literature* 25 (1985): 615–32. Print.

Ogée, Frédéric. "'O, Hogarth, Had I Thy Pencil': Delineations of an Alleged Friendship." Rawson, *Henry Fielding, 1707–1754* 201–29.

Ohmann, Richard. "Use Definite, Specific, Concrete Language." *Politics of Letters.* Middletown: Wesleyan UP, 1987. 241–51. Print.

Opie, Amelia. *Adeline Mowbray*. Ed. Shelley King and John B. Pierce. Oxford: Oxford UP, 1999. Print.

Orrery, Lady (Margaret Hamilton Boyle, countess of Orrery). Letter. Paulson and Lockwood 311.

Osland, Dianne. "Fielding's *Amelia*: Problem Child or Problem Reader?" *Journal of Narrative Technique* 10.1 (1980): 56–67. Print.

Owenson, Sydney (Lady Morgan). *The Missionary*. Ed. Julia M. Wright. Peterborough: Broadview, 2002. Print.

Pagliaro, Harold. *Henry Fielding: A Literary Life*. New York: St. Martin's, 1998. Print.

Pamela Censured. Internet Archive. Internet Archive, 16 Sept. 2010. Web. 25 Sept. 2014.

Parkes, Christopher. "*Joseph Andrews* and the Control of the Poor." *Studies in the Novel* 39 (2007): 17–30. Print.

Paulson, Ronald, ed. *Fielding: A Collection of Critical Essays*. Englewood Cliffs: Prentice, 1962. Print.

———. *Hogarth*. 3 vols. New Brunswick: Rutgers UP, 1991–93. Print.

———. *Hogarth's Graphic Works*. 3rd ed., rev. 2 vols. London: Print Room, 1989. Print.

———. *The Life of Henry Fielding: A Critical Biography.* Malden: Blackwell, 2000. Print.

———. *Popular and Polite Art in the Age of Hogarth and Fielding*. Notre Dame: U of Notre Dame P, 1979. Print.

———. *Satire and the Novel in Eighteenth-Century England*. New Haven: Yale UP, 1967. Print.

Paulson, Ronald, and Thomas Lockwood, eds. *Henry Fielding: The Critical Heritage.* London: Routledge, 1969. Print.

Pettit, Alexander. "What the Drama Does in Fielding's *Jonathan Wild*." *Eighteenth-Century Fiction* 6.2 (1994): 153–68. Print.

Pollak, Ellen. *Incest and the English Novel, 1684–1814*. Baltimore: Johns Hopkins UP, 2003. Print.

Pope, Alexander. "An Essay on Criticism." *The Poems of Alexander Pope*. Ed. John Butt. London: Methuen, 1963. 143–68. Print.

———. *Major Works*. Ed. Pat Rogers. Oxford: Oxford UP, 2006. Print.

Porter, Roy. *English Society in the Eighteenth Century*. London: Penguin, 1990. Print.

Potkay, Adam. "Liberty and Necessity in Fielding's *Amelia*." *Eighteenth-Century Novel* 6–7 (2009): 335–58. Print.

———. *The Story of Joy from the Bible to Late Romanticism*. Cambridge: Cambridge UP, 2007. Print.

Potter, Tiffany. *Honest Sins: Georgian Libertinism and the Plays and Novels of Henry Fielding*. Montreal: McGill-Queen's UP, 1999. Print.

Power, Henry. "Henry Fielding, Richard Bentley, and the 'Sagacious Reader' of *Tom Jones*." *Review of English Studies* 61 (2010): 749–72. Print.

Powers, Lyall. "The Influence of the *Aeneid* on Fielding's *Amelia*." *Modern Language Notes* 71.5 (1956): 330–36. Print.

Prytula, Nina. "'Great-Breasted and Fierce': Fielding's Amazonian Heroines." *Eighteenth-Century Studies* 35 (2002): 173–93. Print.

Rader, Ralph. "*Tom Jones*: The Form in History." Richter, *Ideology* 47–74.

Rawson, Claude. "Avatars of Alexander: Jonathan Wild and the Tyrant Thug, from Voltaire to Brecht." Rawson, *Henry Fielding, 1707–1754* 91–114.

———, ed. *The Cambridge Companion to Henry Fielding*. Cambridge: Cambridge UP, 2007. Print.

———. "Fielding in the Dock." *London Review of Books* 5 Apr. 1990: 20–23. Print.

———. "Fielding's Style." Rawson, *Cambridge Companion* 153–74.

———. "Henry Fielding." Richetti, *Cambridge Companion* 120–52.

———. *Henry Fielding: A Critical Anthology*. Harmondsworth: Penguin, 1973. Print.

———. *Henry Fielding and the Augustan Ideal under Stress*. London: Routledge, 1972. Print.

———, ed. *Henry Fielding, 1707–1754: Novelist, Playwright, Journalist, Magistrate: A Double Anniversary Tribute*. Newark: U of Delaware P, 2008. Print.

———. *Order from Confusion Sprung: Studies in Eighteenth-Century Literature from Swift to Cowper*. London: Allen, 1985. Print.

———. "Some Considerations on Authorial Intrusion in Fielding's Novels and Plays." *Durham University Journal* 33 (1971): 32–44. Print.

Ray, James. *The Acts of the Rebels, Written by an Egyptian*. [London], [1746?]. Print.

———. *A Compleat History of the Rebellion*. York, 1749. Print.

Reeve, Clara. *The Progress of Romance*. 2 vols. Colchester and London, 1785. Print.

Reynolds, Joshua. *Sir Joshua Reynolds*. [1747–49?]. Natl. Portrait Gallery, London. Oil on canvas.

Ribble, Frederick G., and Anne G. Ribble, eds. *Fielding's Library: An Annotated Catalogue*. Charlottesville: Bibliog. Soc. of the U of Virginia, 1996. Print.

Richardson, Samuel. *Clarissa; or, The History of a Young Lady*. Ed. Angus Ross. London: Penguin, 1985. Print.

———. "Letters, 1752." Paulson and Lockwood 334–36.

———. *Letters Written to and for Particular Friends, on the Most Important Occasions*. London, 1741. *Eighteenth-Century Collections Online*. Web. 1 May 2013.

———. *Pamela*. Ed. Thomas Keymer and Alice Wakely. Oxford: Oxford UP, 2001. Print.

Richetti, John, ed. *The Cambridge Companion to the Eighteenth-Century Novel*. Cambridge: Cambridge UP, 1996. Print.

———, ed. *The Columbia History of the British Novel*. New York: Columbia UP, 1994. Print.

———. *The English Novel in History, 1700–1780*. New York: Routledge, 1999. Print.

———. "Ideology and Literary Form in Fielding's *Tom Jones*." Richter, *Ideology* 30–45.

———. Introduction. Richetti, *Cambridge Companion* 1–8.

———. "The Legacy of Ian Watt." *The Profession of Eighteenth-Century Literature*. Ed. Leo Damrosch. Madison: U of Wisconsin P, 1992. 95–112. Print.

———. "Representing the Underclass: Servants and Proletarians in Fielding and Smollett." *The New Eighteenth Century: Theory, Politics, English Literature*. Ed. Felicity Nussbaum and Laura Brown. New York: Methuen, 1987. 84–98. Print.

Richter, David H. "The Closing of Masterpiece Theater: Henry Fielding and the Valorization of Incoherence." Richter, *Ideology* 3–14.

———, ed. *Ideology and Form in Eighteenth-Century Literature*. Lubbock: Texas Tech UP, 1999. Print.

Rivero, Albert, ed. *Critical Essays on Henry Fielding*. Boston: Hall, 1998. Print.

———. *The Plays of Henry Fielding: A Critical Study of His Dramatic Career*. Charlottesville: U of Virginia P, 1989. Print.

Rizzo, Betty. *Companions without Vows: Relations among Eighteenth-Century British Women*. Athens: U of Georgia P, 1994. Print.

Robertson, Scott. *Henry Fielding: Literary and Theological Misplacement*. New York: Lang, 2010. Print.

Rogers, Katherine M. "Sensitive Feminism vs. Conventional Sympathy: Richardson and Fielding and Women." *Novel: A Forum on Fiction* 9 (1976): 256–70. Print.

Rogers, Pat. *Henry Fielding: A Biography*. New York: Scribner's, 1979. Print.

———. "Poacher and Gamekeeper: Fielding, the Law, and the Novels." Rawson, *Henry Fielding, 1701–1754* 233–56.

Rose, Mark. *Authors and Owners: The Invention of Copyright*. Cambridge: Harvard UP, 1993. Print.

Rothstein, Eric. *Systems of Order and Inquiry in Later-Eighteenth-Century Fiction*. Berkeley: U of California P, 1975. Print.

———. "Virtues of Authority in *Tom Jones*." *The Eighteenth Century: Theory and Interpretation* 28 (1987): 99–126. Print.

Roulston, Christine. *Narrating Marriage in Eighteenth-Century England and France*. Burlington: Ashgate, 2010. Print.

Rumbold, Valerie C. "People and Puppets: Fielding's Burlesque of the 'Recognition Scene' in *The Author's Farce*." *Papers on Language and Literature* 11 (1975): 31–38. Print.

Rushdie, Salman. "Is Nothing Sacred?" *Imaginary Homelands*. New York: Penguin, 1991. 415–29. Print.

Ruthven, K. K. "Fielding, Square, and the Fitness of Things." *Eighteenth-Century Studies* 5 (1971–72): 243–55. Print.

Sabor, Peter. "*Amelia*." Rawson, *Cambridge Companion* 94–108.

Sacks, Sheldon. *Fiction and the Shape of Belief: A Study of Henry Fielding*. Berkeley: U of California P, 1964. Print.

Salieri, Antonio, composer. *Prima la musica e poi le parole*. Libretto by Giovanni Batista Casti. 7 Feb. 1786. Concertgebouw Orchestra Amsterdam. KuhlauDilfeng3, 12 Aug. 2013. *YouTube*. YouTube, n.d. Web. 16 July 2015.

Sambrook, James. *The Eighteenth Century: The Intellectual and Cultural Context of English Literature, 1700–1789*. 2nd ed. New York: Longman, 1993. Print.

Sartre, Jean-Paul. *What Is Literature?* 1948. Trans. Bernard Frechtman. What Is Literature? *and Other Essays*. Introd. Steven Ungar. Cambridge: Harvard UP, 1988. 21–246. Print.

Scarron, Paul. *Scarron's Comical Romance*. *The Whole Comical Works of Mon. Scarron*. Trans. Thomas Brown et al. 3rd ed. London, 1712. 1–336. Print.

Schellenberg, Betty. *The Conversational Circle: Rereading the English Novel, 1740–1775*. Lexington: UP of Kentucky, 1996. Print.

Schmidgen, Wolfram. *Eighteenth-Century Fiction and the Law of Property*. Cambridge: Cambridge UP, 2004. Print.

Scholes, Robert, James Phelan, and Robert Kellogg. *The Nature of Narrative*. Oxford: Oxford UP, 2006. Print.

Schonhorn, Manuel. "Fielding's Ecphrastic Moment: Tom Jones and His Egyptian Majesty." *Studies in Philology* 78 (1981): 305–23. Print.

Schroeder, Brian. "Abraham's Odyssey." *Proximity: Emmanuel Levinas and the Eighteenth Century*. Ed. Melvyn New, Robert Bernasconi, and Richard A. Cohen. Lubbock: Texas Tech UP, 2001. 91–109. Print.

Scouten, Arthur H. *The London Stage, 1729–1747*. Carbondale: Southern Illinois UP, 1968. Print.

Sedgwick, Eve Kosofsky. *Between Men: English Literature and Male Homosocial Desire*. New York: Columbia UP, 1985. Print.

Sennett, Richard. *Authority*. New York: Norton, 1980. Print.

Shakespeare, William. *A Midsummer Night's Dream*. Ed. Madeleine Doran. *The Complete Pelican Shakespeare*. Gen. ed. Alfred Harbage. Baltimore: Penguin, 1969. 146–74. Print.

Shaw, George Bernard. *Pygmalion*. Ed. Dan H. Laurence. New York: Penguin, 2001. Print.

Sherburn, George. "The Dunciad: Book IV." *University of Texas Studies in English* 24 (1944): 174–90. Print.

———. "Fielding's *Amelia*: An Interpretation." *ELH* 3.1 (1936): 1–14. Print.

Sheridan, Frances. *The History of Nourjahad*. *Oriental Tales*. Ed. Robert L. Mack. Oxford: Oxford UP, 1992. 115–94. Print.

Sherman, Sandra. "Reading at Arm's Length: Fielding's Contract with the Reader in *Tom Jones*." *Studies in the Novel* 30 (1998): 232–45. Print.

Shesgreen, Sean, ed. *Engravings by Hogarth*. New York: Dover, 1975. Print.

Shevlin, Eleanor F. "Exploring Context and Canonicity: Lessons from the *ECCO* and *EEBO* Databases." *Eighteenth-Century Intelligencer* 23.3 (2009): 4–13. Print.

———. "Legal Discourse and Novelistic Form." Caserio and Hawes 46–62.

Siskin, Clifford, and William Warner, eds. *This Is Enlightenment*. Chicago: U of Chicago P, 2010. Print.

———. "This Is Enlightenment: An Invitation in the Form of an Argument." Siskin and Warner, *This* 1–33.

Smallwood, Angela J. *Fielding and the Woman Question: The Novels of Henry Fielding and Feminist Debate, 1700–1750*. New York: St. Martin's, 1989. Print.

Spacks, Patricia Meyer. *Desire and Truth: Functions of Plot in Eighteenth-Century English Novels.* Chicago: U of Chicago P, 1990. Print.

———. "Ideology and Form: Novels at Work." Richter, *Ideology* 15–30.

———. *On Rereading.* Cambridge: Harvard UP, 2011. Print.

———. *Privacy: Concealing the Eighteenth-Century Self.* Chicago: U of Chicago P, 2003. Print.

Speck, W. A. *Literature and Society in Eighteenth-Century England, 1680–1820: Ideology, Politics and Culture*. London: Longman, 1998. Print.

———. *Society and Literature in England, 1700–1760*. Dublin: Gill, 1983. Print.

Spedding, Patrick. "'The New Machine': Discovering the Limits of *ECCO*." *Eighteenth-Century Studies* 44.4 (2001): 437–53. Print.

Spencer, Jane. "Fielding and Female Authority." Rawson, *Cambridge Companion* 122–36.

Statute of Anne, London. 1710. *Primary Sources on Copyright, 1450–1900*. Ed. L. Bently and M. Kretschmer. Faculty of Law, U of Cambridge, n.d. Web. 1 May 2013.

Staves, Susan. "Fielding and the Comedy of Attempted Rape." *History, Gender, and Eighteenth-Century Literature.* Ed. Beth Fowkes Tobin. Athens: U of Georgia P, 1994. 86–112. Print.

Sterne, Laurence. *The Life and Opinions of Tristram Shandy, Gentleman*. 9 vols. London, 1759–67. Print.

———. *The Works of Laurence Sterne, A.M. Prebendary of York, and Vicar of Sutton on the Forest, and of Stillington, near York*. 5 vols. London, 1769. Print.

———. *The Works of Laurence Sterne, M.A.: In Seven Volumes*. 7 vols. Dublin: Thomas Armitage, 1774. Print.

Stevenson, John Allen. "Fielding's Mousetrap: *Hamlet*, Partridge, and the '45." *Studies in English Literature, 1500–1900* 37.3 (1997): 553–71. Print.

———. *The Real History of Tom Jones.* Basingstoke: Palgrave, 2005. Print.

———. "*Tom Jones* and the Stuarts." *ELH* 61.3 (1994): 471–595. Print.

Stoler, John A. "Henry Fielding: A Partly Annotated Bibliography of Criticism, 1978–1992." *Bulletin of Bibliography* 50 (1993): 83–101. Print.

Stoler, John A., and Richard D. Fulton. *Henry Fielding: An Annotated Bibliography of Twentieth-Century Criticism, 1900–1977*. New York: Garland, 1980. Print.

Straub, Kristina. *Domestic Affairs: Intimacy, Eroticism, and Violence between Servants and Masters in Eighteenth-Century Britain*. Baltimore: Johns Hopkins UP, 2009. Print.

Swift, Jonathan. "The Battle of the Books." A Tale of a Tub *and Other Works.* Ed. Angus Ross and David Wooley. Oxford: Oxford UP, 2008. 104–25. Print.

———. *Gulliver's Travels*. Ed. Albert J. Rivero. New York: Norton, 2002. Print.

Tanner, Tony. *Adultery in the Novel: Contract and Transgression.* Baltimore: Johns Hopkins UP, 1979. Print.

Taylor, Richard C. "James Harrison, the Novelist's Magazine, and the Early Canonizing of the English Novel." *Studies in English Literature, 1500–1900* 33.3 (1993): 629–43. Print.

Teacle, John. *An Excellent New Song on the Battle of Culloden.* [Edinburgh], 1776. Print.

Temple, Kathryn. *Scandal Nation: Law and Authorship in Britain, 1750–1831.* Ithaca: Cornell UP, 2003. Print.

Tey, Josephine. *The Franchise Affair.* New York: Macmillan, 1949. Print.

Thomas, Donald. *Henry Fielding.* London: Weidenfeld, 1990. Print.

Thompson, E. P. *Whigs and Hunters: The Origins of the Black Act.* Harmondsworth: Penguin, 1977. Print.

Thornton, Bonnell. "A New Chapter in *Amelia.*" Paulson and Lockwood 321–24. Excerpt from *Have at You All; or, The Drury-Lane Journal*, 13 Feb. 1752.

Tom Jones. Dir. Tony Richardson. Perf. Albert Finney, Susannah York, Hugh Griffith, Edith Evans, Diane Cilento, and Joyce Redman. Woodfall Films; MGM, 1963. DVD.

Tompkins, J. M. S. *The Popular Novel in England, 1770–1800.* Lincoln: U of Nebraska P, 1961. Print.

Varey, Simon. *Space and the Eighteenth-Century English Novel.* Cambridge: Cambridge UP, 1990. Print.

Vergil. *Opera.* Ed. R. A. B. Mynors. Oxford: Oxford UP, 1969. Print.

Voltaire. *Candide; or, Optimism.* Trans. Theo Cuffe. New York: Penguin, 2005. Print.

Wall, Cynthia Sundberg. "Domesticities and Novel Narratives." Caserio and Hawes 113–30.

———. *The Prose of Things: Transformations of Description in the Eighteenth Century.* Chicago: U of Chicago P, 2006. Print.

Walpole, Horace. *Horace Walpole's Correspondence with Sir Horace Mann.* 11 vols. Ed. W. S. Lewis et al. New Haven: Yale UP, 1967. Print.

Wanko, Cheryl. "Characterization and the Reader's Quandary in Fielding's *Amelia.*" *Journal of English and Germanic Philology* 90.4 (1991): 505–23. Print.

Warner, William B. "The Elevation of the Novel in England: Hegemony and Literary History." *ELH* 59 (1992): 577–96. Print.

———. *Licensing Entertainment: The Elevation of Novel Reading in Britain, 1684–1750.* Berkeley: U of California P, 1998. Print.

Warren, Leland E. "Fielding's Problem and Ours: Allworthy and Authority in *Tom Jones.*" *Essays in Literature* 5 (1978): 15–25. Print.

———. "History as Literature and the Narrative Stance of Henry Fielding." *Clio* 9.1 (1979): 89–109. Print.

Watt, Ian. *The Rise of the Novel.* Berkeley: U of California P, 1957. Print.

Waugh, Patricia, *Metafiction: The Theory and Practice of Self-Conscious Fiction*. London: Methuen, 1984. Print.

Weeks, Kay. "Fielding Looks Down: Tom Jones and the Lower Orders." *Eighteenth-Century Novel* 3 (2003): 97–127. Print.

Wheeler, Roxann. *The Complexion of Race: Categories of Difference in Eighteenth-Century British Culture*. Philadelphia: U of Pennsylvania P, 2000. Print.

Williams, Aubrey. "Literary Backgrounds to Book Four of the *Dunciad*." *PMLA* 68.4 (1953): 806–13. Print.

Williams, Robin. *The Non-designer's Design and Type Books: Deluxe Edition*. Berkeley: Peachpit, 2008. Print.

Wilner, Arlene. "The Mythology of History, the Truth of Fiction: Henry Fielding and the Cases of Bosavern Penlez and Elizabeth Canning." *Journal of Narrative Technique* 21 (1991): 185–201. Print.

Wilputte, Earla. "Ambiguous Language and Ambiguous Gender: The 'Bisexual' Text of *Shamela*." *Modern Language Review* 89 (1994): 561–71. Print.

———. "The Autodiegetic Power of Mrs. Heartfree in Henry Fielding's *Jonathan Wild*: The Moderately Good Wife." *Durham University Journal* 53.2 (1992): 229–34. Print.

———. "'Women Buried': Henry Fielding and Feminine Absence." *Modern Language Review* 95.2 (2000): 324–36. Print.

Wimsatt, W. K., Jr., and Monroe C. Beardsley. "The Intentional Fallacy." *Sewanee Review* 54 (1946): 468–88. Print.

Wintle, Simon. The Beggar's Opera *Playing Cards, 1728. The World of Playing Cards*. World of Playing Cards, n.d. Web. 21 Jan. 2013.

Wolff, Cynthia Griffin. "Fielding's *Amelia:* Private Virtue and Public Good." *Texas Studies in Literature and Language* 10.1 (1968): 37–55. Print.

Wollstonecraft, Mary. *A Vindication of the Rights of Woman: With Strictures on Political and Moral Subjects*. London: J. Johnson, 1792. *Eighteenth Century Collections Online*. Web. 7 Feb. 2015.

The Woman of Colour. Ed. Lyndon Dominique. Peterborough: Broadview, 2008. Print.

Wright, Andrew. *Henry Fielding: Mask and Feast*. Berkeley: U of California P, 1965. Print.

Young, Edward. *Conjectures on Original Composition: In a Letter to the Author of* Sir Charles Grandison. London, 1759. *Eighteenth-Century Collections Online*. Web. 1 May 2013.

Zimmerman, Everett. *The Boundaries of Fiction: History and the Eighteenth-Century British Novel*. Ithaca: Cornell UP, 1996. Print.

Zirker, Malvin R. *Fielding's Social Pamphlets*. Berkeley: U of California P, 1966. Print.

Zunshine, Lisa. "Cognitive Alternatives to Interiority." Caserio and Hawes 147–62.

———. "Lying Bodies of the Enlightenment: Theory of Mind and Cultural Historicism." *Introduction to Cognitive Cultural Studies*. Ed. Lisa Zunshine. Baltimore: Johns Hopkins UP, 2010. 115–33. Print.

INDEX

Modern Language Association of America

Approaches to Teaching World Literature

To purchase MLA publications, visit www.mla.org/bookstore.

Achebe's Things Fall Apart. Ed. Bernth Lindfors. 1991.
Arthurian Tradition. Ed. Maureen Fries and Jeanie Watson. 1992.
Atwood's The Handmaid's Tale *and Other Works*. Ed. Sharon R. Wilson, Thomas B. Friedman, and Shannon Hengen. 1996.
Austen's Emma. Ed. Marcia McClintock Folsom. 2004.
Austen's Mansfield Park. Ed. Marcia McClintock Folsom and John Wiltshire. 2014.
Austen's Pride and Prejudice. Ed. Marcia McClintock Folsom. 1993.
Balzac's Old Goriot. Ed. Michal Peled Ginsburg. 2000.
Baudelaire's Flowers of Evil. Ed. Laurence M. Porter. 2000.
Beckett's Waiting for Godot. Ed. June Schlueter and Enoch Brater. 1991.
Behn's Oroonoko. Ed. Cynthia Richards and Mary Ann O'Donnell. 2014.
Beowulf. Ed. Jess B. Bessinger, Jr., and Robert F. Yeager. 1984.
Blake's Songs of Innocence and of Experience. Ed. Robert F. Gleckner and Mark L. Greenberg. 1989.
Boccaccio's Decameron. Ed. James H. McGregor. 2000.
British Women Poets of the Romantic Period. Ed. Stephen C. Behrendt and Harriet Kramer Linkin. 1997.
Charlotte Brontë's Jane Eyre. Ed. Diane Long Hoeveler and Beth Lau. 1993.
Emily Brontë's Wuthering Heights. Ed. Sue Lonoff and Terri A. Hasseler. 2006.
Byron's Poetry. Ed. Frederick W. Shilstone. 1991.
Works of Italo Calvino. Ed. Franco Ricci. 2013.
Camus's The Plague. Ed. Steven G. Kellman. 1985.
Cather's My Ántonia. Ed. Susan J. Rosowski. 1989.
Cervantes' Don Quixote. First edition. Ed. Richard Bjornson. 1984.
Cervantes's Don Quixote. Second edition. Ed. James A. Parr and Lisa Vollendorf. 2015.
Chaucer's Canterbury Tales. First edition. Ed. Joseph Gibaldi. 1980.
Chaucer's Canterbury Tales. Second edition. Ed. Peter W. Travis and Frank Grady. 2014.
Chaucer's Troilus and Criseyde *and the Shorter Poems*. Ed. Tison Pugh and Angela Jane Weisl. 2006.
Chopin's The Awakening. Ed. Bernard Koloski. 1988.
Coetzee's Disgrace *and Other Works*. Ed. Laura Wright, Jane Poyner, and Elleke Boehmer. 2014.
Coleridge's Poetry and Prose. Ed. Richard E. Matlak. 1991.
Collodi's Pinocchio *and Its Adaptations*. Ed. Michael Sherberg. 2006.

Conrad's "Heart of Darkness" and "The Secret Sharer." Ed. Hunt Hawkins and Brian W. Shaffer. 2002.

Dante's Divine Comedy. Ed. Carole Slade. 1982.

Defoe's Robinson Crusoe. Ed. Maximillian E. Novak and Carl Fisher. 2005.

DeLillo's White Noise. Ed. Tim Engles and John N. Duvall. 2006.

Dickens's Bleak House. Ed. John O. Jordan and Gordon Bigelow. 2009.

Dickens's David Copperfield. Ed. Richard J. Dunn. 1984.

Dickinson's Poetry. Ed. Robin Riley Fast and Christine Mack Gordon. 1989.

Narrative of the Life of Frederick Douglass. Ed. James C. Hall. 1999.

Works of John Dryden. Ed. Jayne Lewis and Lisa Zunshine. 2013.

Duras's Ourika. Ed. Mary Ellen Birkett and Christopher Rivers. 2009.

Early Modern Spanish Drama. Ed. Laura R. Bass and Margaret R. Greer. 2006.

Eliot's Middlemarch. Ed. Kathleen Blake. 1990.

Eliot's Poetry and Plays. Ed. Jewel Spears Brooker. 1988.

Shorter Elizabethan Poetry. Ed. Patrick Cheney and Anne Lake Prescott. 2000.

Ellison's Invisible Man. Ed. Susan Resneck Parr and Pancho Savery. 1989.

English Renaissance Drama. Ed. Karen Bamford and Alexander Leggatt. 2002.

Works of Louise Erdrich. Ed. Gregg Sarris, Connie A. Jacobs, and James R. Giles. 2004.

Dramas of Euripides. Ed. Robin Mitchell-Boyask. 2002.

Faulkner's As I Lay Dying. Ed. Patrick O'Donnell and Lynda Zwinger. 2011.

Faulkner's The Sound and the Fury. Ed. Stephen Hahn and Arthur F. Kinney. 1996.

Novels of Henry Fielding. Ed. Jennifer Preston Wilson and Elizabeth Kraft. 2015.

Fitzgerald's The Great Gatsby. Ed. Jackson R. Bryer and Nancy P. VanArsdale. 2009.

Flaubert's Madame Bovary. Ed. Laurence M. Porter and Eugene F. Gray. 1995.

García Márquez's One Hundred Years of Solitude. Ed. María Elena de Valdés and Mario J. Valdés. 1990.

Gilman's "The Yellow Wall-Paper" and Herland. Ed. Denise D. Knight and Cynthia J. Davis. 2003.

Goethe's Faust. Ed. Douglas J. McMillan. 1987.

Gothic Fiction: The British and American Traditions. Ed. Diane Long Hoeveler and Tamar Heller. 2003.

Poetry of John Gower. Ed. R. F. Yeager and Brian W. Gastle. 2011.

Grass's The Tin Drum. Ed. Monika Shafi. 2008.

H.D.'s Poetry and Prose. Ed. Annette Debo and Lara Vetter. 2011.

Hebrew Bible as Literature in Translation. Ed. Barry N. Olshen and Yael S. Feldman. 1989.

Homer's Iliad *and* Odyssey. Ed. Kostas Myrsiades. 1987.

Hurston's Their Eyes Were Watching God *and Other Works*. Ed. John Lowe. 2009.

Ibsen's A Doll House. Ed. Yvonne Shafer. 1985.

Henry James's Daisy Miller *and* The Turn of the Screw. Ed. Kimberly C. Reed and Peter G. Beidler. 2005.
Works of Samuel Johnson. Ed. David R. Anderson and Gwin J. Kolb. 1993.
Joyce's Ulysses. Ed. Kathleen McCormick and Erwin R. Steinberg. 1993.
Works of Sor Juana Inés de la Cruz. Ed. Emilie L. Bergmann and Stacey Schlau. 2007.
Kafka's Short Fiction. Ed. Richard T. Gray. 1995.
Keats's Poetry. Ed. Walter H. Evert and Jack W. Rhodes. 1991.
Kingston's The Woman Warrior. Ed. Shirley Geok-lin Lim. 1991.
Lafayette's The Princess of Clèves. Ed. Faith E. Beasley and Katharine Ann Jensen. 1998.
Writings of Bartolomé de Las Casas. Ed. Santa Arias and Eyda M. Merediz. 2008.
Works of D. H. Lawrence. Ed. M. Elizabeth Sargent and Garry Watson. 2001.
Lazarillo de Tormes *and the Picaresque Tradition*. Ed. Anne J. Cruz. 2009.
Lessing's The Golden Notebook. Ed. Carey Kaplan and Ellen Cronan Rose. 1989.
Works of Primo Levi. Ed. Nicholas Patruno and Roberta Ricci. 2014.
Works of Naguib Mahfouz. Ed. Waïl S. Hassan and Susan Muaddi Darraj. 2011.
Mann's Death in Venice *and Other Short Fiction*. Ed. Jeffrey B. Berlin. 1992.
Marguerite de Navarre's Heptameron. Ed. Colette H. Winn. 2007.
Works of Carmen Martín Gaite. Ed. Joan L. Brown. 2013.
Medieval English Drama. Ed. Richard K. Emmerson. 1990.
Melville's Moby-Dick. Ed. Martin Bickman. 1985.
Metaphysical Poets. Ed. Sidney Gottlieb. 1990.
Miller's Death of a Salesman. Ed. Matthew C. Roudané. 1995.
Milton's Paradise Lost. First edition. Ed. Galbraith M. Crump. 1986.
Milton's Paradise Lost. Second edition. Ed. Peter C. Herman. 2012.
Milton's Shorter Poetry and Prose. Ed. Peter C. Herman. 2007.
Molière's Tartuffe *and Other Plays*. Ed. James F. Gaines and Michael S. Koppisch. 1995.
Momaday's The Way to Rainy Mountain. Ed. Kenneth M. Roemer. 1988.
Montaigne's Essays. Ed. Patrick Henry. 1994.
Novels of Toni Morrison. Ed. Nellie Y. McKay and Kathryn Earle. 1997.
Murasaki Shikibu's The Tale of Genji. Ed. Edward Kamens. 1993.
Nabokov's Lolita. Ed. Zoran Kuzmanovich and Galya Diment. 2008.
Works of Ngũgĩwa Thiong'o. Ed. Oliver Lovesey. 2012.
Works of Tim O'Brien. Ed. Alex Vernon and Catherine Calloway. 2010.
Works of Ovid and the Ovidian Tradition. Ed. Barbara Weiden Boyd and Cora Fox. 2010.
Petrarch's Canzoniere *and the Petrarchan Tradition*. Ed. Christopher Kleinhenz and Andrea Dini. 2014.
Poe's Prose and Poetry. Ed. Jeffrey Andrew Weinstock and Tony Magistrale. 2008.
Pope's Poetry. Ed. Wallace Jackson and R. Paul Yoder. 1993.
Proust's Fiction and Criticism. Ed. Elyane Dezon-Jones and Inge Crosman Wimmers. 2003.

Puig's Kiss of the Spider Woman. Ed. Daniel Balderston and Francine Masiello. 2007.
Pynchon's The Crying of Lot 49 *and Other Works*. Ed. Thomas H. Schaub. 2008.
Works of François Rabelais. Ed. Todd W. Reeser and Floyd Gray. 2011.
Novels of Samuel Richardson. Ed. Lisa Zunshine and Jocelyn Harris. 2006.
Rousseau's Confessions *and* Reveries of the Solitary Walker. Ed. John C. O'Neal and Ourida Mostefai. 2003.
Scott's Waverley Novels. Ed. Evan Gottlieb and Ian Duncan. 2009.
Shakespeare's Hamlet. Ed. Bernice W. Kliman. 2001.
Shakespeare's King Lear. Ed. Robert H. Ray. 1986.
Shakespeare's Othello. Ed. Peter Erickson and Maurice Hunt. 2005.
Shakespeare's Romeo and Juliet. Ed. Maurice Hunt. 2000.
Shakespeare's The Taming of the Shrew. Ed. Margaret Dupuis and Grace Tiffany. 2013.
Shakespeare's The Tempest *and Other Late Romances*. Ed. Maurice Hunt. 1992.
Shelley's Frankenstein. Ed. Stephen C. Behrendt. 1990.
Shelley's Poetry. Ed. Spencer Hall. 1990.
Sir Gawain and the Green Knight. Ed. Miriam Youngerman Miller and Jane Chance. 1986.
Song of Roland. Ed. William W. Kibler and Leslie Zarker Morgan. 2006.
Spenser's Faerie Queene. Ed. David Lee Miller and Alexander Dunlop. 1994.
Stendhal's The Red and the Black. Ed. Dean de la Motte and Stirling Haig. 1999.
Sterne's Tristram Shandy. Ed. Melvyn New. 1989.
Works of Robert Louis Stevenson. Ed. Caroline McCracken-Flesher. 2013.
The Story of the Stone (Dream of the Red Chamber). Ed. Andrew Schonebaum and Tina Lu. 2012.
Stowe's Uncle Tom's Cabin. Ed. Elizabeth Ammons and Susan Belasco. 2000.
Swift's Gulliver's Travels. Ed. Edward J. Rielly. 1988.
Teresa of Ávila and the Spanish Mystics. Ed. Alison Weber. 2009.
Thoreau's Walden *and Other Works*. Ed. Richard J. Schneider. 1996.
Tolkien's The Lord of the Rings *and Other Works*. Ed. Leslie A. Donovan. 2015.
Tolstoy's Anna Karenina. Ed. Liza Knapp and Amy Mandelker. 2003.
Vergil's Aeneid. Ed. William S. Anderson and Lorina N. Quartarone. 2002.
Voltaire's Candide. Ed. Renée Waldinger. 1987.
Whitman's Leaves of Grass. Ed. Donald D. Kummings. 1990.
Wiesel's Night. Ed. Alan Rosen. 2007.
Works of Oscar Wilde. Ed. Philip E. Smith II. 2008.
Woolf's Mrs. Dalloway. Ed. Eileen Barrett and Ruth O. Saxton. 2009.
Woolf's To the Lighthouse. Ed. Beth Rigel Daugherty and Mary Beth Pringle. 2001.
Wordsworth's Poetry. Ed. Spencer Hall, with Jonathan Ramsey. 1986.
Wright's Native Son. Ed. James A. Miller. 1997.